18th Conference on Computational Natural Language Learning (CoNLL 2014)

Shared Task

Held in Conjunction with ACL 2014

Baltimore, Maryland, USA
26 – 27 June 2014

ISBN: 978-1-63439-232-7

Printed from e-media with permission by:

Curran Associates, Inc.
57 Morehouse Lane
Red Hook, NY 12571

Some format issues inherent in the e-media version may also appear in this print version.

Printed by Curran Associates, Inc. (2014)

For permission requests, please contact the Association for Computational Linguistics at the address below.

Association for Computational Linguistics
209 N. Eighth Street
Stroudsburg, Pennsylvania 18360

Phone: 1-570-476-8006
Fax: 1-570-476-0860

acl@aclweb.org

Additional copies of this publication are available from:

Curran Associates, Inc.
57 Morehouse Lane
Red Hook, NY 12571 USA
Phone: 845-758-0400
Fax: 845-758-2634
Email: curran@proceedings.com
Web: www.proceedings.com

Introduction

This volume contains papers describing the CoNLL-2014 Shared Task and the participating systems. This year, we continue the tradition of the Conference on Computational Natural Language Learning (CoNLL) of having a high profile shared task in natural language processing, centered on automatic grammatical error correction of English essays. The grammatical error correction task is impactful since it is estimated that hundreds of millions of people in the world are learning English as a second language, and they benefit directly from an automated grammar checker.

This task is a continuation of the CoNLL shared task in 2013. We have only one track in which shared task participants are provided with an annotated training corpus, but are allowed to use additional resources as long as they are publicly available. The training corpus, NUCLE (NUS Corpus of Learner English), is a large collection of English essays written by students at the National University of Singapore (NUS) who are non-native speakers of English. The essays were annotated by professional English instructors at the NUS. As in other shared tasks, we provide a common test set with gold-standard annotations, and a scorer to evaluate the submitted system output.

This year's shared task requires a participating system to correct all error types present in an essay, instead of only the five error types in the CoNLL-2013 shared task. Also, the evaluation metric has been changed to $F_{0.5}$, weighting precision twice as much as recall.

A total of 13 participating teams submitted system output and 12 of them submitted system description papers. Many different approaches were adopted to perform grammatical error correction. We hope that these approaches help to advance the state of the art in grammatical error correction, and that the test set and scorer, which are freely available after the shared task, can be useful resources for those interested in grammatical error correction.

Hwee Tou Ng, Siew Mei Wu, Ted Briscoe, Christian Hadiwinoto, Raymond Hendy Susanto, and Christopher Bryant
Organizers of the CoNLL-2014 Shared Task
May 2014

Organizers:

Hwee Tou Ng, National University of Singapore
Siew Mei Wu, National University of Singapore
Ted Briscoe, University of Cambridge
Christian Hadiwinoto, National University of Singapore
Raymond Hendy Susanto, National University of Singapore
Christopher Bryant, National University of Singapore

Program Committee:

Pushpak Bhattacharyya, Indian Institute of Technology Bombay
Francis Bond, Nanyang Technological University
Aoife Cahill, Educational Testing Service
Martin Chodorow, City University of New York
Daniel Dahlmeier, SAP Singapore
Dan Flickinger, Stanford University
Michael Heilman, Educational Testing Service
Gary Geunbae Lee, Pohang University of Science and Technology
Yuji Matsumoto, Nara Institute of Science and Technology
Detmar Meurers, Universität Tübingen
Alla Rozovskaya, Columbia University
Joel Tetreault, Yahoo! Labs
Antal van den Bosch, Radboud University Nijmegen
Torsten Zesch, University of Duisburg-Essen

Additional Reviewer:

Peter Berck, Tilburg University

Table of Contents

Conference Program

Thursday, June 26, 2014

Session 1: Oral Presentation

11:00–11:30 *The CoNLL-2014 Shared Task on Grammatical Error Correction*
Hwee Tou Ng, Siew Mei Wu, Ted Briscoe, Christian Hadiwinoto, Raymond Hendy Susanto and Christopher Bryant

11:30–11:50 *Grammatical error correction using hybrid systems and type filtering*
Mariano Felice, Zheng Yuan, Øistein E. Andersen, Helen Yannakoudakis and Ekaterina Kochmar

11:50–12:10 *The AMU System in the CoNLL-2014 Shared Task: Grammatical Error Correction by Data-Intensive and Feature-Rich Statistical Machine Translation*
Marcin Junczys-Dowmunt and Roman Grundkiewicz

12:10–12:30 *The Illinois-Columbia System in the CoNLL-2014 Shared Task*
Alla Rozovskaya, Kai-Wei Chang, Mark Sammons, Dan Roth and Nizar Habash

Thursday, June 26, 2014 (continued)

Session 2: Poster Presentation

The CoNLL-2014 Shared Task on Grammatical Error Correction

Hwee Tou Ng[1] Siew Mei Wu[2] Ted Briscoe[3]
Christian Hadiwinoto[1] Raymond Hendy Susanto[1] Christopher Bryant[1]

[1]Department of Computer Science, National University of Singapore
{nght,chrhad,raymondhs,bryant}@comp.nus.edu.sg

[2]Centre for English Language Communication, National University of Singapore
elcwusm@nus.edu.sg

[3]Computer Laboratory, University of Cambridge
Ted.Briscoe@cl.cam.ac.uk

Abstract

The CoNLL-2014 shared task was devoted to grammatical error correction of all error types. In this paper, we give the task definition, present the data sets, and describe the evaluation metric and scorer used in the shared task. We also give an overview of the various approaches adopted by the participating teams, and present the evaluation results. Compared to the CoNLL-2013 shared task, we have introduced the following changes in CoNLL-2014: (1) A participating system is expected to detect and correct grammatical errors of *all* types, instead of just the five error types in CoNLL-2013; (2) The evaluation metric was changed from F_1 to $F_{0.5}$, to emphasize precision over recall; and (3) We have two human annotators who independently annotated the test essays, compared to just one human annotator in CoNLL-2013.

1 Introduction

Grammatical error correction is the shared task of the Eighteenth Conference on Computational Natural Language Learning in 2014 (CoNLL-2014). In this task, given an English essay written by a learner of English as a second language, the goal is to detect and correct the grammatical errors of all error types present in the essay, and return the corrected essay.

This task has attracted much recent research interest, with two shared tasks Helping Our Own (HOO) organized in 2011 and 2012 (Dale and Kilgarriff, 2011; Dale et al., 2012), and a CoNLL shared task on grammatical error correction organized in 2013 (Ng et al., 2013). In contrast to previous CoNLL shared tasks which focused on particular subtasks of natural language processing, such as named entity recognition, semantic role labeling, dependency parsing, or coreference resolution, grammatical error correction aims at building a complete end-to-end application. This task is challenging since for many error types, current grammatical error correction systems do not achieve high performance and much research is still needed. Also, tackling this task has far-reaching impact, since it is estimated that hundreds of millions of people worldwide are learning English and they benefit directly from an automated grammar checker.

The CoNLL-2014 shared task provides a forum for participating teams to work on the same grammatical error correction task, with evaluation on the same blind test set using the same evaluation metric and scorer. This overview paper contains a detailed description of the shared task, and is organized as follows. Section 2 provides the task definition. Section 3 describes the annotated training data provided and the blind test data. Section 4 describes the evaluation metric and the scorer. Section 5 lists the participating teams and outlines the approaches to grammatical error correction used by the teams. Section 6 presents the results of the shared task, including a discussion on cross annotator comparison. Section 7 concludes the paper.

2 Task Definition

The goal of the CoNLL-2014 shared task is to evaluate algorithms and systems for automatically detecting and correcting grammatical errors

Proceedings of the Eighteenth Conference on Computational Natural Language Learning: Shared Task, pages 1–14,
Baltimore, Maryland, 26-27 July 2014. ©2014 Association for Computational Linguistics

present in English essays written by second language learners of English. Each participating team is given training data manually annotated with corrections of grammatical errors. The test data consists of new, blind test essays. Preprocessed test essays, which have been sentence-segmented and tokenized, are also made available to the participating teams. Each team is to submit its system output consisting of the automatically corrected essays, in sentence-segmented and tokenized form.

Grammatical errors consist of many different types, including articles or determiners, prepositions, noun form, verb form, subject-verb agreement, pronouns, word choice, sentence structure, punctuation, capitalization, etc. However, most prior published research on grammatical error correction only focuses on a small number of frequently occurring error types, such as article and preposition errors (Han et al., 2006; Gamon, 2010; Rozovskaya and Roth, 2010; Tetreault et al., 2010; Dahlmeier and Ng, 2011b). Article and preposition errors were also the only error types featured in the HOO 2012 shared task. Likewise, although all error types were included in the HOO 2011 shared task, almost all participating teams dealt with article and preposition errors only (besides spelling and punctuation errors). In the CoNLL-2013 shared task, the error types were extended to include five error types, comprising article or determiner, preposition, noun number, verb form, and subject-verb agreement. Other error types such as word choice errors (Dahlmeier and Ng, 2011a) were not dealt with.

In the CoNLL-2014 shared task, it was felt that the community is now ready to deal with *all* error types. Table 1 shows examples of the 28 error types in the CoNLL-2014 shared task.

Since there are 28 error types in our shared task compared to two in HOO 2012 and five in CoNLL-2013, there is a greater chance of encountering multiple, interacting errors in a sentence in our shared task. This increases the complexity of our shared task. To illustrate, consider the following sentence:

> Social *network plays* a role in providing and also filtering information.

The noun number error *networks* needs to be corrected (network → networks). This necessitates the correction of a subject-verb agreement error (plays → play). A pipeline system in which corrections for subject-verb agreement errors occur strictly before corrections for noun number errors would not be able to arrive at a fully corrected sentence for this example. The ability to correct multiple, interacting errors is thus necessary in our shared task. The recent work of Dahlmeier and Ng (2012a) and Wu and Ng (2013), for example, is designed to deal with multiple, interacting errors.

3 Data

This section describes the training and test data released to each participating team in our shared task.

3.1 Training Data

The training data provided in our shared task is the NUCLE corpus, the NUS Corpus of Learner English (Dahlmeier et al., 2013). As noted by (Leacock et al., 2010), the lack of a manually annotated and corrected corpus of English learner texts has been an impediment to progress in grammatical error correction, since it prevents comparative evaluations on a common benchmark test data set. NUCLE was created precisely to fill this void. It is a collection of 1,414 essays written by students at the National University of Singapore (NUS) who are non-native speakers of English. The essays were written in response to some prompts, and they cover a wide range of topics, such as environmental pollution, health care, etc. The grammatical errors in these essays have been hand-corrected by professional English instructors at NUS. For each grammatical error instance, the start and end character offsets of the erroneous text span are marked, and the error type and the correction string are provided. Manual annotation is carried out using a graphical user interface specifically built for this purpose. The error annotations are saved as stand-off annotations, in SGML format.

To illustrate, consider the following sentence at the start of the sixth paragraph of an essay:

> Nothing is *absolute* right or wrong.

There is a word form error (absolute → absolutely) in this sentence. The error annotation, also called *correction* or *edit*, in SGML format is shown in Figure 1. `start_par` (`end_par`) denotes the paragraph ID of the start (end) of the erroneous

Type	Description	Example
Vt	Verb tense	Medical technology during that time [**is** → was] not advanced enough to cure him.
Vm	Verb modal	Although the problem [**would** → may] not be serious, people [**would** → might] still be afraid.
V0	Missing verb	However, there are also a great number of people [**who** → who are] against this technology.
Vform	Verb form	A study in 2010 [**shown** → showed] that patients recover faster when surrounded by family members.
SVA	Subject-verb agreement	The benefits of disclosing genetic risk information [**outweighs** → outweigh] the costs.
ArtOrDet	Article or determiner	It is obvious to see that [**internet** → the internet] saves people time and also connects people globally.
Nn	Noun number	A carrier may consider not having any [**child** → children] after getting married.
Npos	Noun possessive	Someone should tell the [**carriers** → carrier's] relatives about the genetic problem.
Pform	Pronoun form	A couple should run a few tests to see if [**their** → they] have any genetic diseases beforehand.
Pref	Pronoun reference	It is everyone's duty to ensure that [**he or she** → they] undergo regular health checks.
Prep	Preposition	This essay will [**discuss about** → discuss] whether a carrier should tell his relatives or not.
Wci	Wrong collocation/idiom	Early examination is [**healthy** → advisable] and will cast away unwanted doubts.
Wa	Acronyms	After [**WOWII** → World War II], the population of China decreased rapidly.
Wform	Word form	The sense of [**guilty** → guilt] can be more than expected.
Wtone	Tone (formal/informal)	[**It's** → It is] our family and relatives that bring us up.
Srun	Run-on sentences, comma splices	The issue is highly [**debatable, a** → debatable. A] genetic risk could come from either side of the family.
Smod	Dangling modifiers	[**Undeniable,** → It is undeniable that] it becomes addictive when we spend more time socializing virtually.
Spar	Parallelism	We must pay attention to this information and [**assisting** → assist] those who are at risk.
Sfrag	Sentence fragment	**However, from the ethical point of view.**
Ssub	Subordinate clause	This is an issue [**needs** → that needs] to be addressed.
WOinc	Incorrect word order	[**Someone having what kind of disease** → What kind of disease someone has] is a matter of their own privacy.
WOadv	Incorrect adjective/ adverb order	In conclusion, [**personally I** → I personally] feel that it is important to tell one's family members.
Trans	Linking words/phrases	It is sometimes hard to find [**out** → out if] one has this disease.
Mec	Spelling, punctuation, capitalization, etc.	This knowledge [**maybe relavant** → may be relevant] to them.
Rloc−	Redundancy	It is up to the [**patient's own choice** → patient] to disclose information.
Cit	Citation	Poor citation practice.
Others	Other errors	An error that does not fit into any other category but can still be corrected.
Um	Unclear meaning	Genetic disease has a close relationship with the **born gene.** (i.e., no correction possible without further clarification.)

Table 1: The 28 error types in the shared task.

text span (paragraph ID starts from 0 by convention). `start_off` (`end_off`) denotes the character offset of the start (end) of the erroneous text span (again, character offset starts from 0 by convention). The error tag is `Wform`, and the correction string is `absolutely`.

The NUCLE corpus was first used in (Dahlmeier and Ng, 2011b), and has been publicly available for research purposes since June 2011[1]. All instances of grammatical errors are annotated in NUCLE.

To help participating teams in their preparation for the shared task, we also performed automatic preprocessing of the NUCLE corpus and released the preprocessed form of NUCLE. The preprocessing operations performed on the NUCLE essays include sentence segmentation and word tokenization using the NLTK toolkit (Bird et al., 2009), and part-of-speech (POS) tagging, constituency and dependency tree parsing using the Stanford parser (Klein and Manning, 2003; de Marneffe et al., 2006). The error annotations, which are originally at the character level, are then mapped to error annotations at the word token level. Error annotations at the word token level also facilitate scoring, as we will see in Section 4, since our scorer operates by matching tokens. Note that although we released our own preprocessed version of NUCLE, the participating teams were however free to perform their own preprocessing if they so preferred.

NUCLE release version 3.2 was used in the CoNLL-2014 shared task. In this version, 17 essays were removed from the first release of NUCLE since these essays were duplicates with multiple annotations. In addition, in order to facilitate the detection and correction of article/determiner errors and preposition errors, we performed some automatic mapping of error types in the original NUCLE corpus to arrive at release version 3.2. Ng et al. (2013) gives more details of how the mapping was carried out.

The statistics of the NUCLE corpus (release 3.2 version) are shown in Table 2. The distribution of errors among all error types is shown in Table 3.

While the NUCLE corpus is provided in our shared task, participating teams are free to not use NUCLE, or to use additional resources and tools in building their grammatical error correction systems, as long as these resources and tools are publicly available and not proprietary. For example, participating teams are free to use the Cambridge FCE corpus (Yannakoudakis et al., 2011; Nicholls, 2003) (the training data provided in HOO 2012 (Dale et al., 2012)) as additional training data.

[1]http://www.comp.nus.edu.sg/~nlp/corpora.html

	Training data (NUCLE)	**Test data**
# essays	1,397	50
# sentences	57,151	1,312
# word tokens	1,161,567	30,144

Table 2: Statistics of training and test data.

3.2 Test Data

Similar to CoNLL-2013, 25 NUS students, who are non-native speakers of English, were recruited to write new essays to be used as blind test data in the shared task. Each student wrote two essays in response to the two prompts shown in Table 4, one essay per prompt. The first prompt was also used in the NUCLE training data, but the second prompt is entirely new and not used previously. As a result, 50 new test essays were collected. The statistics of the test essays are also shown in Table 2.

Error annotation on the test essays was carried out independently by two native speakers of English. One of them is a lecturer at the NUS Centre for English Language Communication, and the other is a freelance English linguist with extensive prior experience in error annotation of English learners' essays. The distribution of errors in the test essays among the error types is shown in Table 3. The test essays were then preprocessed in the same manner as the NUCLE corpus. The preprocessed test essays were released to the participating teams. Similar to CoNLL-2013, the test essays and their error annotations in the CoNLL-2014 shared task will be made freely available after the shared task.

4 Evaluation Metric and Scorer

A grammatical error correction system is evaluated by how well its proposed corrections or edits match the gold-standard edits. An essay is first sentence-segmented and tokenized before evaluation is carried out on the essay. To illustrate, consider the following tokenized sentence S written by an English learner:

```
<MISTAKE start_par="5" start_off="11" end_par="5" end_off="19">
<TYPE>Wform</TYPE>
<CORRECTION>absolutely</CORRECTION>
</MISTAKE>
```

Figure 1: An example error annotation.

Error type	Training data (NUCLE)	%	Test data (Annotator 1)	%	Test data (Annotator 2)	%
Vt	3,204	7.1%	133	5.5%	150	4.5%
Vm	431	1.0%	49	2.0%	37	1.1%
V0	414	0.9%	31	1.3%	37	1.1%
Vform	1,443	3.2%	132	5.5%	91	2.7%
SVA	1,524	3.4%	105	4.4%	154	4.6%
ArtOrDet	6,640	14.8%	332	13.9%	444	13.3%
Nn	3,768	8.4%	215	9.0%	228	6.8%
Npos	239	0.5%	19	0.8%	15	0.5%
Pform	186	0.4%	47	2.0%	18	0.5%
Pref	927	2.1%	96	4.0%	153	4.6%
Prep	2,413	5.4%	211	8.8%	390	11.7%
Wci	5,305	11.8%	340	14.2%	479	14.4%
Wa	50	0.1%	0	0.0%	1	0.0%
Wform	2,161	4.8%	77	3.2%	103	3.1%
Wtone	593	1.3%	9	0.4%	15	0.5%
Srun	873	1.9%	7	0.3%	26	0.8%
Smod	51	0.1%	0	0.0%	5	0.2%
Spar	519	1.2%	3	0.1%	24	0.7%
Sfrag	250	0.6%	13	0.5%	5	0.2%
Ssub	362	0.8%	68	2.8%	10	0.3%
WOinc	698	1.6%	22	0.9%	54	1.6%
WOadv	347	0.8%	12	0.5%	27	0.8%
Trans	1,377	3.1%	94	3.9%	79	2.4%
Mec	3,145	7.0%	231	9.6%	496	14.9%
Rloc−	4,703	10.5%	95	4.0%	199	6.0%
Cit	658	1.5%	0	0.0%	0	0.0%
Others	1,467	3.3%	44	1.8%	49	1.5%
Um	1,164	2.6%	12	0.5%	42	1.3%
All types	44,912	100.0%	2,397	100.0%	3,331	100.0%

Table 3: Error type distribution of the training and test data. The test data were annotated independently by two annotators.

ID	Prompt
1	"The decision to undergo genetic testing can only be made by the individual at risk for a disorder. Once a test has been conducted and the results are known, however, a new, family-related ethical dilemma is born: Should a carrier of a known genetic risk be obligated to tell his or her relatives?" Respond to the question above, supporting your argument with concrete examples.
2	While social media sites such as Twitter and Facebook can connect us closely to people in many parts of the world, some argue that the reduction in face-to-face human contact affects interpersonal skills. Explain the advantages and disadvantages of using social media in your daily life/society.

Table 4: The two prompts used for the test essays.

> There is no **a doubt** , tracking **system has** brought many benefits in this information age .

The set of gold-standard edits of a human annotator is $\mathbf{g}$ = {a doubt → doubt, system → systems, has → have}. Suppose the tokenized output sentence H of a grammatical error correction system given the above sentence is:

> There is no doubt , tracking system has brought many benefits in this information age .

That is, the set of system edits is $\mathbf{e}$ = {a doubt → doubt}. The performance of the grammatical error correction system is measured by how well the two sets $\mathbf{g}$ and $\mathbf{e}$ match, in the form of recall R, precision P, and $F_{0.5}$ measure: $R = 1/3, P = 1/1, F_{0.5} = (1 + 0.5^2) \times RP/(R + 0.5^2 \times P) = 5/7$.

More generally, given a set of n sentences, where $\mathbf{g}_i$ is the set of gold-standard edits for sentence i, and $\mathbf{e}_i$ is the set of system edits for sentence i, recall, precision, and $F_{0.5}$ are defined as follows:

$$R = \frac{\sum_{i=1}^{n} |\mathbf{g}_i \cap \mathbf{e}_i|}{\sum_{i=1}^{n} |\mathbf{g}_i|} \quad (1)$$

$$P = \frac{\sum_{i=1}^{n} |\mathbf{g}_i \cap \mathbf{e}_i|}{\sum_{i=1}^{n} |\mathbf{e}_i|} \quad (2)$$

$$F_{0.5} = \frac{(1 + 0.5^2) \times R \times P}{R + 0.5^2 \times P} \quad (3)$$

where the intersection between $\mathbf{g}_i$ and $\mathbf{e}_i$ for sentence i is defined as

$$\mathbf{g}_i \cap \mathbf{e}_i = \{e \in \mathbf{e}_i | \exists g \in \mathbf{g}_i, match(g, e)\} \quad (4)$$

Note that we have adopted $F_{0.5}$ as the evaluation metric in the CoNLL-2014 shared task instead of the standard F_1 used in CoNLL-2013. $F_{0.5}$ emphasizes precision twice as much as recall, while F_1 weighs precision and recall equally. When a grammar checker is put into actual use, it is important that its proposed corrections are highly accurate in order to gain user acceptance. Neglecting to propose a correction is not as bad as proposing an erroneous correction.

Similar to CoNLL-2013, we use the *MaxMatch* (M^2) scorer[2] (Dahlmeier and Ng, 2012b) as the official scorer in CoNLL-2014. The M^2 scorer[3] efficiently searches for a set of system edits that maximally matches the set of gold-standard edits specified by an annotator. It overcomes a limitation of the scorer used in HOO shared tasks, which can return an erroneous score since the system edits are computed deterministically by the HOO scorer without regard to the gold-standard edits.

5 Approaches

45 teams registered to participate in the shared task, out of which 13 teams submitted the output of their grammatical error correction systems. These teams are listed in Table 5. Each team is assigned a 3 to 4-letter team ID. In the remainder of this paper, we will use the assigned team ID to refer to a participating team. Every team submitted a system description paper (the only exception is the NARA team). Four of the 13 teams submitted their system output only after the deadline (they were given up to one week of extension). These four teams (IITB, IPN, PKU, and UFC) have an asterisk affixed after their team names in Table 5.

Each participating team in the CoNLL-2014 shared task tackled the error correction problem in a different way. A full list summarizing each

[2] http://www.comp.nus.edu.sg/~nlp/software.html

[3] A few minor bugs were fixed in the M^2 scorer before it was used in the CoNLL-2014 shared task.

Team ID	Affiliation
AMU	Adam Mickiewicz University
CAMB	University of Cambridge
CUUI	Columbia University and the University of Illinois at Urbana-Champaign
IITB*	Indian Institute of Technology, Bombay
IPN*	Instituto Politécnico Nacional
NARA	Nara Institute of Science and Technology
NTHU	National Tsing Hua University
PKU*	Peking University
POST	Pohang University of Science and Technology
RAC	Research Institute for Artificial Intelligence, Romanian Academy
SJTU	Shanghai Jiao Tong University
UFC*	University of Franche-Comté
UMC	University of Macau

Table 5: The list of 13 participating teams. The teams that submitted their system output after the deadline have an asterisk affixed after their team names. NARA did not submit any system description paper.

team's approach can be found in Table 6. While machine-learnt classifiers for specific error types proved popular in last year's CoNLL-2013 shared task, since this year's task required the correction of all 28 error types, teams tended to prefer methods that could deal with all error types simultaneously. In fact, most teams built hybrid systems that made use of a combination of different approaches to identify and correct errors.

One of the most popular approaches to non-specific error type correction, incorporated to various extents in many teams' systems, was the Language Model (LM) based approach. Specifically, the probability of a learner n-gram is compared with the probability of a candidate corrected n-gram, and if the difference is greater than some threshold, an error was perceived to have been detected and a higher scoring replacement n-gram could be suggested. Some teams used this approach only to detect errors, e.g., IPN (Hernandez and Calvo, 2014), which could then be corrected by other methods, whilst other teams used other methods to detect errors first, and then made corrections based on the alternative highest n-gram probability score, e.g., RAC (Boroş et al., 2014). No single team used a uniquely LM-based solution and the LM approach was always a component in a hybrid system.

An alternative solution to correcting all errors was to use a phrase-based statistical machine translation (MT) system to "translate" learner English into correct English. Teams that followed the MT approach mainly differed in terms of their attitude toward tuning; CAMB (Felice et al., 2014) performed no tuning at all, IITB (Kunchukuttan et al., 2014) and UMC (Wang et al., 2014b) tuned $F_{0.5}$ using MERT, while AMU (Junczys-Dowmunt and Grundkiewicz, 2014) explored a variety of tuning options, ultimately tuning $F_{0.5}$ using a combination of kb-MIRA and MERT. No team used a syntax-based translation model, although UMC did include POS tags and morphology in a factored translation model.

With regard to correcting single error types, rule-based (RB) approaches were also common in most teams' systems. A possible reason for this is that some error types are more regular than others, and so in order to boost accuracy, simple rules can be written to make sure that, for example, the number of a subject agrees with the number of a verb. In contrast, it is a lot harder to write a rule to consistently correct Wci (wrong collocation/idiom) errors. As such, RB methods were often, but not always, used as a preliminary or supplementary stage in a larger hybrid system.

Finally, although there were fewer machine-learnt classifier (ML) approaches than last year, some teams still used various classifiers to correct specific error types. In fact, CUUI (Rozovskaya et al., 2014) *only* built classifiers for specific error types and did not attempt to tackle the whole range of errors. SJTU (Wang et al., 2014a) also preprocessed the training data into more precise error categories using rules (e.g., verb tense (Vt) errors might be subcategorized into present, past, or future tense etc.) and then built a single maximum entropy classifier to correct all error types. See Table 6 to find out which teams tackled which error types.

While every effort has been made to make clear which team used which approach to correct which set of error types, as there were more error types than last year, it was sometimes impractical to fit all this information into Table 6. For more information on the specific methods used to correct a specific error type, we must refer the reader to that team's CoNLL-2014 system description paper.

Table 6 also shows the linguistic features used by the participating teams, which include lexical features (i.e., words, collocations, n-grams), parts-of-speech (POS), constituency parses, and dependency parses.

While all teams in the shared task used the NUCLE corpus, they were also allowed to use additional external resources (both corpora and tools) so long as they were publicly available and not proprietary. Three teams also used last year's CoNLL-2013 test set as a development set in this year's CoNLL-2014 shared task. The external resources used by the teams are also listed in Table 6.

6 Results

All submitted system output was evaluated using the M^2 scorer, based on the error annotations provided by our annotators. The recall (R), precision (P), and $F_{0.5}$ measure of all teams are shown in Table 7. The performance of the teams varies greatly, from little more than five per cent to 37.33% for the top team.

The nature of grammatical error correction is such that multiple, different corrections are often acceptable. In order to allow the participating teams to raise their disagreement with the original gold-standard annotations provided by the annotators, and not understate the performance of the teams, we allow the teams to submit their proposed alternative answers. This was also the practice adopted in HOO 2011, HOO 2012, and CoNLL-2013. Specifically, after the teams submitted their system output and the error annotations on the test essays were released, we allowed the teams to propose alternative answers (gold-standard edits), to be submitted within four days after the initial error annotations were released.

Team ID	Precision	Recall	$F_{0.5}$
CAMB	39.71	30.10	37.33
CUUI	41.78	24.88	36.79
AMU	41.62	21.40	35.01
POST	34.51	21.73	30.88
NTHU	35.08	18.85	29.92
RAC	33.14	14.99	26.68
UMC	31.27	14.46	25.37
PKU*	32.21	13.65	25.32
NARA	21.57	29.38	22.78
SJTU	30.11	5.10	15.19
UFC*	70.00	1.72	7.84
IPN*	11.28	2.85	7.09
IITB*	30.77	1.39	5.90

Table 7: Scores (in %) *without* alternative answers. The teams that submitted their system output after the deadline have an asterisk affixed after their team names.

The same annotators who provided the error annotations on the test essays also judged the alternative answers proposed by the teams, to ensure consistency. In all, three teams (CAMB, CUUI, UMC) submitted alternative answers.

The same submitted system output was then evaluated using the M^2 scorer, with the original annotations augmented with the alternative answers. Table 8 shows the recall (R), precision (P), and $F_{0.5}$ measure of all teams under this new evaluation setting.

The $F_{0.5}$ measure of every team improves when evaluated with alternative answers. Not surprisingly, the teams which submitted alternative answers tend to show the greatest improvements in their $F_{0.5}$ measure. Overall, the CUUI team (Rozovskaya et al., 2014) achieves the best $F_{0.5}$ measure when evaluated with alternative answers, and the CAMB team (Felice et al., 2014) achieves the best $F_{0.5}$ measure when evaluated without alternative answers.

For future research which uses the test data of the CoNLL-2014 shared task, we recommend that evaluation be carried out in the setting that does *not* use alternative answers, to ensure a fairer evaluation. This is because the scores of the teams which submitted alternative answers tend to be higher in a biased way when evaluated with alternative answers.

We are also interested in the analysis of the system performance for each of the error types.

Team	Error	Approach	Description of Approach	Linguistic Features	External Resources
AMU	All	MT	Phrase-based translation optimized for F-score using a combination of kb-MIRA and MERT with augmented language models and task-specific features.	Lexical	Wikipedia, CommonCrawl, Lang-8
CAMB	All	RB/LM/MT	Pipeline: Rule-based → LM ranking → Untuned SMT → LM ranking → Type filtering	Lexical, POS	Cambridge "Write and Improve" SAT system, Cambridge Learner Corpus, CoNLL-2013 Test Set, First Certificate in English corpus, English Vocabulary Profile corpus, Microsoft Web LM
CUUI	ArtOrDet, Mec, Nn, Prep, SVA, Vform, Vt, Wform, Wtone	ML	Different combinations of averaged perceptron, naïve Bayes, and pattern-based learning trained on different data sets for different error types.	Lexical, POS, lemma, shallow parse, dependency parse	CoNLL-2013 Test Set, Google Web 1T
IITB	All	MT/ML	Phrase-based translation optimized for F-score using MERT and supplemented with additional RB modules for SVA errors and ML modules for Nn and ArtOrDet.	Lexical, shallow parse	None
IPN	All except Prep	LM/RB	Low LM score trigrams are identified as errors which are subsequently corrected by rules.	Lexical, lemma, dependency parse	Wikipedia
NTHU	ArtOrDet, Nn, Prep, "Prep+Verb", Spelling and Commas, SVA, Wform	RB/LM/MT	External resources correct spelling errors while a conditional random field model corrects comma errors. SVA errors corrected using a RB approach. All other errors corrected by means of a language model. Interacting errors corrected using an MT system.	Lexical, POS, dependency parse	Aspell, GingerIt, Academic Word List, British National Corpus, Google Web 1T, Google Books Syntactic N-Grams, English Gigaword
PKU	All	LM/ML	A LM is used to find the highest scoring variant of a word with a common stem while maximum entropy classifiers deal with articles and prepositions.	Lexical, POS, stem	Gigaword, Apache Lucene Spellchecker
POST	All	LM/RB	N-gram-based approach finds unlikely n-gram "frames" which are then corrected via high scoring LM alternatives. Rule-based methods then improve the results for certain error types.	Lexical, POS, dependency parse, constituency parse	Google Web 1T, CoNLL-2013 Test Set, PyEnchant Spellchecking Library
RAC	See Footnote[a]	RB/LM	Rule-based methods are used to detect errors which can then be corrected based on LM scores.	Lexical, POS, lemma, shallow parse	Google Web 1T, News CRAWL (2007 – 2012), Europarl, UN French-English Corpus, News Commentary, Wikipedia, LanguageTool.org
SJTU	All	RB/ML	Rule-based system generates more detailed error categories which are then used to train a single maximum entropy model.	Lexical, POS, lemma, dependency parse	None
UFC	SVA, Vform, Wform	RB	Mismatched POS tags generated by two different taggers are treated as errors which are then corrected by rules.	POS	Nodebox English Linguistics Library
UMC	All	MT	Factored translation model using modified POS tags and morphology as features.	Lexical, POS, prefix, suffix, stem	WMT2014 Monolingual Data

Table 6: Profile of the participating teams. The *Error* column lists the error types tackled by a team if not all were corrected. The *Approach* column lists the type of approach used, where LM denotes a Language Modeling based approach, ML a Machine Learning classifier based approach, MT a statistical Machine Translation approach, and RB a Rule-Based approach.

[a]The RAC team uses rules to correct error types that differ from the 28 official error types. They include: "the correction of the verb tense especially in time clauses, the use of the short infinitive after modals, the position of frequency adverbs in a sentence, subject-verb agreement, word order in interrogative sentences, punctuation accompanying certain lexical elements, the use of articles, of correlatives, etc."

Type	AMU	CAMB	CUUI	IITB	IPN	NARA	NTHU	PKU	POST	RAC	SJTU	UFC	UMC
Vt	10.66	19.12	3.79	1.74	0.88	14.18	10.61	12.30	3.76	26.19	4.17	0.00	14.84
Vm	10.81	22.58	0.00	0.00	0.00	29.03	0.00	3.23	0.00	35.90	0.00	0.00	6.45
V0	17.86	25.00	0.00	0.00	0.00	36.67	0.00	0.00	0.00	0.00	0.00	0.00	25.93
Vform	22.76	24.37	21.43	1.85	4.63	27.62	24.30	25.64	1.89	27.35	3.67	0.95	14.68
SVA	24.30	31.36	70.34	1.06	14.14	27.50	62.67	17.31	20.56	30.36	14.85	28.70	14.41
ArtOrDet	15.52	49.48	58.85	0.68	0.33	50.89	33.63	8.20	54.45	0.63	12.54	0.00	24.05
Nn	58.74	54.11	56.10	4.49	10.36	57.32	46.76	41.78	55.60	36.45	10.11	0.00	17.03
Npos	14.29	7.69	4.76	0.00	0.00	20.00	0.00	0.00	0.00	4.76	4.55	0.00	5.26
Pform	22.22	22.58	7.14	0.00	0.00	14.81	16.13	12.00	0.00	3.70	0.00	0.00	17.24
Pref	9.33	19.35	1.32	0.00	0.00	10.00	1.20	1.35	1.32	0.00	0.00	0.00	12.05
Prep	18.41	38.26	15.45	2.12	0.00	29.72	19.42	0.00	2.28	0.00	7.92	0.00	14.55
Wci	12.00	9.17	0.94	0.36	0.35	7.55	0.63	1.65	1.27	0.34	0.00	0.00	3.23
Wa	0.00	0.00	0.00	0.00	0.00	0.00	0.00	0.00	0.00	0.00	0.00	0.00	0.00
Wform	45.56	45.05	17.24	4.05	2.60	39.08	14.81	25.88	6.49	11.25	1.39	1.30	16.46
Wtone	81.82	36.36	36.36	0.00	0.00	14.29	0.00	0.00	28.57	0.00	16.67	0.00	44.44
Srun	0.00	0.00	0.00	0.00	0.00	0.00	0.00	0.00	0.00	0.00	0.00	0.00	0.00
Smod	0.00	0.00	0.00	0.00	0.00	0.00	0.00	0.00	0.00	0.00	0.00	0.00	0.00
Spar	0.00	0.00	0.00	0.00	0.00	0.00	0.00	0.00	0.00	50.00	0.00	0.00	0.00
Sfrag	0.00	0.00	0.00	0.00	0.00	20.00	0.00	0.00	0.00	0.00	25.00	0.00	25.00
Ssub	7.89	14.63	0.00	0.00	2.27	15.38	0.00	0.00	9.52	2.38	2.27	0.00	6.98
WOinc	0.00	3.03	0.00	3.57	0.00	3.03	0.00	0.00	0.00	0.00	0.00	0.00	6.67
WOadv	0.00	47.62	0.00	12.50	0.00	43.75	0.00	0.00	0.00	0.00	0.00	0.00	44.44
Trans	13.43	21.43	2.86	1.43	0.00	11.25	1.41	1.52	2.67	0.00	0.00	0.00	12.16
Mec	29.35	28.75	15.79	1.02	4.33	36.69	6.67	30.28	36.61	43.51	0.51	0.00	16.80
Rloc−	5.41	20.16	7.76	0.00	5.56	18.64	9.68	10.48	9.26	9.09	2.50	0.00	15.84
Cit	0.00	0.00	0.00	0.00	0.00	0.00	0.00	0.00	0.00	0.00	0.00	0.00	0.00
Others	0.00	0.00	0.00	0.00	0.00	0.00	0.00	0.00	0.00	3.12	0.00	0.00	0.00
Um	7.69	9.09	0.00	0.00	0.00	4.00	0.00	15.79	8.70	8.33	0.00	0.00	0.00

Table 9: Recall (in %) for each error type *without* alternative answers, indicating how well each team performs against a particular error type.

Type	AMU	CAMB	CUUI	IITB	IPN	NARA	NTHU	PKU	POST	RAC	SJTU	UFC	UMC
Vt	11.61	20.00	5.79	1.90	0.98	16.18	12.90	14.16	3.31	29.17	4.59	0.00	17.60
Vm	11.11	23.33	0.00	0.00	0.00	29.03	0.00	3.33	0.00	39.47	0.00	0.00	7.69
V0	19.23	29.63	0.00	0.00	0.00	38.71	0.00	0.00	0.00	0.00	0.00	0.00	30.77
Vform	23.93	27.42	21.05	1.92	4.85	29.09	24.07	26.79	2.83	26.96	3.77	0.98	15.32
SVA	25.00	33.90	72.41	1.11	14.74	28.57	63.76	17.82	22.86	32.43	15.46	30.09	14.95
ArtOrDet	18.75	54.74	67.38	1.81	0.36	54.42	37.96	9.65	59.41	0.66	14.63	0.00	33.42
Nn	62.14	62.03	65.53	4.91	12.29	62.69	52.89	51.01	64.14	42.67	11.93	0.00	22.22
Npos	23.33	40.00	4.35	0.00	0.00	29.17	0.00	0.00	0.00	9.52	4.55	0.00	13.64
Pform	22.22	23.33	7.69	0.00	0.00	14.81	17.86	12.50	0.00	4.00	0.00	0.00	22.22
Pref	9.59	18.56	1.32	0.00	0.00	9.80	1.25	1.33	1.37	0.00	0.00	0.00	11.11
Prep	18.41	38.63	18.22	2.21	0.00	30.28	20.42	0.00	2.25	0.00	8.95	0.00	16.98
Wci	15.26	15.18	0.96	0.79	0.38	8.05	1.33	3.17	1.94	0.36	0.00	0.00	9.57
Wa	0.00	0.00	0.00	0.00	0.00	0.00	0.00	0.00	0.00	0.00	0.00	0.00	0.00
Wform	45.45	46.59	21.11	2.90	2.67	40.91	15.58	27.38	6.49	12.50	1.47	1.37	17.11
Wtone	88.24	38.46	52.63	0.00	0.00	12.50	0.00	0.00	50.00	0.00	33.33	0.00	55.56
Srun	0.00	0.00	0.00	0.00	0.00	0.00	0.00	0.00	0.00	0.00	0.00	0.00	0.00
Smod	0.00	0.00	0.00	0.00	0.00	0.00	0.00	0.00	0.00	0.00	0.00	0.00	0.00
Spar	0.00	0.00	0.00	0.00	0.00	0.00	0.00	0.00	0.00	50.00	0.00	0.00	0.00
Sfrag	0.00	0.00	0.00	0.00	0.00	16.67	0.00	0.00	0.00	0.00	25.00	0.00	20.00
Ssub	7.89	14.29	0.00	0.00	2.33	15.38	0.00	0.00	9.76	2.44	2.33	0.00	6.98
WOinc	0.00	3.45	0.00	4.00	0.00	3.33	0.00	0.00	0.00	0.00	0.00	0.00	7.14
WOadv	0.00	50.00	0.00	16.67	0.00	44.44	0.00	0.00	0.00	0.00	0.00	0.00	50.00
Trans	14.52	22.39	3.08	1.67	0.00	11.84	1.56	1.64	2.82	0.00	0.00	0.00	20.78
Mec	31.56	30.67	17.47	1.13	4.79	37.28	7.17	31.69	37.88	45.82	1.10	0.00	22.31
Rloc−	5.45	26.47	7.38	0.00	5.62	21.43	11.34	12.38	11.82	10.00	3.66	0.00	29.66
Cit	0.00	0.00	0.00	0.00	0.00	0.00	0.00	0.00	0.00	0.00	0.00	0.00	0.00
Others	0.00	3.03	0.00	0.00	0.00	0.00	0.00	0.00	0.00	3.33	0.00	0.00	0.00
Um	7.69	9.09	0.00	0.00	0.00	4.35	0.00	15.00	4.55	8.70	0.00	0.00	0.00

Table 10: Recall (in %) for each error type *with* alternative answers, indicating how well each team performs against a particular error type.

Team ID	Precision	Recall	$F_{0.5}$
CUUI	52.44	29.89	45.57
CAMB	46.70	34.30	43.55
AMU	45.68	23.78	38.58
POST	41.28	25.59	36.77
UMC	43.17	19.72	34.88
NTHU	38.34	21.12	32.97
PKU*	36.64	15.96	29.10
RAC	35.63	16.73	29.06
NARA	23.83	31.95	25.11
SJTU	32.95	5.95	17.28
UFC*	72.00	1.90	8.60
IPN*	11.66	3.17	7.59
IITB*	34.07	1.66	6.94

Table 8: Scores (in %) *with* alternative answers. The teams that submitted their system output after the deadline have an asterisk affixed after their team names.

Computing the recall of an error type is straightforward as the error type of each gold-standard edit is provided. Conversely, computing the precision of each of the 28 error types is difficult as the error type of each system edit is not available since the submitted system output only contains corrected sentences with no indication of the error type of the system edits. Predicting the error type out of the 28 types for a particular system edit not found in gold-standard annotation can be tricky and error-prone. Therefore, we decided to compute the per-type performance based on recall. The recall scores when distinguished by error type are shown in Tables 9 and 10.

6.1 Cross Annotator Comparison

To measure the agreement between our two annotators, we computed Cohen's Kappa coefficient (Cohen, 1960) for identification, which measures the extent to which annotators agreed which words needed correction and which did not, regardless of the error type or correction. We obtained a Kappa coefficient value of 0.43, indicating moderate agreement (since it falls between 0.40 and 0.60). While this may seem low, it is worth pointing out that the Kappa coefficient does not take into account the fact that there is often more than one valid way to correct a sentence.

In addition to computing the performance of each team against the gold standard annotations of both annotators with and without alternative annotations, we also had an opportunity to compare the performance of each team's system against each annotator individually.

A recent concern is that there can be a high degree of variability between individual annotators which can dramatically affect a system's output score. For example, in a much simplified error correction task concerning only the correction of prepositions, Tetreault and Chodorow (2008) showed an actual difference of 10% precision and 5% recall between two annotators. Table 11 hence shows the precision (P), recall (R), and $F_{0.5}$ scores for *all* error types against the gold standard annotations of each CoNLL-2014 annotator individually.

The results show that there can indeed be a high amount of disagreement between two annotators, the most noticeable being precision in the UFC system: precision was 70% for Annotator 2 but only 28% for Annotator 1. This 42% difference is, however, likely to be an extreme case, and most teams show little more than 10% variation in precision and 5% variation in $F_{0.5}$. Recall remained fairly constant between annotators. 10% is still a large margin however, and these results reinforce the idea that error correction systems should be judged against the gold-standard annotations of multiple annotators.

Table 12 additionally shows how each annotator compares against each other; i.e., what score Annotator 1 gets if Annotator 2 was the gold standard (part (a) of Table 12) and vice versa (part (b)).

The low $F_{0.5}$ scores of 45.36% and 38.54% represent an upper bound for system performance on this data set and again emphasize the difficulty of the task. The low human $F_{0.5}$ scores imply that there are many ways to correct a sentence.

7 Conclusions

The CoNLL-2014 shared task saw the participation of 13 teams worldwide to evaluate their grammatical error correction systems on a common test set, using a common evaluation metric and scorer. The best systems in the shared task achieve an $F_{0.5}$ score of 37.33% when it is scored without alternative answers, and 45.57% with alternative answers. There is still much room for improvement in the accuracy of grammatical error correction systems. The evaluation data sets and scorer used in our shared task serve as a benchmark for

Team ID	Annotator 1			Annotator 2		
	P	**R**	**$F_{0.5}$**	**P**	**R**	**$F_{0.5}$**
AMU	27.30	13.55	22.69	35.49	12.90	26.29
CAMB	24.96	19.62	23.67	35.22	20.29	30.70
CUUI	26.05	15.60	22.97	36.91	16.37	29.51
IITB	23.33	0.88	3.82	24.18	0.66	2.99
IPN	5.80	1.25	3.36	9.62	1.51	4.63
NARA	13.54	19.20	14.38	18.74	19.69	18.92
NTHU	22.19	11.38	18.64	31.48	11.79	23.60
PKU	21.53	8.36	16.37	27.47	7.72	18.17
POST	22.39	13.89	19.94	29.53	13.42	23.81
RAC	19.68	8.28	15.43	28.52	8.80	19.70
SJTU	21.08	3.09	9.75	24.64	2.59	9.12
UFC	28.00	0.59	2.70	70.00	1.06	4.98
UMC	20.41	8.78	16.14	26.63	8.38	18.55

Table 11: Performance (in %) for each team's output scored against the annotations of a single annotator.

P	**R**	**$F_{0.5}$**
50.47	32.29	45.36

(a)

P	**R**	**$F_{0.5}$**
37.14	45.38	38.54

(b)

Table 12: Performance (in %) for output of one gold standard annotation scored against the other gold standard annotation: (a) The score of Annotator 1 if Annotator 2 was the gold standard, (b) The score of Annotator 2 if Annotator 1 was the gold standard.

future research on grammatical error correction[4].

Acknowledgments

This research is supported by the Singapore National Research Foundation under its International Research Centre @ Singapore Funding Initiative and administered by the IDM Programme Office. We thank our two annotators Mark Brooke and Diane Nicholls who provided the gold-standard annotations.

References

Steven Bird, Ewan Klein, and Edward Loper. 2009. *Natural Language Processing with Python*. O'Reilly Media.

Tiberiu Boroş, Stefan Daniel Dumitrescu, Adrian Zafiu, Dan Tufiş, Verginica Mititelu Barbu, and Paul Ionuţ Văduva. 2014. RACAI GEC – a hybrid approach to grammatical error correction. In *Proceedings of the Eighteenth Conference on Computational Natural Language Learning: Shared Task*.

Jacob Cohen. 1960. A coefficient of agreement for nominal scales. *Educational and Psychological Measurement*, 20(1):37–46.

[4]http://www.comp.nus.edu.sg/~nlp/conll14st.html

Daniel Dahlmeier and Hwee Tou Ng. 2011a. Correcting semantic collocation errors with L1-induced paraphrases. In *Proceedings of the 2011 Conference on Empirical Methods in Natural Language Processing*, pages 107–117.

Daniel Dahlmeier and Hwee Tou Ng. 2011b. Grammatical error correction with alternating structure optimization. In *Proceedings of the 49th Annual Meeting of the Association for Computational Linguistics*, pages 915–923.

Daniel Dahlmeier and Hwee Tou Ng. 2012a. A beam-search decoder for grammatical error correction. In *Proceedings of the 2012 Joint Conference on Empirical Methods in Natural Language Processing and Computational Natural Language Learning*, pages 568–578.

Daniel Dahlmeier and Hwee Tou Ng. 2012b. Better evaluation for grammatical error correction. In *Proceedings of the 2012 Conference of the North American Chapter of the Association for Computational Linguistics: Human Language Technologies*, pages 568–572.

Daniel Dahlmeier, Hwee Tou Ng, and Siew Mei Wu. 2013. Building a large annotated corpus of learner English: The NUS Corpus of Learner English. In *Proceedings of the Eighth Workshop on Innovative Use of NLP for Building Educational Applications*, pages 22–31.

Robert Dale and Adam Kilgarriff. 2011. Helping Our Own: The HOO 2011 pilot shared task. In *Proceedings of the 13th European Workshop on Natural Language Generation*, pages 242–249.

Robert Dale, Ilya Anisimoff, and George Narroway. 2012. HOO 2012: A report on the preposition and determiner error correction shared task. In *Proceedings of the 7th Workshop on the Innovative Use of NLP for Building Educational Applications*, pages 54–62.

Marie-Catherine de Marneffe, Bill MacCartney, and Christopher D. Manning. 2006. Generating typed dependency parses from phrase structure parses. In *Proceedings of the Fifth Conference on Language Resources and Evaluation*, pages 449–454.

Mariano Felice, Zheng Yuan, Øistein E. Andersen, Helen Yannakoudakis, and Ekaterina Kochmar. 2014. Grammatical error correction using hybrid systems and type filtering. In *Proceedings of the Eighteenth Conference on Computational Natural Language Learning: Shared Task.*

Michael Gamon. 2010. Using mostly native data to correct errors in learners' writing: A meta-classifier approach. In *Proceedings of the Annual Meeting of the North American Chapter of the Association for Computational Linguistics*, pages 163–171.

Na-Rae Han, Martin Chodorow, and Claudia Leacock. 2006. Detecting errors in English article usage by non-native speakers. *Natural Language Engineering*, 12(2):115–129.

S. David Hernandez and Hiram Calvo. 2014. CoNLL 2014 shared task: Grammatical error correction with a syntactic n-gram language model from a big corpora. In *Proceedings of the Eighteenth Conference on Computational Natural Language Learning: Shared Task.*

Marcin Junczys-Dowmunt and Roman Grundkiewicz. 2014. The AMU system in the CoNLL-2014 shared task: Grammatical error correction by data-intensive and feature-rich statistical machine translation. In *Proceedings of the Eighteenth Conference on Computational Natural Language Learning: Shared Task.*

Dan Klein and Christopher D. Manning. 2003. Accurate unlexicalized parsing. In *Proceedings of the 41st Annual Meeting of the Association for Computational Linguistics*, pages 423–430.

Anoop Kunchukuttan, Sriram Chaudhury, and Pushpak Bhattacharyya. 2014. Tuning a grammar correction system for increased precision. In *Proceedings of the Eighteenth Conference on Computational Natural Language Learning: Shared Task.*

Claudia Leacock, Martin Chodorow, Michael Gamon, and Joel Tetreault. 2010. *Automated Grammatical Error Detection for Language Learners.* Morgan & Claypool Publishers.

Hwee Tou Ng, Siew Mei Wu, Yuanbin Wu, Christian Hadiwinoto, and Joel Tetreault. 2013. The CoNLL-2013 shared task on grammatical error correction. In *Proceedings of the Seventeenth Conference on Computational Natural Language Learning: Shared Task*, pages 1–12.

Diane Nicholls. 2003. The Cambridge Learner Corpus: Error coding and analysis for lexicography and ELT. In *Proceedings of the Corpus Linguistics 2003 Conference*, pages 572–581.

Alla Rozovskaya and Dan Roth. 2010. Generating confusion sets for context-sensitive error correction. In *Proceedings of the 2010 Conference on Empirical Methods in Natural Language Processing*, pages 961–970.

Alla Rozovskaya, Kai-Wei Chang, Mark Sammons, Dan Roth, and Nizar Habash. 2014. The Illinois-Columbia system in the CoNLL-2014 shared task. In *Proceedings of the Eighteenth Conference on Computational Natural Language Learning: Shared Task.*

Joel R. Tetreault and Martin Chodorow. 2008. Native judgments of non-native usage: Experiments in preposition error detection. In *COLING Workshop on Human Judgments in Computational Linguistics*, Manchester, UK.

Joel Tetreault, Jennifer Foster, and Martin Chodorow. 2010. Using parse features for preposition selection and error detection. In *Proceedings of the ACL 2010 Conference Short Papers*, pages 353–358.

Peilu Wang, Zhongye Jia, and Hai Zhao. 2014a. Grammatical error detection and correction using a single maximum entropy model. In *Proceedings of the Eighteenth Conference on Computational Natural Language Learning: Shared Task.*

Yiming Wang, Longyue Wang, Derek F. Wong, Lidia S. Chao, Xiaodong Zeng, and Yi Lu. 2014b. Factored statistical machine translation for grammatical error correction. In *Proceedings of the Eighteenth Conference on Computational Natural Language Learning: Shared Task.*

Yuanbin Wu and Hwee Tou Ng. 2013. Grammatical error correction using integer linear programming. In *Proceedings of the 51st Annual Meeting of the Association for Computational Linguistics*, pages 1456–1465.

Helen Yannakoudakis, Ted Briscoe, and Ben Medlock. 2011. A new dataset and method for automatically grading ESOL texts. In *Proceedings of the 49th Annual Meeting of the Association for Computational Linguistics*, pages 180–189.

Grammatical error correction using hybrid systems and type filtering

Mariano Felice **Zheng Yuan** **Øistein E. Andersen**
Helen Yannakoudakis **Ekaterina Kochmar**
Computer Laboratory, University of Cambridge, United Kingdom
{mf501,zy249,oa223,hy260,ek358}@cl.cam.ac.uk

Abstract

This paper describes our submission to the CoNLL 2014 shared task on grammatical error correction using a hybrid approach, which includes both a rule-based and an SMT system augmented by a large web-based language model. Furthermore, we demonstrate that correction type estimation can be used to remove unnecessary corrections, improving precision without harming recall. Our best hybrid system achieves state-of-the-art results, ranking first on the original test set and second on the test set with alternative annotations.

1 Introduction

Grammatical error correction has attracted considerable interest in the last few years, especially through a series of 'shared tasks'. These efforts have helped to provide a common ground for evaluating and comparing systems while encouraging research in the field. These shared tasks have primarily focused on English as a second or foreign language and addressed different error types. The HOO 2011 task (Dale and Kilgarriff, 2011), for example, included all error types whereas HOO 2012 (Dale et al., 2012) and the CoNLL 2013 shared task (Ng et al., 2013) were restricted to only two and five types respectively.

In this paper, we describe our submission to the CoNLL 2014 shared task (Ng et al., 2014), which involves correcting all the errors in essays written in English by students at the National University of Singapore. An all-type task poses a greater challenge, since correcting open-class types (such as spelling or collocation errors) requires different correction strategies than those in closed classes (such as determiners or prepositions).

In this scenario, hybrid systems or combinations of correction modules seem more appropriate and typically produce good results. In fact, most of the participating teams in previous shared tasks have used a combination of modules or systems for their submissions, even for correcting closed-class types (Dahlmeier et al., 2011; Bhaskar et al., 2011; Rozovskaya et al., 2011; Ivanova et al., 2011; Rozovskaya et al., 2013; Yoshimoto et al., 2013; Xing et al., 2013; Kunchukuttan et al., 2013; Putra and Szabo, 2013; Xiang et al., 2013).

In line with previous research, we present a hybrid approach that employs a rule-based error correction system and an ad-hoc statistical machine translation (SMT) system, as well as a large-scale language model to rank alternative corrections and an error type filtering technique.

The remainder of this paper is organised as follows: Section 2 describes our approach and each component in detail, Section 3 presents our experiments using the CoNLL 2014 shared task development set and Section 4 reports our official results on the test set. Finally, we discuss the performance of our system and present an error analysis in Section 5 and conclude in Section 6.

2 Approach

We tackle the error correction task using a pipeline of processes that combines results from multiple systems. Figure 1 shows the interaction of the components in our final hybrid system, producing the results submitted to the CoNLL 2014 shared task. The following sections describe each of these components in detail.

2.1 Rule-based error correction system (RBS)

The rule-based system is a component of the Self-Assessment and Tutoring (SAT) system, a web service developed at the University of Cambridge aimed at helping intermediate learners of English

Proceedings of the Eighteenth Conference on Computational Natural Language Learning: Shared Task, pages 15–24,
Baltimore, Maryland, 26-27 July 2014.

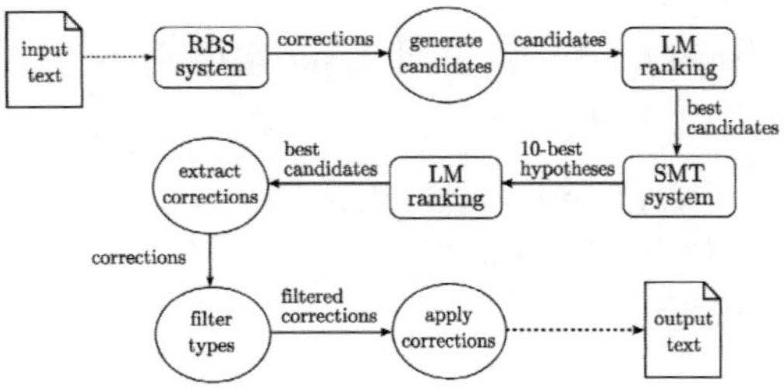

Figure 1: Overview of components and interactions in our final hybrid system.

in their writing tasks[1] (Andersen et al., 2013). The original SAT system provides three main functionalities: 1) *text assessment*, producing an overall score for a piece of text, 2) *sentence evaluation*, producing a sentence-level quality score, and 3) *word-level feedback*, suggesting specific corrections for frequent errors. Since the focus of the shared task is on strict correction (as opposed to detection), we only used the word-level feedback component of the SAT system.

This module uses rules automatically derived from the Cambridge Learner Corpus[2] (CLC) (Nicholls, 2003) that are aimed at detecting errorful unigrams, bigrams and trigrams. In order to ensure high precision, rules are based on n-grams that have been annotated as incorrect at least five times and at least ninety per cent of the times they occur. In addition to these corpus-derived rules, many cases of incorrect but plausible derivational and inflectional morphology are detected by means of rules derived from a machine-readable dictionary. For further details on specific components, we refer the reader to the aforementioned paper.

Given an input text, the rule-based system produces an XML file containing a list of suggested corrections. These corrections can either be applied to the original text or used to generate multiple correction candidates, as described in Section 2.3.

2.2 SMT system

We follow a similar approach to the one described by Yuan and Felice (2013) in order to train an SMT system that can 'translate' from incorrect into correct English. Our training data comprises a set of different parallel corpora, where the original (incorrect) sentences constitute the source side and corrected versions based on gold standard annotations constitute the target side. These corpora include:

- the NUCLE v3.1 corpus (Dahlmeier et al., 2013), containing around 1,400 essays written in English by students at the National University of Singapore (approx. 1,220,257 tokens in 57,152 sentences),
- phrase alignments involving corrections extracted automatically from the NUCLE corpus (with up to 7 tokens per side), which are used to boost the probability of phrase alignments that involve corrections so as to improve recall,
- the CoNLL 2014 shared task development set, containing 50 essays from the previous year's test set (approx. 29,207 tokens in 1,382 sentences),
- the First Certificate in English (FCE) corpus (Yannakoudakis et al., 2011), containing 1,244 exam scripts and 2 essays per script (approx. 532,033 tokens in 16,068 sentences),
- a subset of the International English Language Testing System (IELTS) examination dataset extracted from the CLC corpus, containing 2,498 exam scripts and 2 essays per script (approx. 1,361,841 tokens in 64,628 sentences), and
- a set of sentences from the English Vocabulary Profile[3] (EVP), which have been modified to include artificially generated errors (approx. 351,517 tokens in 18,830 sentences). The original correct sentences are a subset of the CLC and come from examinations at different proficiency levels. The artificial error generation method aims at replicating frequent error patterns observed in the NUCLE corpus on error-free sentences, as described by Yuan and Felice (2013).

[1]The latest version of the system, called 'Write & Improve', is available at http://www.cambridgeenglish.org/writeandimprovebeta/.

[2]More information at http://www.cambridge.org/elt/catalogue/subject/custom/item3646603/

[3]Sentences were automatically scraped from http://www.englishprofile.org/index.php?option=com_content&view=article&id=4&Itemid=5

Word alignment was carried out using pialign (Neubig et al., 2011), after we found it outperformed GIZA++ (Och and Ney, 2000; Och and Ney, 2003) and Berkeley Aligner (Liang et al., 2006; DeNero and Klein, 2007) in terms of precision and $F_{0.5}$ on the development set. Instead of using heuristics to extract phrases from the word alignments learnt by GIZA++ or Berkeley Aligner, pialign created a phrase table directly from model probabilities.

In addition to the features already defined by pialign, we added character-level Levenshtein distance to each mapping in the phrase table. This was done to allow for the fact that, in error correction, most words translate into themselves and errors are often similar to their correct forms. Equal weights were assigned to these features.

We then built a lexical reordering model using the alignments created by pialign. The maximum phrase length was set to 7, as recommended in the SMT literature (Koehn et al., 2003; Koehn, 2014).

The IRSTLM Toolkit (Federico et al., 2008) was used to build a 4-gram target language model with Kneser–Ney smoothing (Kneser and Ney, 1995) on the correct sentences from the NUCLE, full CLC and EVP corpora.

Decoding was performed with Moses (Koehn et al., 2007), using the default settings and weights. No tuning process was applied. The resulting system was used to produce the 10 best correction candidates for each sentence in the dataset, which were further processed by other modules.

Segmentation, tokenisation and part-of-speech tagging were performed using NLTK (Bird et al., 2009) for consistency with the shared task datasets.

2.3 Candidate generation

In order to integrate corrections from multiple systems, we developed a method to generate all the possible corrected versions of a sentence (*candidates*). Candidates are generated by computing all possible combinations of corrections (irrespective of the system from which they originate), including the original tokens to allow for a 'no correction' option. The list of candidates produced for each sentence always includes the original (unmodified) sentence plus any other versions derived from system corrections.

In order for a combination of corrections to generate a valid candidate, all the corrections must be *compatible*; otherwise, the candidate is discarded. We consider two or more corrections to be compatible if they do not overlap, in an attempt to avoid introducing accidental errors. In addition, if different correction sets produce the same candidate, we only keep one. Figure 2 illustrates the candidate generation process.

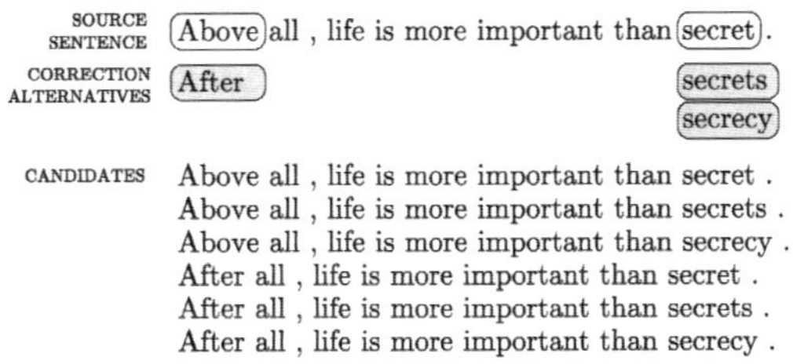

Figure 2: An example showing the candidate generation process.

Model	CE	ME	UE	P	R	$F_{0.5}$
SMT IRSTLM	651	2766	1832	0.2621	0.1905	0.2438
Microsoft Web N-grams	666	2751	1344	0.3313	0.1949	0.2907

Table 1: Performance of language models on the development set after ranking the SMT system's 10-best candidates per sentence. CE: correct edits, ME: missed edits, UE: unnecessary edits, P: precision, R: recall.

2.4 Language model ranking

Generated candidates are ranked using a language model (LM), with the most probable candidate being selected as the final corrected version.

We tried two different alternatives for ranking: 1) using the target LM embedded in our SMT system (described in Section 2.2) and 2) using a large n-gram LM built from web data. In the latter case, we used Microsoft Web N-gram Services, which provide access to large smoothed n-gram language models (with n=2,3,4,5) built from web documents (Gao et al., 2010). All our experiments are based on the 5-gram 'bing-body:apr10' model.

The ranking performance of these two models was evaluated on the 10-best hypotheses generated by the SMT system for each sentence in the development set. Table 1 shows the results from the M^2 Scorer (Dahlmeier and Ng, 2012), the official scorer for the shared task that, unlike previous versions, weights precision twice as much as recall.

Results show that using Microsoft's Web LM yields better performance, which is unsurprising given the vast amounts of data used to build that

System	CE	ME	UE	P	R	$F_{0.5}$
RBS	95	3322	107	0.4703	0.0278	0.1124
SMT	452	2965	690	0.3958	0.1323	0.2830

Table 2: Results of individual systems on the development set.

model. For this reason, we adopt Microsoft's model for all further experiments.

We also note that without normalisation, higher probabilities may be assigned to shorter sentences, which can introduce a bias towards preferring deletions or skipping insertions.

2.5 Type filtering

Analysing performance by error type is very valuable for system development and tuning. However, this can only be performed for corrections in the gold standard (either matched or missed). To estimate types for unnecessary corrections, we defined a set of heuristics that analyse differences in word forms and part-of-speech tags between the original phrases and their system corrections, based on common patterns observed in the training data. We had previously used a similar strategy to classify errors in our CoNLL 2013 shared task submission (Yuan and Felice, 2013) but have now included a few improvements and rules for new types. Estimation accuracy is 50.92% on the training set and 67.57% on the development set, which we consider to be acceptable for our purposes given that the final test set is more similar to the development set.

Identifying types for system corrections is not only useful during system development but can also be exploited to filter out and reduce the number of proposed corrections. More specifically, if a system proposes a much higher number of unnecessary corrections than correct suggestions for a specific error type, we can assume the system is actually degrading the quality of the original text, in which case it is preferable to filter out those error types. Such decisions will lower the total number of unnecessary edits, thus improving overall precision. However, they will also harm recall, unless the number of matched corrections for the error type is zero (i.e. unless $P_{type} = 0$). To avoid this, only corrections for types having zero precision should be removed.

3 Experiments and results

We carried out a series of experiments on the development set using different pipelines and combinations of systems in order to find an optimal setting. The following sections describe them in detail.

3.1 Individual system performance

Our first set of experiments were aimed at investigating individual system performance on the development set, which is reported in Table 2. Results show that the SMT system has much better performance, which is expected given that it has been trained on texts similar to those in the test set.

3.2 Pipelines

Since corrections from the RBS and SMT systems are often complementary, we set out to explore combination schemes that would integrate corrections from both systems. Table 3 shows results for different combinations, where RBS and SMT indicate all corrections from the respective systems, subscript 'c' indicates candidates generated from a system's individual corrections, subscript '10-best' indicates the 10-best list of candidates produced by the SMT system, '>' indicates a pipeline where the output of one system is the input to the other and '+' indicates a combination of candidates from different systems. All these pipelines use the RBS system as the first processing step in order to perform an initial correction, which is extremely beneficial for the SMT system.

Results reveal that the differences between these pipelines are small in terms of $F_{0.5}$, although there are noticeable variations in precision and recall. The best results are achieved when the 10 best hypotheses from the SMT system are ranked with Microsoft's LM, which confirms our results in Table 1 showing that the SMT LM is outperformed by a larger web-based model.

A simple pipeline using the RBS system first and the SMT system second (#3) yields performance that is better than (or comparable to) pipelines #1, #2 and #4, suggesting that there is no real benefit in using more sophisticated pipelines when only the best hypothesis from the SMT system is used. However, performance is improved when the 10 best SMT hypotheses are considered. The only difference between pipelines #5 and #6 lies in the way corrections from the RBS system

#	Pipeline	CE	ME	UE	P	R	$F_{0.5}$ ↑
1	RBS > SMT_c > LM	372	3045	481	0.4361	0.1088	0.2723
2	RBS_c + SMT_c > LM	400	3017	485	**0.4520**	0.1171	0.2875
3	RBS > SMT	476	2941	738	0.3921	0.1393	0.2877
4	RBS_c > LM > SMT	471	2946	718	0.3961	0.1378	0.2881
5	RBS > $SMT_{10\text{-best}}$ > LM	678	2739	1368	0.3314	0.1984	0.2922
6	RBS_c > LM > $SMT_{10\text{-best}}$ > LM	681	2736	1366	0.3327	**0.1993**	**0.2934**

Table 3: Results for different system pipelines on the development set.

System	CE	ME	UE	P	R	$F_{0.5}$
RBS_c > LM > $SMT_{10\text{-best}}$ > LM	681	2736	1366	0.3327	0.1993	0.2934
RBS_c > LM > $SMT_{10\text{-best}}$ > LM > Filter	681	2736	1350	**0.3353**	**0.1993**	**0.2950**

Table 4: Results for individual systems on the development set.

are handled. In the first case, all corrections are applied at once whereas in the second, the suggested corrections are used to generate candidates that are subsequently ranked by our LM, often discarding some of the suggested corrections.

3.3 Filtering

As described in Section 2.5, we can evaluate performance by error type in order to identify and remove unnecessary corrections. In particular, we tried to optimise our best hybrid system (#6) by filtering out types with zero precision. Table 5 shows type-specific performance for this system, where three zero-precision types can be identified: *Reordering* (a subset of *Others* that we treat separately), *Srun* (run-ons/comma splices) and *Wa* (acronyms). Although reordering was explicitly disabled in our SMT system, a translation table can still include this type of mappings if they are observed in the training data (e.g. 'you also can' → 'you can also').

In order to remove such undesired corrections, the following procedure was applied: first, individual corrections were extracted by comparing the original and corrected sentences; second, the type of each extracted correction was predicted, subsequently deleting those that matched unwanted types (i.e. reordering, Srun or Wa); finally, the set of remaining corrections was applied to the original text. This method improves precision while preserving recall (see Table 4), although the resulting improvement is not statistically significant (paired t-test, $p > 0.05$).

4 Official evaluation results

Our submission to the CoNLL 2014 shared task is the result of our best hybrid system, described in the previous section and summarised in Figure 1. The official test set comprised 50 new essays (approx. 30,144 tokens in 1,312 sentences) written in response to two prompts, one of which was also included in the training data.

Systems were evaluated using the M^2 Scorer, which uses $F_{0.5}$ as its overall measure. As in previous years, there were two evaluation rounds. The first one was based on the original gold-standard annotations provided by the shared-task organisers whereas the second was based on a revised version including alternative annotations submitted by the participating teams. Our submitted system achieved the first and second place respectively. The official results of our submission in both evaluation rounds are reported in Table 6.

5 Discussion and error analysis

In order to assess how our system performed per error type on the test set, we ran our type estimation script and obtained the results shown in Table 7. Although these results are estimated and therefore not completely accurate,[4] they can still provide valuable insights, at least at a coarse level. The following sections discuss our main findings.

5.1 Type performance

According to Table 7, our system achieves the best performance for types *WOadv* (adverb/adjective position) and *Wtone* (tone), but these results are

[4]Estimation accuracy was found to be 57.90% on the test set.

Error type	CE	ME	UE	P	R	$F_{0.5}$
ArtOrDet	222	465	225	0.4966	0.3231	0.4485
Cit	0	6	0	–	0.0000	–
Mec	31	151	15	0.6739	0.1703	0.4235
Nn	138	256	136	0.5036	0.3503	0.4631
Npos	4	25	45	0.0816	0.1379	0.0889
Others	1	34	12	0.0769	0.0286	0.0575
Pform	1	25	22	0.0435	0.0385	0.0424
Pref	1	38	5	0.1667	0.0256	0.0794
Prep	61	249	177	0.2563	0.1968	0.2417
Reordering	0	1	12	**0.0000**	0.0000	–
Rloc-	13	115	80	0.1398	0.1016	0.1300
SVA	32	86	25	0.5614	0.2712	0.4624
Sfrag	0	4	0	–	0.0000	–
Smod	0	16	0	–	0.0000	–
Spar	4	30	0	1.0000	0.1176	0.4000
Srun	0	55	28	**0.0000**	0.0000	–
Ssub	7	64	15	0.3182	0.0986	0.2201
Trans	13	128	36	0.2653	0.0922	0.1929
Um	0	34	0	–	0.0000	–
V0	2	16	3	0.4000	0.1111	0.2632
Vform	28	90	68	0.2917	0.2373	0.2789
Vm	9	86	41	0.1800	0.0947	0.1525
Vt	18	137	53	0.2535	0.1161	0.2050
WOadv	0	12	0	–	0.0000	–
WOinc	2	35	71	0.0274	0.0541	0.0304
Wa	0	5	2	**0.0000**	0.0000	–
Wci	28	400	241	0.1041	0.0654	0.0931
Wform	65	161	54	0.5462	0.2876	0.4630
Wtone	1	12	0	1.0000	0.0769	0.2941
TOTAL	681	2736	1366	0.3327	0.1993	0.2934

Table 5: Type-specific performance of our best hybrid system on the development set. Types with zero precision are marked in bold.

Test set	CE	ME	UE	P	R	$F_{0.5}$
Original	772	1793	1172	0.3971	0.3010	0.3733
Revised	913	1749	1042	0.4670	0.3430	0.4355

Table 6: Official results of our system on the original and revised test sets.

not truly representative as they only account for a small fraction of the test data (0.64% and 0.36% respectively).

The third best performing type is *Mec*, which comprises mechanical errors (such as punctuation, capitalisation and spelling mistakes) and represents 11.58% of the errors in the data. The remarkably high precision obtained for this error type suggests that our system is especially suitable for correcting such errors.

We also found that our system was particularly good at enforcing different types of agreement, as demonstrated by the results for SVA (subject–verb agreement), Pref (pronoun reference), Nn (noun number) and Vform (verb form) types, which add up to 22.80% of the errors. The following example shows a successful correction:

Error type	CE	ME	UE	P	R	$F_{0.5}$
ArtOrDet	185	192	206	0.4731	0.4907	0.4766
Mec	86	219	16	0.8431	0.2820	0.6031
Nn	122	106	143	0.4604	0.5351	0.4736
Npos	2	13	59	0.0328	0.1333	0.0386
Others	0	30	10	**0.0000**	0.0000	–
Pform	8	26	21	0.2759	0.2353	0.2667
Pref	19	77	12	0.6129	0.1979	0.4318
Prep	100	159	144	0.4098	0.3861	0.4049
Reordering	0	0	7	**0.0000**	–	–
Rloc-	23	89	116	0.1655	0.2054	0.1722
SVA	38	85	31	0.5507	0.3089	0.4762
Sfrag	0	4	0	–	0.0000	–
Smod	0	2	0	–	0.0000	–
Spar	0	10	0	–	0.0000	–
Srun	0	14	1	**0.0000**	0.0000	–
Ssub	8	39	19	0.2963	0.1702	0.2581
Trans	17	54	39	0.3036	0.2394	0.2881
Um	2	21	0	1.0000	0.0870	0.3226
V0	8	20	15	0.3478	0.2857	0.3333
Vform	31	93	46	0.4026	0.2500	0.3588
Vm	7	27	35	0.1667	0.2059	0.1733
Vt	26	108	40	0.3939	0.1940	0.3266
WOadv	10	11	0	1.0000	0.4762	0.8197
WOinc	1	33	37	0.0263	0.0294	0.0269
Wci	33	305	146	0.1844	0.0976	0.1565
Wform	42	49	29	0.5915	0.4615	0.5600
Wtone	4	7	0	1.0000	0.3636	0.7407
TOTAL	772	1793	1172	0.3971	0.3010	0.3733

Table 7: Type-specific performance of our submitted system on the original test set.

ORIGINAL SENTENCE:
He or she has *the right not to tell anyone .*

SYSTEM HYPOTHESIS:
They have *the right not to tell anyone .*

GOLD STANDARD:
They have *the right not to tell anyone .*

In other cases, our system seems to do a good job despite gold-standard annotations:

ORIGINAL SENTENCE:
This is because ***his or her*** *relatives have the right to know about this .*

SYSTEM HYPOTHESIS:
This is because ***their*** *relatives have the right to know about this .*

GOLD STANDARD:
This is because ***his or her*** *relatives have the right to know about this .* (unchanged)

The worst performance is observed for *Others* (including *Reordering*) and *Srun*, which only account for 1.69% of the errors. We also note that *Reordering* and *Srun* errors, which had explicitly been filtered out, still appear in our final results, which is due to differences in the edit extraction algorithms used by the M^2 Scorer and our own implementation. According to our estimations, our system has poor performance on the *Wci* type (the second most frequent), suggesting it is not very successful at correcting idioms and collocations.

Corrections for more complex error types such as *Um* (unclear meaning), which are beyond the scope of this shared task, are inevitably missed.

5.2 Deletions

We have also observed that many mismatches between our system's corrections and the gold standard are caused by unnecessary deletions, as in the following example:

ORIGINAL SENTENCE:
*I **could** understand the feeling of the carrier .*

SYSTEM HYPOTHESIS:
I understand the feeling of the carrier .

GOLD STANDARD:
*I **could** understand the feeling of the carrier .* (unchanged)

This effect is the result of using 10-best hypotheses from the SMT system together with LM ranking. Hypotheses from an SMT system can include many malformed sentences which are effectively discarded by the embedded target language model and additional heuristics. However, ranking these raw hypotheses with external systems can favour deletions, as language models will generally assign higher probabilities to shorter sentences. A common remedy for this is normalisation but we found it made no difference in our experiments.

In other cases, deletions can be ascribed to differences in the domain of the training and test sets, as observed in this example:

ORIGINAL SENTENCE:
*Nowadays , **social** media are able to disseminate information faster than any other media .*

SYSTEM HYPOTHESIS:
*Nowadays , **the** media are able to disseminate information faster than any other media .*

GOLD STANDARD:
*Nowadays , **social** media are able to disseminate information faster than any other media .* (unchanged)

5.3 Uncredited corrections

Our analysis also reveals a number of cases where the system introduces changes that are not included in the gold standard but we consider improve the quality of a sentence. For example:

ORIGINAL SENTENCE:
***Demon** is not easily to be defeated and it **is required much of** energy and psychological support .*

SYSTEM HYPOTHESIS:
***Demon** is not easily defeated and it **requires a lot of** energy and psychological support .*

GOLD STANDARD:
***The demon** is not easily defeated and it **requires much** energy and psychological support .*

Adding alternative corrections to the gold standard alleviates this problem, although the list of alternatives will inevitably be incomplete.

There are also a number of cases where the sentences are considered incorrect as part of a longer text but are acceptable when they are evaluated in isolation. Consider the following examples:

ORIGINAL SENTENCE:
*The opposite is **also** true .*

SYSTEM HYPOTHESIS:
The opposite is true .

GOLD STANDARD:
*The opposite is **also** true .* (unchanged)

ORIGINAL SENTENCE:
***It has** erased the boundaries of distance and time .*

SYSTEM HYPOTHESIS:
***It has** erased the boundaries of distance and time .* (unchanged)

GOLD STANDARD:
***They have** erased the boundaries of distance and time .*

In both cases, system hypotheses are perfectly grammatical but they are considered incorrect when analysed in context. Such mismatch is the result of discrepancies between the annotation and evaluation criteria: while the gold standard is annotated taking discourse into account, system corrections are proposed in isolation, completely devoid of discursive context.

Finally, the inability of the M^2 Scorer to combine corrections from different annotators (as opposed to selecting only one annotator's corrections for the whole sentence) can also result in underestimations of performance. However, it is clear that exploring these combinations during evaluation is a challenging task itself.

6 Conclusions

We have presented a hybrid approach to error correction that combines a rule-based and an SMT error correction system. We have explored different combination strategies, including sequential pipelines, candidate generation and ranking. In addition, we have demonstrated that error type estimations can be used to filter out unnecessary corrections and improve precision without harming recall.

Results of our best hybrid system on the official CoNLL 2014 test set yield $F_{0.5}$=0.3733 for the original annotations and $F_{0.5}$=0.4355 for alternative corrections, placing our system in the first and second place respectively.

Error analysis reveals that our system is particularly good at correcting mechanical errors and agreement but is often penalised for unnecessary deletions. However, a thorough inspection shows that the system tends to produce very fluent sentences, even if they do not match gold standard annotations.

Acknowledgements

We would like to thank Marek Rei for his valuable feedback and suggestions as well as Cambridge English Language Assessment, a division of Cambridge Assessment, for supporting this research.

References

Øistein E. Andersen, Helen Yannakoudakis, Fiona Barker, and Tim Parish. 2013. Developing and testing a self-assessment and tutoring system. In *Proceedings of the Eighth Workshop on Innovative Use of NLP for Building Educational Applications*, BEA 2013, pages 32–41, Atlanta, GA, USA, June. Association for Computational Linguistics.

Pinaki Bhaskar, Aniruddha Ghosh, Santanu Pal, and Sivaji Bandyopadhyay. 2011. May I check the English of your paper!!! In *Proceedings of the Generation Challenges Session at the 13th European Workshop on Natural Language Generation*, pages 250–253, Nancy, France, September. Association for Computational Linguistics.

Steven Bird, Edward Loper, and Ewan Klein. 2009. *Natural Language Processing with Python*. O'Reilly Media Inc.

Daniel Dahlmeier and Hwee Tou Ng. 2012. Better evaluation for grammatical error correction. In *Proceedings of the 2012 Conference of the North American Chapter of the Association for Computational Linguistics: Human Language Technologies*, NAACL 2012, pages 568–572, Montreal, Canada.

Daniel Dahlmeier, Hwee Tou Ng, and Thanh Phu Tran. 2011. NUS at the HOO 2011 Pilot Shared Task. In *Proceedings of the Generation Challenges Session at the 13th European Workshop on Natural Language Generation*, pages 257–259, Nancy, France, September. Association for Computational Linguistics.

Daniel Dahlmeier, Hwee Tou Ng, and Siew Mei Wu. 2013. Building a Large Annotated Corpus of Learner English: The NUS Corpus of Learner English. In *Proceedings of the 8th Workshop on Innovative Use of NLP for Building Educational Applications*, BEA 2013, pages 22–31, Atlanta, Georgia, USA, June.

Robert Dale and Adam Kilgarriff. 2011. Helping Our Own: The HOO 2011 Pilot Shared Task. In *Proceedings of the Generation Challenges Session at the 13th European Workshop on Natural Language Generation*, pages 242–249, Nancy, France, September. Association for Computational Linguistics.

Robert Dale, Ilya Anisimoff, and George Narroway. 2012. HOO 2012: A Report on the Preposition and Determiner Error Correction Shared Task. In *Proceedings of the Seventh Workshop on Building Educational Applications Using NLP*, pages 54–62, Montréal, Canada, June. Association for Computational Linguistics.

John DeNero and Dan Klein. 2007. Tailoring word alignments to syntactic machine translation. In *Proceedings of the 45th Annual Meeting of the Association of Computational Linguistics*, pages 17–24, Prague, Czech Republic, June. Association for Computational Linguistics.

Marcello Federico, Nicola Bertoldi, and Mauro Cettolo. 2008. IRSTLM: an open source toolkit for handling large scale language models. In *Proceedings of the 9th Annual Conference of the International Speech Communication Association*, INTERSPEECH 2008, pages 1618–1621, Brisbane, Australia, September. ISCA.

Jianfeng Gao, Patrick Nguyen, Xiaolong Li, Chris Thrasher, Mu Li, and Kuansan Wang. 2010. A Comparative Study of Bing Web N-gram Language Models for Web Search and Natural Language Processing. In *Web N-gram Workshop, Workshop of the*

33rd Annual International ACM SIGIR Conference (SIGIR 2010), pages 16–21, Geneva, Switzerland, July.

Elitza Ivanova, Delphine Bernhard, and Cyril Grouin. 2011. Handling Outlandish Occurrences: Using Rules and Lexicons for Correcting NLP Articles. In *Proceedings of the Generation Challenges Session at the 13th European Workshop on Natural Language Generation*, pages 254–256, Nancy, France, September. Association for Computational Linguistics.

Reinhard Kneser and Hermann Ney. 1995. Improved backing-off for m-gram language modeling. In *Proceedings of the IEEE International Conference on Acoustics, Speech and Signal Processing*, volume I, pages 181–184, Detroit, Michigan, May.

Philipp Koehn, Franz Josef Och, and Daniel Marcu. 2003. Statistical phrase-based translation. In *Proceedings of the 2003 Conference of the North American Chapter of the Association for Computational Linguistics on Human Language Technology*, volume 1 of *NAACL '03*, pages 48–54, Edmonton, Canada. Association for Computational Linguistics.

Philipp Koehn, Hieu Hoang, Alexandra Birch, Chris Callison-Burch, Marcello Federico, Nicola Bertoldi, Brooke Cowan, Wade Shen, Christine Moran, Richard Zens, Chris Dyer, Ondřej Bojar, Alexandra Constantin, and Evan Herbst. 2007. Moses: open source toolkit for statistical machine translation. In *Proceedings of the 45th Annual Meeting of the ACL on Interactive Poster and Demonstration Sessions*, ACL '07, pages 177–180, Prague, Czech Republic. Association for Computational Linguistics.

Philipp Koehn, 2014. *Moses: Statistical Machine Translation System – User Manual and Code Guide*. University of Edinburgh, April. Available online at `http://www.statmt.org/moses/manual/manual.pdf`.

Anoop Kunchukuttan, Ritesh Shah, and Pushpak Bhattacharyya. 2013. IITB System for CoNLL 2013 Shared Task: A Hybrid Approach to Grammatical Error Correction. In *Proceedings of the Seventeenth Conference on Computational Natural Language Learning: Shared Task*, pages 82–87, Sofia, Bulgaria, August. Association for Computational Linguistics.

Percy Liang, Ben Taskar, and Dan Klein. 2006. Alignment by agreement. In *Proceedings of the Human Language Technology Conference of the NAACL, Main Conference*, pages 104–111, New York City, USA, June. Association for Computational Linguistics.

Graham Neubig, Taro Watanabe, Eiichiro Sumita, Shinsuke Mori, and Tatsuya Kawahara. 2011. An unsupervised model for joint phrase alignment and extraction. In *Proceedings of the 49th Annual Meeting of the Association for Computational Linguistics: Human Language Technologies*, pages 632–641, Portland, Oregon, USA, June. Association for Computational Linguistics.

Hwee Tou Ng, Siew Mei Wu, Yuanbin Wu, Christian Hadiwinoto, and Joel Tetreault. 2013. The CoNLL-2013 Shared Task on Grammatical Error Correction. In *Proceedings of the Seventeenth Conference on Computational Natural Language Learning: Shared Task*, pages 1–12, Sofia, Bulgaria, August. Association for Computational Linguistics.

Hwee Tou Ng, Siew Mei Wu, Ted Briscoe, Christian Hadiwinoto, Raymond Hendy Susanto, and Christopher Bryant. 2014. The CoNLL-2014 Shared Task on Grammatical Error Correction. In *Proceedings of the Eighteenth Conference on Computational Natural Language Learning: Shared Task (CoNLL-2014 Shared Task)*, Baltimore, Maryland, USA, June. Association for Computational Linguistics. To appear.

Diane Nicholls. 2003. The Cambridge Learner Corpus: Error coding and analysis for lexicography and ELT. In Dawn Archer, Paul Rayson, Andrew Wilson, and Tony McEnery, editors, *Proceedings of the Corpus Linguistics 2003 conference*, pages 572–581, Lancaster, UK. University Centre for Computer Corpus Research on Language, Lancaster University.

Franz Josef Och and Hermann Ney. 2000. Improved statistical alignment models. In *Proceedings of the 38th Annual Meeting on Association for Computational Linguistics*, ACL '00, pages 440–447, Hong Kong, October. Association for Computational Linguistics.

Franz Josef Och and Hermann Ney. 2003. A systematic comparison of various statistical alignment models. *Comput. Linguist.*, 29(1):19–51, March.

Desmond Darma Putra and Lili Szabo. 2013. UdS at CoNLL 2013 Shared Task. In *Proceedings of the Seventeenth Conference on Computational Natural Language Learning: Shared Task*, pages 88–95, Sofia, Bulgaria, August. Association for Computational Linguistics.

Alla Rozovskaya, Mark Sammons, Joshua Gioja, and Dan Roth. 2011. University of Illinois System in HOO Text Correction Shared Task. In *Proceedings of the Generation Challenges Session at the 13th European Workshop on Natural Language Generation*, pages 263–266, Nancy, France, September. Association for Computational Linguistics.

Alla Rozovskaya, Kai-Wei Chang, Mark Sammons, and Dan Roth. 2013. The University of Illinois System in the CoNLL-2013 Shared Task. In *Proceedings of the Seventeenth Conference on Computational Natural Language Learning: Shared Task*, pages 13–19, Sofia, Bulgaria, August. Association for Computational Linguistics.

Yang Xiang, Bo Yuan, Yaoyun Zhang, Xiaolong Wang, Wen Zheng, and Chongqiang Wei. 2013. A hybrid model for grammatical error correction. In *Proceedings of the Seventeenth Conference on Computational Natural Language Learning: Shared Task*, pages 115–122, Sofia, Bulgaria, August. Association for Computational Linguistics.

Junwen Xing, Longyue Wang, Derek F. Wong, Lidia S. Chao, and Xiaodong Zeng. 2013. UM-Checker: A Hybrid System for English Grammatical Error Correction. In *Proceedings of the Seventeenth Conference on Computational Natural Language Learning: Shared Task*, pages 34–42, Sofia, Bulgaria, August. Association for Computational Linguistics.

Helen Yannakoudakis, Ted Briscoe, and Ben Medlock. 2011. A new dataset and method for automatically grading esol texts. In *Proceedings of the 49th Annual Meeting of the Association for Computational Linguistics: Human Language Technologies*, pages 180–189, Portland, Oregon, USA, June. Association for Computational Linguistics.

Ippei Yoshimoto, Tomoya Kose, Kensuke Mitsuzawa, Keisuke Sakaguchi, Tomoya Mizumoto, Yuta Hayashibe, Mamoru Komachi, and Yuji Matsumoto. 2013. NAIST at 2013 CoNLL Grammatical Error Correction Shared Task. In *Proceedings of the Seventeenth Conference on Computational Natural Language Learning: Shared Task*, pages 26–33, Sofia, Bulgaria, August. Association for Computational Linguistics.

Zheng Yuan and Mariano Felice. 2013. Constrained grammatical error correction using statistical machine translation. In *Proceedings of the Seventeenth Conference on Computational Natural Language Learning: Shared Task*, pages 52–61, Sofia, Bulgaria, August. Association for Computational Linguistics.

The AMU System in the CoNLL-2014 Shared Task: Grammatical Error Correction by Data-Intensive and Feature-Rich Statistical Machine Translation

Marcin Junczys-Dowmunt **Roman Grundkiewicz**
Information Systems Laboratory
Adam Mickiewicz University
ul. Umultowska 87, 61-614 Poznań, Poland
{junczys,romang}@amu.edu.pl

Abstract

Statistical machine translation toolkits like Moses have not been designed with grammatical error correction in mind. In order to achieve competitive results in this area, it is not enough to simply add more data. Optimization procedures need to be customized, task-specific features should be introduced. Only then can the decoder take advantage of relevant data.

We demonstrate the validity of the above claims by combining web-scale language models and large-scale error-corrected texts with parameter tuning according to the task metric and correction-specific features. Our system achieves a result of 35.0% $F_{0.5}$ on the blind CoNLL-2014 test set, ranking on third place. A similar system, equipped with identical models but without tuned parameters and specialized features, stagnates at 25.4%.

1 Introduction

There has been an increasing interest in using statistical machine translation (SMT) for the task of grammatical error correction. Among the 16 teams that took part in the CoNLL-2013 Shared Task (Ng et al., 2013), four teams described approaches that fully or partially used SMT in their system. While in the previous year the correction task was restricted to just five error types, the CoNLL-2014 Shared Task (Ng et al., 2014) now requires a participating system to correct all 28 error types present in NUCLE (Dahlmeier et al., 2013). Since the high number of error types has made it harder to target each error category with dedicated components, SMT with its ability to learn generic text transformations is now an even more appealing approach.

With out-of-the-box machine translation toolkits like Moses (Koehn et al., 2007) being freely available, the application of SMT to grammatical error correction seems straightforward. However, Moses has not been designed as a grammar correction system, the standard features and optimization methods are geared towards translation performance measured by the metrics used in the SMT field. Training Moses on data that is relevant for grammatical error correction is a step in the right direction, but data alone is not enough. The decoder needs to be able to judge the data based on relevant features, parameter optimization needs to be performed according to relevant metrics.

This paper constitutes the description of the Adam Mickiewicz University (AMU) submission to the CoNLL-2014 Shared Task on Grammatical Error Correction. We explore the interaction of large-scale data, parameter optimization, and task-specific features in a Moses-based system. Related work is presented in the next section, the system setup is shortly described in Section 3. Sections 4 to 7 contain our main contributions.

In Section 4, we describe our implementation of feature weights tuning according to the MaxMatch (M^2) metric by Dahlmeier and Ng (2012b) which is the evaluation metric of the current CoNLL-2014 Shared Task. Sections 5 and 6 deal with the data-intensive aspects of our paper. We start by extending the baseline system with a Wikipedia-based language model and finish with a web-scale language model estimated from CommonCrawl data. Uncorrected/corrected data from the social language learner's platform Lang-8 is used to extend the translation models of our system.

Task-specific dense and sparse features are introduced in Section 7. These features are meant to raise the "awareness" of the decoder for grammatical error correction. In Section 8, we discuss the results of our submission and several intermediate systems on the blind CoNLL-2014 test set.

Proceedings of the Eighteenth Conference on Computational Natural Language Learning: Shared Task, pages 25–33,
Baltimore, Maryland, 26-27 July 2014.

2 Related Work

Brockett et al. (2006) use SMT to correct countability errors for a set of 14 mass nouns that pose problems to Chinese ESL learners. For this very restricted task they achieve a results of 61.81% corrected mistakes. This work mentions minimum error rate tuning according to BLEU.

A Moses-based system is described by Mizumoto et al. (2011) who correct grammatical errors of learners of Japanese. This work is continued for English in Mizumoto et al. (2012). The effect of learner corpus size on various types of grammatical errors is investigated. The additional large-scale data originates from the social learner's platform Lang-8. We use similar resources.

Very interesting work is presented by Dahlmeier and Ng (2012a). A custom beam-search decoder for grammatical error correction is introduced that incorporates discriminative classifiers for specific error categories such as articles and prepositions. The authors perform parameter tuning and find PRO to work better with M^2_1 than MERT[1]. The specialized decoder tuned with M^2_1 is compared to Moses that has been tuned with BLEU. As we show in Section 4.2, this cannot be a fair comparison.

The CoNLL-2013 Shared Task (Ng et al., 2013) saw a number of systems based entirely or partially on translation approaches. Most notable are Yuan and Felice (2013) and Yoshimoto et al. (2013). Yuan and Felice (2013) apply Moses to all five error types of the shared task and extend the provided training data by adding other learner's corpora. They also experiment with generating artificial errors. Improvement over the baseline are small, but their approach to generate errors shows promise. We successfully re-implement their baseline. Yoshimoto et al. (2013) use Moses for two error classes, prepositions and determiners, for other classes they find classifier-based approaches and treelet language models to perform better. None of the CoNLL-2013 SMT-based systems seems to use parameter tuning.

3 General System Setup

Our system is based on the phrase-based part of the statistical machine translation system Moses (Koehn et al., 2007). Only plain text data is used for language model and translation model training. External linguistic knowledge is introduced during parameter tuning as the tuning metric relies on the error annotation present in NUCLE. Phrase tables are binarized with the compact phrase table (Junczys-Dowmunt, 2012), no reordering models are used, the distortion limit is set to 0, effectively prohibiting any reordering. Apart from that, our basic setup is very similar to that of Yuan and Felice (2013). We adapted their 4-fold cross validation scheme on NUCLE to our needs and use a similar baseline, now with 28 error types.

4 Parameter Tuning

The training of feature functions like translation models or language models is only half the work required to produce a state-of-the-art statistical machine translation system. The other half relies on parameter tuning.

During translation, Moses scores translations e of string f by a log-linear model

$$\log p(e|f) = \sum_i \lambda_i \log(h_i(e, f))$$

where h_i are feature functions and λ_i are feature weights. Without parameter tuning, results may be questionable as the choice of feature function weights (everything else being identical) can turn a mediocre system into a high-scoring system or render a good system useless. This is illustrated in Section 4.2 and by examples throughout the paper.

All our modifications to MERT, PRO, kb-MIRA discussed in this section are publicly available[2].

4.1 Tuning Scheme

To accommodate for parameter tuning, we modify the standard 4-fold cross validation procedure. The test set in each of the four training/testing runs is again divided into two halves. The first half is treated as a tuning set, the second half as a test set. Next, tuning set and test set are inverted in order to tune and test a second time. Altogether, we perform four separate translation model training steps and eight tuning/testing steps. Each tuning/test set consists of ca. 7,000 sentences. We call this procedure 4×2-fold cross validation (4×2-CV). This way the entire NUCLE corpus serves as training, test, and tuning set. We also evaluate all our results on the CoNLL-2013 gold standard (ST-2013) which has been made available with 28 error types after the previous shared task.

[1] This is different from our findings for Moses, but may be a property of their custom decoder.

[2] `https://github.com/moses-smt/mosesdecoder/fscorer`

Tuned with	4×2-CV BLEU	4×2-CV $M^2_{0.5}$	ST-2013 BLEU	ST-2013 $M^2_{0.5}$
Untuned	85.52	14.02	70.38	19.05
BLEU	88.31	1.27	72.62	1.12
$M^2_{0.5}$	87.76	15.43	71.99	16.73
Original	89.51	0.00	72.67	0.00

Table 1: Tuning with BLEU and M^2

System	Concat.	Average
NUCLE	15.16	15.43
NUCLE+CCLM	22.03	22.19
Final	25.93	26.26

Table 2: Effects of parameter weight smoothing on three selected systems for 4×2-CV (CoNLL-2014)

4.2 Tuning Metric

We refer to $F_{0.5}$ computed by the M^2 metric as $M^2_{0.5}$. Moses is bundled with several tuning tools that can tune parameter vectors according to different MT tuning metrics. The most widely used is BLEU (Papineni et al., 2002). We first attempt minimum error rate tuning (MERT) (Och, 2003) with BLEU, results are shown in Table 1. While BLEU scores increase on both, 4×2-CV and ST-2013, the effect on $M^2_{0.5}$ is catastrophic[3] though not surprising. The baseline is so weak that it introduces more errors than corrections, thus lowering the similarity of the output and the reference below the level of the similarity of the input and the reference. MERT learns parameter weights that disable nearly all correction attempts.

The obvious solution is to tune directly with M^2. M^2 provides per-sentence sufficient statistics and can easily[4] be integrated with MERT. We re-tune with M^2 and see an improvement on 4×2-CV but a significant decrease for ST-2013. BLEU increases for this system despite the drop in M^2.

This seems contradictory, but actually proves our point about the necessity of parameter tuning. Good luck should not be a basis for choosing parameters, in the case of a blind submission we have a much better chance to reach good results betting on optimized parameters. As we see later, this situation does not occur again for the more advanced systems, tuned parameters do generally better.

4.3 Parameter Smoothing

Based on the results of Clark et al. (2011), it has become good practice to tune systems between three and five times and report average results in order to cope with optimizer instability. Cettolo et al. (2011) expand on this work and explore parameter smoothing methods for different parameter vectors obtained on the same tuning sets. They report that parameter vector centroids averaged over several tuning runs yield better than average results and reduce variation. Tuning three to five times would require 24 to 40 tuning runs in our setup. However, we already have eight parameter vectors obtained from distinct tuning sets and decide to average these parameters. This way we hope to obtain a single vector of smoothed parameters that represents the entire NUCLE corpus.

Eventually, we retranslate the test sets according to 4-fold cross validation using the respective training data with this parameter vector. The same parameters are later used with the full training data to translate the CoNLL-2013 test set and the blind CoNLL-2014 test set. As it turns out, averaging parameter vectors across all parts has a consistently positive effect for M^2. This is shown in Table 2, systems mentioned in the table are introduced in Section 5 and Section 7.2.

4.4 Tuning Sparse Feature Weights

Tuning sparse features (Section 7.2) with M^2 poses an unexpected challenge. Moses implements two methods for feature-rich tuning: PRO (Hopkins and May, 2011) and Batch k-best MIRA (kb-MIRA) (Cherry and Foster, 2012) that both function as drop-in replacements for MERT. MERT cannot be used directly with sparse features. When BLEU is used as a tuning metric, Koehn and Haddow (2012) report results for PRO on a par with MERT for a system with only dense features. Unfortunately, this cannot be confirmed for M^2; we consistently see worse results than for MERT using PRO or kb-MIRA.

PRO and kb-MIRA operate on sentence-level while MERT computes M^2 for the complete corpus. Similar to Dahlmeier and Ng (2012a), we use sentence-level M^2 as an approximation. We suspect that M^2 might not be distinctive enough in a

[3]Which might explain why none of the Moses-based CoNLL-2013 systems used parameter tuning.

[4]We run the original m2scorer Python code with an embedded Python interpreter in MERT's C++ source code.

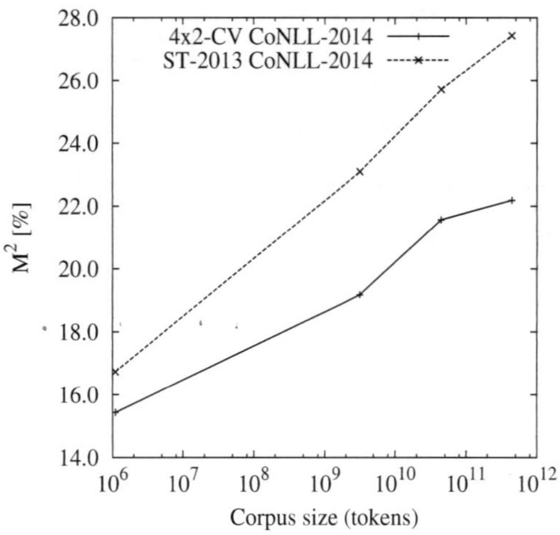

Figure 1: Language model corpus size versus M^2

sentence-based scenario.

Koehn and Haddow (2012) also explore a method they call "PRO-MERT" where PRO and MERT are run in turns. The parameter vector calculated by PRO serves as a starting point for MERT which optimizes dense features and in the case of existing sparse features a scalar weight that is multiplied with all sparse feature weights.

While this method does not seem to have any advantage for BLEU-based tuning in a MT setting it has a positive effect on tuning with M^2. Results for sparse features are now not worse than when tuned with MERT alone in a dense feature scenario. Additionally to "PRO-MERT", we implemented "kb-MIRA-MERT" which seems to display better convergence. As in the case of dense feature functions, we smooth sparse feature weights by averaging over all eight tuning steps.

All reported results in this paper have been tuned according to $M^2_{0.5}$, systems with dense features use MERT, systems with sparse features kb-MIRA-MERT. All results are given for parameter vectors that have been smoothed over eight optimizer runs from 4×2-CV.

5 Adding Language Model Data

With parameter tuning working, we can now explore the effects of adding feature functions to our system, starting with bigger language models.

All systems use one 5-gram language model that has been estimated from the target side of the parallel data available for training. In this section, only NUCLE is used as parallel data, four times 3/4 of NUCLE for 4×2-CV and complete NUCLE for ST-2013. If additional parallel data is added to the training process (see Section 6), the target data is concatenated with NUCLE and a new 5-gram language model is estimated.

System	4×2-CV	ST-2013
NUCLE	15.43	16.73
+WikiLM	19.18	23.10
+CCLM$_{10\%}$	21.57	25.71
+CCLM	22.19	27.43

Table 3: Results for increasing language models size on both shared task scenarios

The additional language models discussed in this section form separate feature functions, i.e. they are weighted separately from the target data language model. We experiment with three models that have been estimated using KenLM's (Heafield, 2011) modified Kneser-Ney estimation tool (Heafield et al., 2013):

WikiLM – a 3-gram model estimated from the entire English Wikipedia (2014-01-02). The raw text corpus consists of 3.2×10^9 tokens.

CCLM$_{10\%}$ – a 3-gram model estimated from 10% of the English CommonCrawl data (4.4×10^{10} tokens) described by Buck et al. (2014). The full corpus data has been made publicly available by the authors.

CCLM – a 5-gram model estimated from the entire CommonCrawl data (4.4×10^{11} tokens). This model has been created and made available to us by Kenneth Heafield. A newer version is publicly available (Buck et al., 2014).

Results are shown in Table 3. Improvements seem to be proportionate to the order of magnitude of the language model training corpora (Figure 1). $M^2_{0.5}$ improves by nearly 7% for 4×2-CV and by more than 10% on ST-2013.

6 Adding Translation Model Data

SMT systems for grammatical error correction can be trained on unannotated data. For the 28 error-type task from CoNLL-2014, we do not need the linguistically rich error annotations present in NUCLE to add more training data. It suffices to have parallel data in which the source text contains errors and the target text has been corrected. For English, such data is available.

System	4×2-CV	ST-2013
NUCLE+CCLM	22.19	27.43
+L8-NAIST	23.34	31.20
+L8	25.02	33.52
NUCLE+CCLM	17.50	29.01
+L8-NAIST	14.54	30.84
+L8	17.48	30.14

Table 4: Adding parallel data from Lang-8. Top results are for tuned systems, bottom results for untuned systems.

6.1 Lang-8

Mizumoto et al. (2011) published[5] a list of learner's corpora that were scraped from the social language learning site Lang-8 (`http://lang-8.com`). For our first experiments we use entries from "Lang-8 Learner Corpora v1.0" with English as the learned language, we do not care for the native language of the user. Only entries for which at least one sentence has been corrected are taken into account. Sentences without corrections from such entries are treated as error-free and mirrored on the target side of the corpus. Eventually, we obtain a corpus of 2,567,969 sentence pairs with 28,506,540 tokens on the uncorrected source side. No noise-filtering is applied. We call this resource L8-NAIST. Yoshimoto et al. (2013) use this resource for sub-elements of their system at the CoNLL-2013 Shared Task, but end up with half the number of sentences. This seems to be caused by noise-reduction.

We further investigate the effect of adding even greater parallel resources. Lang-8 is scraped for additional entries and we manage to nearly double the size of the corpus to 3,733,116 sentences with 51,259,679 tokens on the source side. This joint resource is labeled L8.

During training, the additional data is concatenated with all training corpora in our setup (3/4 of NUCLE for 4×2-CV and all of NUCLE for the final system).

Results are presented in Table 4. We extend the previous best system NUCLE+CCLM with L8-NAIST and L8. For tuned systems (top), results improve for both evaluation settings with growing corpus size. In the case of untuned systems (bottom) results are entirely inconclusive.

[5] `http://cl.naist.jp/nldata/lang-8`

6.2 Error Selection

Yuan and Felice (2013) generate artificial errors to add more training data to their system. We prefer actual errors, but the Lang-8 data may be too error-prone as the general level of proficiency seems to be lower than that of the NUCLE essays. We therefore select errors that match NUCLE error types and replace all other errors with their corresponding corrections.

For each pair of sentences, a sequence of deletions and insertions is computed with the LCS algorithm (Maier, 1978) that transform the source sentence into the target sentence. Adjacent deleted words are concatenated, adjacent inserted words result in a phrase insertion. A deleted phrase followed directly by a phrase insertion is interpreted as a phrase substitution. Substitutions are generalized if they consist of common substrings. Generalizations are encoded by the regular expression `(\w{3,})` and a back-reference, e.g. `\1`. Table 5 contains the 20 most frequent patterns extracted from NUCLE, 666 patterns with a frequency of five or higher remain. Next, we perform the same computation for the to-be-adapted data. Edits that match patterns from our list are kept, other edits are replaced with their corrections.

Although results (Table 6) with error selection increase for 4×2-CV, the NUCLE+CCLM+L8A seems to generalize poorly to new data, there is a significant drop for the external test set. Compared to NUCLE+CCLM+L8 (prec.: 59.80, rec.: 15.95) the error adapted (prec.: 70.07, rec.: 8.52) is much more conservative.

Inspired by this, we also try a combination (NUCLE+CCLM+L8AT as in Adapted Tuning) of both systems by tuning with the adapted NUCLE+CCLM+L8A, but applying the weights to the unadapted system NUCLE+CCLM+L8. This results in a gain of 5% for ST-2013. It seems that the unadapted Lang8 data introduces a substantial amount of noise that interferes with the tuning process. Weights obtained from the cleaned data seem to better approximate the true weight vector and also work with unadapted data without sacrificing recall. In the remainder of the paper we use this training/tuning scheme for all newly introduced systems.

7 Task-Specific Features

The systems presented so far relied on default features available in Moses. In this section we will

Pattern	Freq.	Pattern	Freq.
`sub(«(\w{3,})»,«\1s»)`	2441	`ins(«an»)`	222
`ins(«the»)`	2364	`sub(«(\w{3,})d»,«\1»)`	181
`del(«the»)`	1624	`del(«of»)`	178
`sub(«(\w{3,})s»,«\1»)`	1110	`sub(«is»,«are»)`	166
`ins(«,»)`	961	`ins(«of»)`	166
`ins(«a»)`	663	`del(«a»)`	160
`sub(«(\w{3,})»,«\1d»)`	253	`sub(«(\w{3,})y»,«\1ies»)`	150
`del(«,»)`	244	`ins(«to»)`	148
`del(«.»)`	227	`sub(«is»,«was»)`	147
`sub(«(\w{3,})»,«\1ed»)`	222	`sub(«the»,«a»)`	132

Table 5: 20 most frequent patterns extracted from NUCLE 3.0

System	4×2-CV	ST-2013
NUCLE+CCLM+L8	25.02	33.52
NUCLE+CCLM+L8A	26.82	28.67
NUCLE+CCLM+L8AT	26.82	38.59

Table 6: Results of error selection

Source (s)	Target (t)	$e^{d(s,t)}$
a short time .	short term only .	20.0855
a situation	into a situation	2.7183
a supermarket .	a supermarket .	1.0000
able	unable	2.7183

Table 7: Dense Levenshtein feature examples.

extend the translation model with features tailored to the task of grammatical error correction.

7.1 Dense Features

In Moses, translation models are described by a set of dense features: phrase translation probabilities, lexical scores, and a phrase penalty (Koehn et al., 2003). In the grammatical error correction scenario where source and target phrases are often identical or similar, it might be useful to inform the decoder about the differences in a phrase pair.

We extend translation models with a word-based Levenshtein distance feature (Levenshtein, 1966) that captures the number of edit operations required to turn the source phrase into the target phrase. Each phrase pair in the phrase table is scored with $e^{d(s,t)}$ where d is the word-based distance function, s is the source phrase, t is the target phrase. The exponential function is used because Moses relies on a log-linear model. In the log-linear model, the edit distances of all phrase pairs used to translate a sentence sum to the total number of edits that have been applied to produce the target sentence. Note that the Lang-8 data has not been processed for noise-reduction, this feature should take care of the problem and penalize sentences that have diverged to much from the source. Table 7 contains examples of phrase pairs and their Levenshtein distance feature.

We extend the currently best system NUCLE+CCLM+L8AT with the Levenshtein distance feature. Results are shown in Table 8 (+LD). For 4×2-CV small improvements can be observed, the effect is more significant for ST-2013. It can be concluded that this very simple modification of the standard translation model is a beneficial extension of SMT for grammatical correction.

7.2 Sparse Features

Sparse features are a relatively new addition to Moses (Hasler et al., 2012). Unlike dense features, they are optional and unrestricted in number, thousands of different sparse features may be used. A verbose version of the above mentioned LD feature is implemented as a sparse feature. Each edit operation is annotated with the operation type and the words that take part in the operation. The decoder can now learn to favor or penalize specific edits during tuning. As before in the case of error adaption patterns from Section 6.2, we generalize substitution operations if common substrings of a length equal to or greater than three characters appear in corresponding source and target phrases. In the end,

System	4×2-CV	ST-2013
NUCLE+CCLM+L8AT	26.82	38.59
+LD	27.34	40.21
+SF	**27.58**	**40.60**

Table 8: Results for dense Levenshtein distance (LD) and sparse pattern features (SF). Each component extends the previous system cumulatively.

we obtain sparse features that look exactly like these patterns. Features that correspond to patterns that had a frequency below 5 in NUCLE are mapped to `del(OTHER)`, `ins(OTHER)`, and `sub(OTHER1,OTHER2)`. Contrary to the Levenshtein distance feature, the sparse features are computed during decoding.

Sparse features are added to the system which has already been extended with the dense Levenshtein feature. Results in Table 8 (+SF) show small, but consistent gains. LD and SF are linearly dependent as the total sum of triggered sparse features should be equal to the value of LD for a sentence, but we still observe positive effects. Sparse feature tuning is currently a work-around with dubious effects, it can be expected that results might be more significant once this problem is solved. Based on these results, we choose the last system NUCLE+CCLM+L8AT+LD+SF as our final system for the CoNLL-2014 Shared Task.

8 Results for blind CoNLL-2014 test set

Our final system achieves an official result of 35.01% $M^2_{0,5}$ ("Submission" in Table 9) on the blind CoNLL-2014 Shared Task test set (ST-2014). Due to a tight time frame, this system suffered from missing words in an incorrectly filtered language model and too few tuning iterations. After the submission we retrained the same system and achieve a score of 35.38% $M^2_{0,5}$. Table 9 contains the results for incrementally added features, starting with the baseline, ending with the final system. The addition of a web-scale language model results in similar improvements as for 4×2-CV and ST-2013. Additional unadapted parallel training data from Lang-8 (+L8) has a very modest effect on ST-2014. This improves with the mixed tuning scheme (+L8AT) which shows that the gains for ST-2013 are not a one-time effect. Surprising are the substantial gains due to the dense Levenshtein feature and the sparse features.

System	P	R	$M^2_{0.5}$
Submission	**41.62**	**21.40**	**35.01**
NUCLE	49.85	5.19	18.32
+CCLM	50.39	9.90	27.72
+L8	37.67	14.07	28.21
+L8AT	37.02	17.94	30.53
+LD	39.41	22.15	34.10
+SF	**41.72**	**22.00**	**35.38**
NUCLE	36.59	9.96	23.84
+CCLM	27.92	18.68	25.41
+L8	25.06	26.75	25.38
+L8AT	24.49	34.89	26.04
+LD	25.94	36.41	27.52
+SF	25.94	36.41	27.52

Table 9: Performance of chosen systems on the CoNLL-2014 test set. Bottom results are untuned.

We suspect that the task-specific features allow the decoder to better exploit the potential of the Lang-8 data. This is verified by training NUCLE+CCLM+LD+SF which scores only 25.82%.

To support our claim concerning the importance of parameter tuning, we also provide the performance of the same systems on ST-2014 with standard parameters (bottom of Table 9). With one exception, we see significant improvements with tuning. The untuned systems display very similar results which would make it difficult to choose among the configurations (untuned +LD and +LD+SF are actually the same system). One might conclude incorrectly that the new features and additional resources have very little effect on the final results and miss a gain of ca. 8%.

Table 10 contains the ranking for all participating systems. Our system ranks on third place (see the Shared Task proceedings (Ng et al., 2014) for more information on the other systems), loosing by 2.32% and 1.78% against the first two teams. We win with a quite significant margin of 4.13% over the next best system. Compared to the top-two systems we suffer from lower recall, a problem which should be attacked in the future.

Participants were invited to submit alternative answers for evaluation, i.e. answers that were generated by their system and considered to be correct alternatives to the provided gold standard. These answers were checked by human annotators. Only three teams submitted alternative an-

Rank	Team ID	P	R	$M^2_{0.5}$
1	CAMB	39.71	30.10	37.33
2	CUUI	41.78	24.88	36.79
3	**AMU**	**41.62**	**21.40**	**35.01**
4	POST	34.51	21.73	30.88
5	NTHU	35.08	18.85	29.92
6	RAC	33.14	14.99	26.68
7	UMC	31.27	14.46	25.37
8	PKU	32.21	13.65	25.32
9	NARA	21.57	29.38	22.78
10	SJTU	30.11	5.10	15.19
11	UFC	70.00	1.72	7.84
12	IPN	11.28	2.85	7.09
13	IITB	30.77	1.39	5.90

Table 10: Shared Task results for submission without alternative answers. **AMU** is our result.

swers: CAMB, CUUI, and UMC. The results for all teams improved when evaluated on these additional answers, naturally those teams that submitted answers had the greatest gains. Our result with additional answers is 38.58%, we remain on third place after CUUI (45.57%) and CAMB (43.55%) which switched places. However, we do not consider the evaluation on alternative answers to be meaningful as it is strongly biased.[6]

9 Conclusions

We have shown that pure-surface phrase-based SMT can be used to achieve state-of-the-art results for grammatical error correction if sufficiently large resources are combined with correctly executed parameter tuning and task-specific features. For noisy data, it seems beneficial to tune on cleaned data, but noise can be useful when correcting unseen texts.

Most of the previous work that we reviewed lacked the detail of parameter tuning that is commonly applied in SMT. In consequence, potentially useful contributions rarely improved over the baselines or were beaten by classifier-based approaches. Many good features might have been overlooked or dismissed as unhelpful. Our findings invite to re-evaluate these previous results. The tools we extended for parameter tuning according to the M^2 metric are publicly available and we strongly suggest to use them in the future or to adapt them to the particular task at hand. Parameter tuning of sparse features according to the M^2 metric is ongoing research, but it seems the proposed work-around is a viable option.

Since it is quite simple to implement the task-specific features introduced in this paper, we recommend to use them whenever Moses is applied in a similar setting.

[6] We would accept alternative answers if all original system submissions were to be analyzed by annotators not associated with any team. If this is not possible due to considerable costs and efforts, we would advocate to abandon the current practice altogether.

References

Chris Brockett, William B. Dolan, and Michael Gamon. 2006. Correcting ESL errors using phrasal SMT techniques. In *Proceedings of the 21st International Conference on Computational Linguistics and the 44th Annual Meeting of the Association for Computational Linguistics*, pages 249–256, Stroudsburg, USA. Association for Computational Linguistics.

Christian Buck, Kenneth Heafield, and Bas van Ooyen. 2014. N-gram counts and language models from the Common Crawl. In *Proceedings of the Language Resources and Evaluation Conference*, pages 3579–3584, Reykjavík, Iceland.

Mauro Cettolo, Nicola Bertoldi, and Marcello Federico. 2011. Methods for smoothing the optimizer instability in SMT. In *MT Summit XIII: the Thirteenth Machine Translation Summit*, pages 32–39.

Colin Cherry and George Foster. 2012. Batch tuning strategies for statistical machine translation. In *Proceedings of the 2012 Conference of the North American Chapter of the Association for Computational Linguistics: Human Language Technologies*, pages 427–436, Stroudsburg, USA. Association for Computational Linguistics.

Jonathan H. Clark, Chris Dyer, Alon Lavie, and Noah A. Smith. 2011. Better hypothesis testing for statistical machine translation: Controlling for optimizer instability. In *Proceedings of the 49th Annual Meeting of the Association for Computational Linguistics: Human Language Technologies*, HLT '11, pages 176–181, Stroudsburg, USA. Association for Computational Linguistics.

Daniel Dahlmeier and Hwee Tou Ng. 2012a. A beam-search decoder for grammatical error correction. In *Proceedings of the 2012 Joint Conference on Empirical Methods in Natural Language Processing and Computational Natural Language Learning*, EMNLP-CoNLL '12, pages 568–578, Stroudsburg, USA. Association for Computational Linguistics.

Daniel Dahlmeier and Hwee Tou Ng. 2012b. Better evaluation for grammatical error correction. In *Proceedings of the 2012 Conference of the North American Chapter of the Association for Computational*

Linguistics: Human Language Technologies, pages 568–572, Stroudsburg, USA. Association for Computational Linguistics.

Daniel Dahlmeier, Hwee Tou Ng, and Siew Mei Wu. 2013. Building a large annotated corpus of learner english: The NUS Corpus of Learner English. In *Proceedings of the Eighth Workshop on Innovative Use of NLP for Building Educational Applications*, pages 22–31, Atlanta, Georgia. Association for Computational Linguistics.

Eva Hasler, Barry Haddow, and Philipp Koehn. 2012. Sparse lexicalised features and topic adaptation for SMT. In *Proceedings of the 7th International Workshop on Spoken Language Translation (IWSLT)*, pages 268–275.

Kenneth Heafield, Ivan Pouzyrevsky, Jonathan H. Clark, and Philipp Koehn. 2013. Scalable modified Kneser-Ney language model estimation. In *Proceedings of the 51st Annual Meeting of the Association for Computational Linguistics*, pages 690–696, Sofia, Bulgaria.

Kenneth Heafield. 2011. KenLM: Faster and smaller language model queries. In *Proceedings of the Sixth Workshop on Statistical Machine Translation*, WMT '11, pages 187–197, Stroudsburg, USA. Association for Computational Linguistics.

Mark Hopkins and Jonathan May. 2011. Tuning as ranking. In *Proceedings of the Conference on Empirical Methods in Natural Language Processing*, EMNLP '11, pages 1352–1362, Stroudsburg, USA. Association for Computational Linguistics.

Marcin Junczys-Dowmunt. 2012. Phrasal rank-encoding: Exploiting phrase redundancy and translational relations for phrase table compression. *Prague Bull. Math. Linguistics*, 98:63–74.

Philipp Koehn and Barry Haddow. 2012. Towards effective use of training data in statistical machine translation. In *Proceedings of the 7th Workshop on Statistical Machine Translation*, WMT '12, pages 317–321, Stroudsburg, USA. Association for Computational Linguistics.

Philipp Koehn, Franz Josef Och, and Daniel Marcu. 2003. Statistical phrase-based translation. In *Proceedings of the 2003 Conference of the North American Chapter of the Association for Computational Linguistics on Human Language Technology - Volume 1*, pages 48–54, Stroudsburg, USA. Association for Computational Linguistics.

Philipp Koehn, Hieu Hoang, Alexandra Birch, Chris Callison-Burch, Marcello Federico, Nicola Bertoldi, Brooke Cowan, Wade Shen, Christine Moran, Richard Zens, Chris Dyer, Ondrej Bojar, Alexandra Constantin, and Evan Herbst. 2007. Moses: Open source toolkit for statistical machine translation. In *Annual Meeting of the Association for Computational Linguistics*. The Association for Computer Linguistics.

Vladimir I. Levenshtein. 1966. Binary codes capable of correcting deletions, insertions and reversals. *Soviet Physics Doklady*, 10:707–710.

David Maier. 1978. The complexity of some problems on subsequences and supersequences. *Journal of the ACM*, 25(2):322–336.

Tomoya Mizumoto, Mamoru Komachi, Masaaki Nagata, and Yuji Matsumoto. 2011. Mining revision log of language learning SNS for automated japanese error correction of second language learners. In *The 5th International Joint Conference on Natural Language Processing*, pages 147–155.

Tomoya Mizumoto, Yuta Hayashibe, Mamoru Komachi, Masaaki Nagata, and Yu Matsumoto. 2012. The effect of learner corpus size in grammatical error correction of ESL writings. In *Proceedings of COLING 2012*, pages 863–872.

Hwee Tou Ng, Siew Mei Wu, Yuanbin Wu, Christian Hadiwinoto, and Joel Tetreault. 2013. The CoNLL-2013 shared task on grammatical error correction. In *Proceedings of the 17th Conference on Computational Natural Language Learning: Shared Task*, pages 1–12, Sofia, Bulgaria. Association for Computational Linguistics.

Hwee Tou Ng, Siew Mei Wu, Ted Briscoe, Christian Hadiwinoto, Raymond Hendy Susanto, , and Christopher Bryant. 2014. The CoNLL-2014 shared task on grammatical error correction. In *Proceedings of the Eighteenth Conference on Computational Natural Language Learning: Shared Task (CoNLL-2014 Shared Task)*, pages 1–14, Baltimore, USA. Association for Computational Linguistics.

Franz Josef Och. 2003. Minimum error rate training in statistical machine translation. In *Proceedings of the 41st Annual Meeting on Association for Computational Linguistics - Volume 1*, ACL '03, pages 160–167, Stroudsburg, USA. Association for Computational Linguistics.

Kishore Papineni, Salim Roukos, Todd Ward, and Wei-Jing Zhu. 2002. BLEU: A method for automatic evaluation of machine translation. In *Proceedings of the 40th Annual Meeting on Association for Computational Linguistics*, pages 311–318, Stroudsburg, USA. Association for Computational Linguistics.

Ippei Yoshimoto, Tomoya Kose, Kensuke Mitsuzawa, Keisuke Sakaguchi, Tomoya Mizumoto, Yuta Hayashibe, Mamoru Komachi, and Yuji Matsumoto. 2013. NAIST at 2013 CoNLL grammatical error correction shared task. In *Proceedings of the 17th Conference on Computational Natural Language Learning: Shared Task*, pages 26–33, Sofia, Bulgaria. Association for Computational Linguistics.

Zheng Yuan and Mariano Felice. 2013. Constrained grammatical error correction using statistical machine translation. In *Proceedings of the 17th Conference on Computational Natural Language Learning: Shared Task*, pages 52–61, Sofia, Bulgaria. Association for Computational Linguistics.

The Illinois-Columbia System in the CoNLL-2014 Shared Task

Alla Rozovskaya[1] Kai-Wei Chang[2] Mark Sammons[2] Dan Roth[2] Nizar Habash[1]

[1]Center for Computational Learning Systems, Columbia University
{alla,habash}@ccls.columbia.edu
[2] Cognitive Computation Group, University of Illinois at Urbana-Champaign
{kchang10,mssammon,danr}@illinois.edu

Abstract

The CoNLL-2014 shared task is an extension of last year's shared task and focuses on correcting grammatical errors in essays written by non-native learners of English. In this paper, we describe the Illinois-Columbia system that participated in the shared task. Our system ranked second on the original annotations and first on the revised annotations.

The core of the system is based on the University of Illinois model that placed first in the CoNLL-2013 shared task. This baseline model has been improved and expanded for this year's competition in several respects. We describe our underlying approach, which relates to our previous work, and describe the novel aspects of the system in more detail.

1 Introduction

The topic of text correction has seen a lot of interest in the past several years, with a focus on correcting grammatical errors made by English as a Second Language (ESL) learners. ESL error correction is an important problem since most writers of English are not native English speakers. The increased interest in this topic can be seen not only from the number of papers published on the topic but also from the three competitions devoted to grammatical error correction for non-native writers that have recently taken place: HOO-2011 (Dale and Kilgarriff, 2011), HOO-2012 (Dale et al., 2012), and the CoNLL-2013 shared task (Ng et al., 2013).

In all three shared tasks, the participating systems performed at a level that is considered extremely low compared to performance obtained in other areas of NLP: even the best systems attained F1 scores in the range of 20-30 points.

The key reason that text correction is a difficult task is that even for non-native English speakers, writing accuracy is very high, as *errors are very sparse*. Even for some of the most common types of errors, such as article and preposition usage, the majority of the words in these categories (over 90%) are used correctly. For instance, in the CoNLL training data, only 2% of prepositions are incorrectly used. Because errors are so sparse, it is more difficult for a system to identify a mistake accurately and without introducing many false alarms.

The CoNLL-2014 shared task (Ng et al., 2014) is an extension of the CoNLL-2013 shared task (Ng et al., 2013). Both competitions make use of essays written by ESL learners at the National University of Singapore. However, while the first one focused on five kinds of mistakes that are commonly made by ESL writers – article, preposition, noun number, verb agreement, and verb form – this year's competition covers all errors occurring in the data. Errors outside the target group were present in the task corpora last year as well, but were not evaluated.

Our system extends the one developed by the University of Illinois (Rozovskaya et al., 2013) that placed first in the CoNLL-2013 competition. For this year's shared task, the system has been extended and improved in several respects: we extended the set of errors addressed by the system, developed a general approach for improving the error-specific models, and added a joint inference component to address interaction among errors. See Rozovskaya and Roth (2013) for more detail.

We briefly discuss the task (Section 2) and give an overview of the baseline Illinois system (Section 3). Section 4 presents the novel aspects of the system. In Section 5, we evaluate the complete system on the development data and show the results obtained on test. We offer error analysis and a brief discussion in Section 6. Section 7 concludes.

Proceedings of the Eighteenth Conference on Computational Natural Language Learning: Shared Task, pages 34–42,
Baltimore, Maryland, 26-27 July 2014.

Error type	Rel. freq.	Examples
Article (*ArtOrDet*)	14.98%	*∅/*The* government should help encourage *the/∅ breakthroughs as well as *a/∅ complete medication system .
Wrong collocation (*Wci*)	11.94%	Some people started to **think/wonder* if electronic products can replace human beings for better performances .
Local redundancy (*Rloc-*)	10.52%	Some solutions *{*as examples*}/∅ would be to design plants/fertilizers that give higher yield ...
Noun number (*Nn*)	8.49%	There are many reports around the internet and on newspaper stating that some users ' **iPhone/iPhones* exploded .
Verb tense (*Vt*)	7.21%	Through the thousands of years , most Chinese scholars **are*/{*have been*} greatly affected by Confucianism .
Orthography/punctuation (*Mec*)	6.88%	Even British Prime Minister , Gordon Brown *∅/, has urged that all cars in **britain/Britain* to be green by 2020 .
Preposition (*Prep*)	5.43%	I do not agree **on/with* this argument that surveillance technology should not be used to track people .
Word form (*Wform*)	4.87%	On the other hand , the application of surveillance technology serves as a warning to the **murders/murderers* and they might not commit more murder .
Subject-verb agreement (*SVA*)	3.44%	However , tracking people **are/is* difficult and different from tracking goods .
Verb form (*Vform*)	3.25%	Travelers survive in desert thanks to GPS **guide/guiding* them .
Tone (*Wtone*)	1.29%	Hence , as technology especially in the medical field continues to get developed and updated , people {*do n't*}/{*do not*} risk their lives anymore .

Table 1: **Example errors.** In the parentheses, the error codes used in the shared task are shown. Note that only the errors exemplifying the relevant phenomena are marked in the table; the sentences may contain other mistakes. Errors marked as verb form include multiple grammatical phenomena that may characterize verbs. Our system addresses all of the error types except "Wrong Collocation" and "Local Redundancy".

2 Task Description

Both the training and the test data of the CoNLL-2014 shared task consist of essays written by students at the National University of Singapore. The training data contains 1.2 million words from the NUCLE corpus (Dahlmeier et al., 2013) corrected by English teachers, and an additional set of about 30,000 words that was released last year as a test set for the CoNLL-2013 shared task. We use last year's test data as a *development* set; the results in the subsequent sections are reported on this subset.

The CoNLL corpus error tagset includes 28 error categories. Table 1 illustrates the most common error categories in the training data; errors are marked with an asterisk, and ∅ denotes a missing word. Our system targets all of these, with the exception of collocation and local redundancy errors. Among the less commonly occurring error types, our system addresses tone (style) errors; these are illustrated in the table.

It should be noted that the proportion of erroneous instances is several times higher in the development data than in the training data for all of the error categories. For example, while only 2.4% of noun phrases in the training data have determiner errors, in the development data 10% of noun phrases have determiner errors.

"Hence, the environmental ***factor/factors** also ***contributes/contribute** to various difficulties, ***included/including** problems in nuclear technology."	
Error type	**Confusion set**
Noun number	{factor, factors}
Verb Agreement	{contribute, contributes}
Verb Form	{included, including, includes, include}

Table 2: **Sample confusion sets for noun number, verb agreement, and verb form.**

3 The Baseline System

In this section, we briefly describe the University of Illinois system (henceforth *Illinois*; in the overview paper of the shared task the system is referred to as UI) that achieved the best result in the CoNLL-2013 shared task and which we use as our baseline model. For a complete description, we refer the reader to Rozovskaya et al. (2013).

The Illinois system implements five independently-trained machine-learning classifiers that follow the popular approach to ESL error correction borrowed from the context-sensitive spelling correction task (Golding and Roth, 1999; Carlson et al., 2001). A *confusion set* is defined as a list of confusable words. Each occurrence of a confusable word in text is represented as a vector of features derived from a context window around the target. The problem is cast as a multi-class classification task and a classifier is trained on native or learner data. At prediction time, the model selects the most likely candidate from the confusion set.

The confusion set for prepositions includes the top 12 most frequent English prepositions (this year, we extend the confusion set and also target extraneous preposition usage). The article confusion set is as follows: {a, the, ∅}.[1] The confusion sets for *noun*, *agreement*, and *form* modules depend on the target word and include its morphological variants. Table 2 shows sample confusion sets for *noun*, *agreement*, and *form* errors.

Each classifier takes as input the corpus documents preprocessed with a part-of-speech tagger[2] and shallow parser[3] (Punyakanok and Roth, 2001). The other system components use the preprocessing tools only as part of candidate generation (e.g., to identify all nouns in the data for the noun classifier).

The choice of learning algorithm for each classifier is motivated by earlier findings showing that discriminative classifiers outperform other machine-learning methods on error correction tasks (Rozovskaya and Roth, 2011). Thus, the classifiers trained on the learner data make use of a discriminative model. Because the Google corpus does not contain complete sentences but only n-gram counts of length up to five, training a discriminative model is not desirable, and we thus use NB (details in Rozovskaya and Roth (2011)).

The *article* classifier is a discriminative model that draws on the state-of-the-art approach described in Rozovskaya et al. (2012). The model makes use of the Averaged Perceptron (AP) algorithm (Freund and Schapire, 1996) and is trained on the training data of the shared task with rich features. The article module uses the POS and chunker output to generate some of its features and candidates (likely contexts for missing articles).

The original word choice (the source article) used by the writer is also used as a feature. Since the errors are sparse, this feature causes the model to abstain from flagging mistakes, resulting in low recall. To avoid this problem, we adopt the approach proposed in Rozovskaya et al. (2012), the *error inflation* method, and add artificial article errors to the training data based on the error distribution on the training set. This method prevents the source feature from dominating the context features, and improves the recall of the system.

The other classifiers in the baseline system – noun number, verb agreement, verb form, and preposition – are trained on native English data, the Google Web 1T 5-gram corpus (henceforth, Google, (Brants and Franz, 2006)) with the Naïve Bayes (NB) algorithm. All models use word n-gram features derived from the 4-word window around the target word. In the *preposition* model, priors for preposition preferences are learned from the shared task training data (Rozovskaya and Roth, 2011).

The modules targeting *verb agreement* and

[1]∅ denotes noun-phrase-initial contexts where an article is likely to have been omitted. The variants "a" and "an" are conflated and are restored later.

[2]`http://cogcomp.cs.illinois.edu/page/software_view/POS`

[3]`http://cogcomp.cs.illinois.edu/page/software_view/Chunker`

verb form mistakes draw on the linguistically-motivated approach to correcting verb errors proposed in Rozovskaya et. al (2014).

4 The CoNLL-2014 System

The system in the CoNLL-2014 shared task is improved in three ways: 1) Additional error-specific classifiers: word form, orthography/punctuation, and style; 2) Model combination; and 3) Joint inference to address interacting errors. Table 3 summarizes the Illinois and the Illinois-Columbia systems.

4.1 Targeting Additional Errors

The Illinois-Columbia system implements several new classifiers to address word form, orthography and punctuation, and style errors (Table 1).

4.1.1 Word Form Errors

Word form (*Wform*) errors are grammatical errors that involve confusing words that share a base form but differ in derivational morphology, e.g. "use" and "usage" (see also Table 1). Confusion sets for word form errors thus should include words that differ derivationally but share the same base form. In contrast to verb form errors where confusion sets specify all possible inflectional forms for a given verb, here, the associated parts-of-speech may vary more widely. An example of a confusion set is {technique, technical, technology, technological}.

Because word form errors encompass a wide range of misuse, one approach is to consider every word as an error candidate. We follow a more conservative method and only attempt to correct those words that occurred in the training data and were tagged as word form errors (we cleaned up that list by removing noisy annotations).

A further challenge in addressing word form errors is generating confusion sets. We found that about 45% of corrections for word form errors in the development data are covered by the confusion sets from the training data for the same word. We thus derive the confusion sets using the training data. Specifically, for every source word that is tagged as a word form error in the training data, the confusion set includes all labels to which that word is mapped in the training data. In addition, plural and singular forms are added for all words tagged as nouns, and inflectional forms are added for words tagged as verbs. For more detail on correcting verb errors, we refer the reader to Rozovskaya et al. (2014).

4.1.2 Orthography and Punctuation Errors

The *Mec* error category includes errors in spelling, context-sensitive spelling, capitalization, and punctuation. Our system addresses punctuation errors and capitalization errors.

To correct capitalization errors, we collected words that are always capitalized in the training and development data when not occurring sentence-initially.

The punctuation classifier includes two modules: a learned component targets missing and extraneous comma usage and is an AP classifier trained on the learner data with error inflation. A second, pattern-based component, complements the AP model: it inserts missing commas by using a set of patterns that overwhelmingly prefer the usage of a comma, e.g. when a sentence starts with the word "hence". The patterns are learned automatically over the training data: specifically, using a sliding window of three words on each side, we compiled a list of word n-gram contexts that are strongly associated with the usage of a comma. This list is then used to insert missing commas in the test data.

4.1.3 Style Errors

The style (*Wtone*) errors marked in the corpus are diverse, and the annotations are often not consistent. We constructed a pattern-based system to deal with two types of *style* errors that are commonly annotated. The first type of *style* edit avoids using contractions of negated auxiliary verbs. For example, it changes "do n't" to "do not". We use a pattern-based classifier to identify such errors and replace the contractions. The second type of *style* edit encourages the use of a semi-colon to join two independent clauses when a conjunctive adverb is used. For example, it edits "[clause], however, [clause]" to "[clause]; however, [clause]". To identify such errors, we use a part-of-speech tagger to recognize conjunctive adverbs signifying independent clauses: if two clauses are joined by the pattern ", [conjunctive adverb],", we will replace it with "; [conjunctive adverb],".

4.2 Modules not Included in the Final System

In addition to the modules described above, we attempted to address two other common error categories: spelling errors and collocation errors. We

Illinois		
Classifiers	**Training data**	**Algorithm**
Article	Learner	AP with inflation
Preposition	Native	NB-priors
Noun number	Native	NB
Verb agreement	Native	NB
Verb form	Native	NB

Illinois-Columbia		
Classifiers	**Training data**	**Algorithm**
Article	Learner and native	AP with infl. (learner) and NB-priors (native)
Preposition	Learner and native	AP with infl. (learner) and NB-priors (native)
Noun number	Learner and native	AP with infl. (learner) and NB (native)
Verb agreement	Native	AP with infl. (learner) and NB (native)
Verb form	Native	NB-priors
Word form	Native	NB-priors
Orthography/punctuation	Learner	AP and pattern-based
Style	Learner	Pattern-based
Model combination	Section 4.3	
Global inference	Section 4.4	

Table 3: **The baseline (Illinois) system vs. the Illinois-Columbia system.** AP stands for Averaged Perceptron, and NB stands for the Naïve Bayes algorithm.

describe these below even though they were not included in the final system.

Regular spelling errors are noticeable but not very frequent, and a number are not marked in the corpus (for example, the word "dictronary" instead of "dictionary" is not tagged as an error). We used an open source package – "Jazzy"[4] – to attempt to automatically correct these errors to improve context signals for other modules. However, there are often multiple similar words that can be proposed as corrections, and Jazzy uses phonetic guidelines that sometimes lead to unintuitive proposals (such as "doctrinaire" for "dictronary"). It would be possible to extend the system with a filter on candidate answers that uses n-grams or some other context model to choose better candidates, but the relatively small number of such errors limits the potential impact of such a system.

Collocation errors are the second most common error category accounting for 11.94% of all errors in the training data (Table 1). We tried using the Illinois context-sensitive spelling system[5] to detect these errors, but this system requires predefined confusion sets to detect possible errors and to propose valid corrections. The coverage of the pre-existing confusion sets was poor – the system could potentially correct only 2.5% of collocation errors – and it is difficult to generate new confusion sets that generalize well, which requires a great deal of annotated training data. The system performance was relatively poor because it proposed many spurious corrections: we believe this is due to the relatively limited context it uses, which makes it particularly susceptible to making mistakes when there are multiple errors in close proximity.

4.3 Model Combination

Model combination is another key extension of the Illinois system.

In the Illinois-Columbia system, article, preposition, noun, and verb agreement errors are each addressed via a model that combines error predictions made by a classifier trained on the learner data with the AP algorithm and those made by the NB model trained on the Google corpus. The AP classifiers all make use of richer sets of features than the native-trained classifiers: the article, noun number, and preposition classifiers employ features that use POS information, while the verb agreement classifier also makes use of dependency features extracted using a parser (de Marneffe et al., 2008). For more detail on the features used in the agreement module, we refer the reader to

[4]http://jazzy.sourceforge.net

[5]http://cogcomp.cs.illinois.edu/cssc/

Rozovskaya et al. (2014). Finally, all of the AP models use the source word of the author as a feature and, similar to the article AP classifier (Section 3), implement the error inflation method. The combined model generates a union of corrections produced by the components.

We found that for every error type, the combined model is superior to each of the single classifiers, as it combines the advantages of both of the classifiers so that they complement one another. In particular, while each of the learner and native components have similar precision, since the predictions made differ, the recall of the combined model improves.

4.4 Joint Inference

One of the mistakes typical for Illinois system were inconsistent predictions. Inconsistent predictions occur when the classifiers address grammatical phenomena that interact at the sentence level, e.g. noun number and verb agreement. To address this problem, the Illinois-Columbia system makes use of global inference via an Integer Linear Programming formulation (Rozovskaya and Roth, 2013). Note that Rozovskaya and Roth (2013) also describe a joint learning model that performs better than the joint inference approach. However, the joint learning model is based on training a joint model on the Google corpus, and is not as strong as the individually-trained classifiers of the Illinois-Columbia system that combine predictions from two components – NB classifiers trained on the native data from the Google corpus and AP models trained on the learner data (Section 4.3).

5 Experimental Results

In Sections 3 and 4, we described the individual system components that address different types of errors. In this section, we show how the system improves when each component is added into the system. In this year's competition, systems are compared using F0.5 measure instead of F1. This is because in error correction good precision is more important than having a high recall, and the F0.5 reflects that by weighing precision twice as much as recall. System output is scored with the M2 scorer (Dahlmeier and Ng, 2012).

Table 4 reports performance results of each individual classifier. In the final system, the article, preposition, noun number, and verb agree-

Model	**P**	**R**	**F0.5**
Articles (AP)	38.97	8.85	23.19
Articles (NB-priors)	47.34	6.01	19.93
Articles (Comb.)	38.73	10.93	25.67
Prep. (AP)	34.00	0.5	2.35
Prep. (NB-priors)	33.33	0.79	3.61
Prep. (Comb.)	30.06	1.17	5.13
Noun number (NB)	44.74	5.48	18.39
Noun number (AP)	82.35	0.41	2.01
Noun number (Comb.)	45.02	5.57	18.63
Verb agr. (AP)	38.56	1.23	5.46
Verb agr. (NB)	63.41	0.76	3.64
Verb agr. (Comb.)	41.09	1.55	6.75
Verb form (NB-priors)	59.26	1.41	6.42
Word form (NB-priors)	57.54	3.02	12.48
Mec (AP; patterns)	48.48	0.47	2.26
Style (patterns)	84.62	0.64	3.13

Table 4: **Performance of classifiers targeting specific errors.**

Model	**P**	**R**	**F0.5**
The baseline (Illinois) system			
Articles	38.97	8.85	23.19
+Prepositions	39.24	9.35	23.93
+Noun number	42.13	14.83	30.79
+Subject-verb agr.	42.25	16.06	31.86
+Verb form	43.19	17.20	33.17
Model Combination			
+Model combination	42.72	20.19	34.92
Additional Classifiers			
+Word form	43.39	21.54	36.07
+Mec	43.70	22.04	36.52
+Style	44.22	21.54	37.09
Joint Inference			
+Joint Inference	44.28	22.57	37.13

Table 5: **Results on the development data**. The top part of the table shows the performance of the baseline (Illinois) system from last year.

P	**R**	**F0.5**
Scores based on the original annotations		
41.78	24.88	36.79
Scores based on the revised annotations		
52.44	29.89	45.57

Table 6: **Results on Test.**

ment classifiers use combined models, each consisting of a classifier trained on the learner data and a classifier trained on native data. We report performance of each such component separately and when they are combined. The results show that combining models boosts the performance of each classifier: for example, the performance of the article classifier improves by more than 2 F0.5 points. It should be noted that results are computed with respect to all errors present in the data. For this reason, recall is low.

Next, in Table 5, we show the contribution of the novel components over the baseline system on the development set. As described in Section 3, the baseline Illinois system consists of five individual components; their performance is shown in the top part of the table. Note that although for the development set we make use of last year's test set, these results are not comparable to the performance results reported in last year's competition that used the F1 measure. Overall, the baseline system achieves an F0.5 score of 33.17 on the development set.

Then, by applying the model combination technique introduced in Section 4.3, the performance is improved to 34.92. By adding modules to target three additional error types, the overall performance becomes 37.09. Finally, the joint inference technique (see Section 4.4) slightly improves the performance further. The final system achieves an F0.5 score of 37.13.

Table 6 shows the results on the test set provided by the organizers. As was done previously, the organizers also offered another set of annotations based on the combination of revised official annotations and accepted alternative annotations proposed by participants. Performance results on this set are also shown in Table 6.

6 Discussion and Error Analysis

Here, we present some interesting errors that our system makes on the development set and discuss our observations on the competition. We analyze both the false positive errors and those cases that are missed by our system.

6.1 Error Analysis

Stylistic preference *Surveillance* ***technology*** *such as RFID (radio-frequency identification) is one type of examples that has currently been implemented.*

Here, our system proposes a change to plural for the noun "technology". The gold standard solution instead proposes a large number of corrections throughout that work with the choice of the singular "technology". However, using the plural "technologies" as proposed by the Illinois-Columbia system is quite acceptable, and a comparable number of corrections would make the rest of the sentence compatible. Note also that the gold standard proposes the use of commas around the phrase "such as RFID (radio-frequency identification)", which could also be omitted based on stylistic considerations alone.

Word choice *The high accuracy in utilizing surveillance technology eliminates the* *amount/number *of disagreements among people.*

The use of "amount" versus "number" depends on the noun to which the term attaches. This could conceivably be achieved by using a rule and word list, but many such rules would be needed and each would have relatively low coverage. Our system does not detect this error.

Presence of multiple errors *Not only the details of location will be provided, but also may lead to find out the root of this kind of children trading agency and it helps to prevent more this kind of tragedy to happen* ***on*** *any family.*

The writer has made numerous errors in this sentence. To determine the correct preposition in the marked location requires at least the preceding verb phrase to be corrected to "from happening"; the extraneous "more" after "prevent" in turn makes the verb phrase correction more unlikely as it perturbs the contextual clues that a system might learn to make that correction. Our system proposes a different preposition – "in" – that is better than the original in the local context, but which is not correct in the wider context.

Locally coherent, globally incorrect *People's lives become* ***from*** *increasingly convenient to almost luxury, thanks to the implementation of increasingly technology available for the Man's life.*

In this example, the system proposes to delete the preposition "from". This correctiom improves the local coherency of the sentence. However, the resulting construction is not consistent with "to almost luxury", suggesting a more complex correction (changing the word "become" to "are going").

Cascading NLP errors *In this, I mean that we can input this device* ***implant*** *into an animal or birds species, for us to track their movements and actions relating to our human research that can bring us to a new regime.*

The word "implant" in the example sentence has been identified as a verb by the system and not a noun due to the unusual use as part of the phrase "device implant". As a result, the system incorrectly proposes the verb form correction "implanted".

6.2 Discussion

The error analysis suggests that there are three significant challenges to developing a better grammar correction system for the CoNLL-2014 shared task: identifying candidate errors; modeling the context of possible errors widely enough to capture long-distance cues where necessary; and modeling stylistic preferences involving word choice, selection of plural or singular, standards for punctuation, use of a definite or indefinite article (or no article at all), and so on. For ESL writers, the tendency for multiple errors to be made in close proximity means that global decisions must be made about sets of possible mistakes, and a system must therefore have a quite sophisticated abstract model to generate the basis for consistent sets of corrections to be proposed.

7 Conclusion

We have described our system that participated in the shared task on grammatical error correction. The system builds on the elements of the Illinois system that participated in last year's shared task. We extended and improved the Illinois system in three key dimensions, which we presented and evaluated in this paper. We have also presented error analysis of the system output and discussed possible directions for future work.

Acknowledgments

This material is based on research sponsored by DARPA under agreement number FA8750-13-2-0008. The U.S. Government is authorized to reproduce and distribute reprints for Governmental purposes notwithstanding any copyright notation thereon. The views and conclusions contained herein are those of the authors and should not be interpreted as necessarily representing the official policies or endorsements, either expressed or implied, of DARPA or the U.S. Government. This research is also supported by a grant from the U.S. Department of Education and by the DARPA Machine Reading Program under Air Force Research Laboratory (AFRL) prime contract no. FA8750-09-C-018. The first and last authors were partially funded by grant NPRP-4-1058-1-168 from the Qatar National Research Fund (a member of the Qatar Foundation). The statements made herein are solely the responsibility of the authors.

References

T. Brants and A. Franz. 2006. *Web 1T 5-gram Version 1*. Linguistic Data Consortium, Philadelphia, PA.

A. J. Carlson, J. Rosen, and D. Roth. 2001. Scaling up context sensitive text correction. In *IAAI*.

D. Dahlmeier and H.T. Ng. 2012. Better evaluation for grammatical error correction. In *NAACL*, pages 568–572, Montréal, Canada, June. Association for Computational Linguistics.

D. Dahlmeier, H.T. Ng, and S.M. Wu. 2013. Building a large annotated corpus of learner english: The nus corpus of learner english. In *Proc. of the NAACL HLT 2013 Eighth Workshop on Innovative Use of NLP for Building Educational Applications*, Atlanta, Georgia, June. Association for Computational Linguistics.

R. Dale and A. Kilgarriff. 2011. Helping Our Own: The HOO 2011 pilot shared task. In *Proceedings of the 13th European Workshop on Natural Language Generation*.

R. Dale, I. Anisimoff, and G. Narroway. 2012. A report on the preposition and determiner error correction shared task. In *Proc. of the NAACL HLT 2012 Seventh Workshop on Innovative Use of NLP for Building Educational Applications*, Montreal, Canada, June. Association for Computational Linguistics.

Marie-Catherine de Marneffe, Anna N. Rafferty, and Christopher D. Manning. 2008. Finding contradictions in text. In *ACL*.

Yoav Freund and Robert E. Schapire. 1996. Experiments with a new boosting algorithm. In *Proc. 13th International Conference on Machine Learning*.

A. R. Golding and D. Roth. 1999. A Winnow based approach to context-sensitive spelling correction. *Machine Learning*.

H.T. Ng, S.M. Wu, Y. Wu, C. Hadiwinoto, and J. Tetreault. 2013. The conll-2013 shared task on grammatical error correction. In *Proceedings of the Seventeenth Conference on Computational Natural Language Learning: Shared Task*, pages 1–12, Sofia, Bulgaria, August. Association for Computational Linguistics.

H. T. Ng, S. M. Wu, T. Briscoe, C. Hadiwinoto, R. H. Susanto, and C. Bryant. 2014. The CoNLL-2014 shared task on grammatical error correction. In *Proceedings of the Eighteenth Conference on Computational Natural Language Learning: Shared Task*, Baltimore, Maryland, USA, June. Association for Computational Linguistics.

V. Punyakanok and D. Roth. 2001. The use of classifiers in sequential inference. In *NIPS*.

A. Rozovskaya and D. Roth. 2011. Algorithm selection and model adaptation for esl correction tasks. In *ACL*.

A. Rozovskaya and D. Roth. 2013. Joint learning and inference for grammatical error correction. In *EMNLP*, 10.

A. Rozovskaya, M. Sammons, and D. Roth. 2012. The UI system in the HOO 2012 shared task on error correction. In *Proc. of the Annual Conference of the North American Chapter of the Association for Computational Linguistics (NAACL) Workshop on Innovative Use of NLP for Building Educational Applications*.

A. Rozovskaya, K.-W. Chang, M. Sammons, and D. Roth. 2013. The University of Illinois system in the CoNLL-2013 shared task. In *CoNLL Shared Task*.

A. Rozovskaya, D. Roth, and V. Srikumar. 2014. Correcting grammatical verb errors. In *EACL*.

RACAI GEC – A hybrid approach to Grammatical Error Correction

Tiberiu Boroş
Calea 13 Septembrie, 13
Bucharest
RACAI
tibi@racai.ro

Stefan Daniel Dumitrescu
Calea 13 Septembrie,13
Bucharest
RACAI
sdumitrescu@racai.ro

Adrian Zafiu
Str. Targul din Vale, 1
Pitesti
UPIT - FECC
adrian.zafiu@comin.ro

Dan Tufiş
Calea 13 Septembrie, 13
Bucharest
RACAI
tufis@racai.ro

Verginica Mititelu Barbu
Calea 13 Septembrie, 13
Bucharest
RACAI
vergi@racai.ro

Paul Ionuţ Văduva
Calea 13 Septembrie, 13
Bucharest
RACAI
ionut@racai.ro

Abstract

This paper describes RACAI's (Research Institute for Artificial Intelligence) hybrid grammatical error correction system. This system was validated during the participation into the CONLL'14 Shared Task on Grammatical Error Correction. We offer an analysis of the types of errors detected and corrected by our system, we present the necessary steps to reproduce our experiment and also the results we obtained.

1 Introduction

Grammatical error correction (GEC) is a complex task mainly because of the natural dependencies between the words of a sentence both at the lexical and the semantic levels, leave it aside the morphologic and syntactic levels, an intrinsic and complex attribute specific to the human language. Grammatical error detection and correction received a significant level of interest from various research groups both from the academic and commercial environments. A testament to the importance of this task is the long history of challenges (e.g. Microsoft Speller Challenge and CONLL Shared Task) (Hwee et al., 2014) that had the primary objective of proving a common testing ground (i.e. resources, tools and gold standards) in order to assess the performance of various methods and tools for GEC, when applied to identical input data.

In the task of GEC, one can easily distinguish two separate tasks: grammatical error detection and grammatical error correction. Typically, there are three types of approaches: statistical, rule-based and hybrid. The difficulty of detecting and correcting an error depends on its class.

(a) **Statistical approaches** rely on building statistical models (using surface forms or syntactic labels) that are used for detecting and correcting local errors. The typical statistical approach is to model how likely the occurrence of an event is, given a history of preceding events. Thus, statistical approaches easily adaptable to any language (requiring only training data in the form of raw or syntactically labeled text) are very good guessers when it comes to detecting and correcting collocations, idioms, typos and small grammatical inadvertences such as the local gender and case agreements. The main impediments of such systems are two-fold: (1) they are resource consuming techniques (memory/storage) and they are highly dependent on data – large and domain adapted datasets are required in order to avoid the data-scarceness specific issue and currently they rely only on a limited horizon of events; (2) they usually lack semantic information and favoring high-occurring events is not always the best way of detecting and correcting grammatical errors.

(b) **Rule-based approaches** embed linguistic knowledge in the form of machine parsable rules that are used to detect errors and

Proceedings of the Eighteenth Conference on Computational Natural Language Learning: Shared Task, pages 43–48,
Baltimore, Maryland, 26-27 July 2014.

describe via transformations how various error types should be corrected. The drawbacks to rule-based system are (1) the extensive effort required to build the rule-set, (2) regardless of the size of the rule-set, given the variability of the human language it is virtually impossible to capture all possible errors and (3) the large number of exceptions to rules.

(c) **Hybrid systems** that combine both rule-based and statistical approaches are plausible to overcome the weaknesses of the two methodologies if the mixture of the two components is done properly. Detection of errors can be achieved statistically and rule-based, the task of the hybrid approach being to resolve any conflicts that arise between the outputs of the two approaches.

However, even the most advanced systems are only able to distinguish between a limited number of error types and the task of correcting an error is even more difficult. Along the typical set of errors that are handled by typical correction systems (punctuation, capitalization, spelling, typos, verb tense, missing verb, etc.), CONLL's GEC task introduces some hard cases which require a level of semantic analysis: local redundancy, unclear meaning, parallelism, etc.

2 External tools and resources

One step in the preparation phase was the analysis of the types of errors. The training set was automatically processed with our Bermuda tool (Boroș et al., 2013): it underwent sentence splitting, tokenization, part of speech tagging, lemmatization and also chunking. Comparing the original and the corrected sentences, we could rank the types of mistakes.

The most frequent ones, i.e. occurring more than 1000 times, are presented in the following table:

Type of error	Occurrences	Percent
use of articles and determiners	6647	14.98
wrong collocations or idioms	5300	11.94
local redundancies	4668	10.52
noun number	3770	8.49
tenses	3200	7.21
punctuation and orthography	3054	6.88
use of prepositions	2412	5.43
word form	2160	4.87
subject-verb agreement	1527	3.44
Verb form	1444	3.25
Link word/phrases	1349	3.04

Table 1. The most frequent types of mistakes in the training data

There are also some less frequent errors: pronoun form, noun possessive form, word order of adjectives and adverbs, etc. Some of these can be solved by means of rules, others by accessing lexical resources and others are extremely difficult to deal with.

As far as the test data are concerned, the error distribution according to their types is the following:

Type of error	Occurrences in official-2014.0.m2	Occurrences in official-2014.1.m2
use of articles and determiners	332	437
wrong collocations or idioms	339	462
local redundancies	94	194
noun number	214	222
tenses	133	146
punctuation and orthography	227	474
use of prepositions	95	152
word form	76	104
subject-verb agreement	107	148
Verb form	132	88
Link word/phrases	93	78

Table 2. The most frequent types of mistakes in the test data

Roughly, the same types of mistakes are more frequent in the test set, just like as in the training set.

For collocations and idioms, as well as for correct prepositions use, we consider that only lexical resources can be of help. They can take the form of a corpus or lists of words that subcategorize for prepositional phrases obligatorily headed by a certain preposition (see section 3.2). We adopted the former solution: we used Google 1T n-grams corpus (see section 2.2) from which the selectional restrictions can be learned quite successfully. However, dealing with collocations is difficult, as correction does not involve only syntax, but also semantics. Changing a word in a sentence usually implies changing the meaning of the sentence as a whole. Nevertheless, a solution can be found: as mistakes in collocations involve the use of a related word (synonyms), a resource such as the WordNet can be of help. When the word used in the sentence and the one occurring in the corpus can be found in the same synset (or even in synsets in direct relation), the correction could be made. Otherwise, it is risky to try. In any scenario, this remains as future work for us.

2.1 RACAI NLP Tools

We have used our in-house Bermuda software suite (Boroş et al., 2013), (Boroş and Dumitrescu, 2013) to perform text pre-processing. As the tool is well documented in the cited papers above, we summarize its main functionalities concerning the task at hand and the algorithms behind them.

Tokenization. A basic necessary preprocessing step that needs to be applied from the beginning as most tools work on a certain tokenization format. Bermuda uses a custom-built, language dependent tokenizer. Based on regular expressions, it detects and splits words such as [haven't] into [have] and [n't]; [boy's] into [boy] and ['s], while leaving abbreviations like [dr.] or [N.Y.] as a single token.

Part-of-speech (POS) tagger. Tagging is essential to determine each word's part of speech and thus its role in the sentence. Each word is tagged with a morpho-syntactic descriptor, called MSD. The English language has around 100 MSDs defined, while more inflected languages, like Romanian – a Latin-derived language, uses over 600. An MSD completely characterizes the word morphologically and syntactically[1]. For example, 'Np' refers to a proper noun while 'Ncns' refers to a common (c) noun (N) that has a neuter (n) gender and is in singular form (ex: zoo, zone). Our tagger is based on a neural network, introduced in (Boroş et al., 2013). Overall, the Bermuda POS Tagger obtains very high accuracy rates (>98%) even on the more difficult, highly inflected languages.

Lemmatization. The Bermuda Lemmatizer is based on the MIRA algorithm (Margin Infused Relaxed Algorithm) (Crammer and Singer, 2003). We treat lemmatization as a tagging task, in which each individual letter of the surface word is tagged as either remaining unchanged, being removed or transformed to another letter. The lemmatizer was trained and tested on an English lexicon containing a number of around 120K surface-lemma-MSD entries.

[1] Full description of MSDs can be found at : http://nl.ijs.si/ME/V4/msd/html/msd-en.html

2.2 Google 1T corpus

A good performing language model is a very important resource for the current task, as it allows discriminating between similar phrases by comparing their perplexities.

Although we had several corpora available to extract surface-based language models from, we preferred to use a significantly larger model than we could create: Google 1T n-gram corpus (Brants and Franz, 2006). This 4 billion n-gram corpus should provide high-quality perplexity estimations. However, loading 4*10^9 n-grams without any compression scheme would require, even by today's standards, a large amount of memory. For example, using SRILM (Stolcke, 2002) which uses 33 bytes per n-gram, would require a total of ~116GB of RAM. The article by Adam Pauls and Dan Klein (2011) describes an ingenious way to create a data structure that reduces the amount of RAM needed to load the 1T corpus. However, the system they propose is written in Java, a language that is object-oriented, and which, for any object, introduces an additional overhead. Furthermore, they do not implement any smoothing method for the 1T corpus, defaulting to the +1 "stupid smoothing" as they themselves named it, relying on the fact that smoothing is less relevant with a very large corpus. For these reasons, coupled with the difficulty to understand and modify other persons' code, we wrote our language model software. We based our implementation around Pauls and Klein's sorted array idea, with a few modifications. Firstly, we encoded the unigrams in a simple HashMap instead of a value-rank array. Secondly, we wrote a multi-step n-gram reader and loader. Thirdly, we implemented the Jelinek-Mercer smoothing method instead of the simple +1 smoothing. Using deleted interpolation we computed the lambda parameters for the JM smoothing; we further built a stand-alone server that would load the smoothed n-gram probabilities and could be queried over TCP-IP either for an n-gram (max 5-gram – direct probability) or for an entire sentence (compute its perplexity). The entire software was written in C++ to avoid Java's overhead problems. Overall, the simplified ranked array encoding allowed us to obtain very fast response times (under a millisecond per query) with a moderate memory usage: the entire 1T corpus was loaded in around 60GB of RAM, well below our development server memory limit.

We are aware of the limitations of this corpus: as data was collected from the web, mistakes will occur in it.

We also need a language model that can estimate the probability of parts of speech. By learning a model from the parts of speech we can learn to discriminate between words different forms. Grantedly, a part of speech language model can promote a grammatically "more" correct but semantically inferior sentence over a semantically sound one, due to assigning a higher probability to a more common part of speech sequence in the sentence. Our experiments show that, generally, a part of speech language model helps text quality overall.

Our initial idea for this POS language model was to use the same 1T corpus that we could annotate using our tagging tools. However, given the limited context, performance would have been acceptable at the 5-gram level, decreasing to the point of simply picking the most common part of speech for the unigrams, as no context exists for them. As such, we used the following available monolingual resources for English: the News CRAWL corpus (2007-2012 editions), Europarl, UN French-English Corpus, the News Commentary, our own cleaned English Wikipedia dump. The total size of the raw text was around 20GB. We joined and annotated the files and extracted all the 1-5 grams, using the same format as the 1T corpus. We then used another instance of the language model software to load this POS LM and await the main system perplexity estimation requests. Overall, the part of speech language model turned out to be rather small (a hard-disk footprint of only 315MB of binary part of speech LM compared to the 57GB of surface model compressed data). This is normal, as the entire part of speech MSD vocabulary for English is around 100 tags, compared to the more than 13 million surface forms (unigrams) in the 1T corpus.

3 RACAI's Hybrid Grammatical Error Correction System

3.1 An overview of the system

In many cases, statistical methods are preferable over rule-based systems since they only rely on large available raw corpora instead of handcrafted rules that are difficult to design and are limited by the effort invested by human experts in their endeavor.

However, a purely statistical method is not always able to validate rarely used expressions and always favors frequency over fine grained compositions.

As a rule of thumb, hybrid systems are always a good choice in tasks where the complexity exceeds the capacity of converting knowledge into formal rules and large scale training data is available for developing statistical models.

Our GEC system has three cascaded phases divided between two modules: (a) in the first phase, a statistical surface based and a POS LM are used to solve orthographic errors inside the input sentences, thus enhancing the quality of the NLP processing for the second stage; (b) a rule-based system is used to detect typical grammatical errors, which are labeled and then (c) corrected using a statistical method to validate between automatically generated candidates.

3.2 The statistical component

Typos are a distinctive class of errors found in texts written by both native and non-native English speakers which do not violate any explicit (local agreement related) grammatical constraints. Most POS tagging systems handle previously unseen words through suffix analysis and are able (using the local context) to assign a tag which is conformant with the tags of the surrounding words. Such errors cannot be detected by applying rules, since it is impossible to have lexicons that cover the entire possible vocabulary of a language.

The typical approach is to generate spelling alternatives for words that are outside the vocabulary and to use a LM to determine the most likely correct word form. However, when relying on simple distance functions such as the unmodified Levenstein it is extremely difficult to differentiate between spelling alternatives even with the help of contextual information. There are multiple causes for this type of errors, starting from the lack of language knowledge (typically non-native speakers rely on phonetic similarity when spelling words) to speed (usually results in missing letters) or keyboard related (multiple keys touched at once). The distance function we used for scoring alternatives uses a weighted Levenstein algorithm, which was tuned on the TREC dataset.

3.3 The rule based error detection and correction

As previously mentioned, not all grammatical errors are automatically detectable by pure statistical methods. In our experiments we noticed frequent cases where the LM does not provide sufficient support to distinguish between true grammatical errors and simply unusual but grammatically correct expressions.

For the present shared task we concentrated on a subset of potential errors. Our rules aimed the correction of the verb tense especially in time clauses, the use of the short infinitive after modals, the position of frequency adverbs in a sentence, subject-verb agreement, word order in interrogative sentences, punctuation accompanying certain lexical elements, the use of articles, of correlatives, etc.

For the sake of an easier understanding of our rule-based component of the GEC system, we will start by introducing some technical details about how the rule interpreter works, emphasizing on the structure of the configuration file, the input modality and the general pointers on writing rules. In our approach we treat error detection and error correction separately, in a two-stage system. The configuration file contains a set of language dependent rules, each rule being uniquely identified by the label and its body. The role of using labels is two-fold: (1) they provide guidance and assistance to the user in navigating through the structure of the configuration file (when editing or creating new rules); (2) they play a crucial role in the error correction process and serve as common denominators for different classes of errors.

Our rule description system is inspired after the time-independent logic function (combinational logic) paradigm, which stipulates that a fixed input size logical function, described through a stochastic list of input/output dependence sequence, through a process of logical minimization, this function can be implemented as an array of "AND" gates, followed by an array of "OR" gates. Thus, in our configuration file, each rule is described by a set of string pairs (i_0 r_0, i_1 r_1… i_n r_n) which act as "AND" gates – we refer to this as a sub-instance of a rule. At this point, a sub-instance is activated only if all constraints are met. The "OR" gate array is simulated by adding rules with the same label. This way, if any sub-instance is active then the rule is considered active and we proceed to the errror correction step.

Every pair (i_k r_k) is a single Boolean input of a sub-instance. A rule is checked against every token inside an utterance, from left to right. r_k is a regular expression which, depending on the value of i_k, is applied to the word's surface form (s), the word's lemma (l) or the word's MSD (m). i_k can also select if the regular expression should be applied to a neighboring token. To exemplify, we have extracted two sections from our configuration file: (a) the modal infinitive common error for non-native English speakers (also found in the development set of CONLL) (lines 1 to 7) and (b) the possible missing comma case (line 8):

```
1) modal_infinitive: s must   s+1 to s-1 ^!a
2) modal_infinitive: s could  s+1 to
3) modal_infinitive: s can    s+1 to
4) modal_infinitive: s might  s+1 to
5) modal_infinitive: s may    s+1 to
6) modal_infinitive: s would  s+1 to
7) modal_infinitive: s should s+1 to
8) pmc: s which m-1 ^((?!COMMA).)*$
```

Table 3: a sample of error detection rules

The "modal_infinitive" rule is complex and it is described using 7 sub-instances, which share an identical label. Line 1 of the configuration excerpt contains three pairs as opposed to the other sub-instances. This does not contradict the combinational logic paradigm, since we can consider this rule as having a fixed input size of three and, as a result of logic minimization, the third parameter for 6 of the seven instances falls into the "DON'T CARE" special input class. The first $i_k r_k$ pair ("s must") is used to check if the surface form ("s") of the current word is "must". The second pair ("s+1 to") checks if the word form of the next token is "to". The third pair ("s-1 ^!a") verifies that the collocation "a must to" does not accidentally trigger this rule. This rule will detect the error in "I must to go...", but will licence a sequence like "This book is a must to read...".

The error detection rules that we designed for the CONLL shared task are created, as an external resource for the program, on the basis of the mistakes observed in the training set and can be updated/extended any time .

In the error correction phase, for every error type we encompass, we provide the necessary transformations (at token level) through which the initial word sequence that generated this error should be corrected. The configuration file of this module is straightforward: rule-labels are marked as strings at the beginning of a new line; for each label, we provide a set of transformation rules, that are contained in the following tab-indented lines; once a new line does not start with a TAB character, it should either be empty or contain the label for a different error type. the correction phase, multiple sentence candidates are automatically generated (based on the transformation rules) and they are checked against the language model to see which one yields the lowest perplexity. That is, once an error is found, its correction way tends to be applied provided that the language model offers another solution.

As an example, suppose that the rule for detecting a possible missing comma (pmc in Table 3, line 8) was fired. The corresponding correction rule is described as below:

```
pmc:
   $w-1 , $w
   $w-1 $w
```

The "pmc" rule is activated if the word "which" is not preceded by a comma. Since it is not always the case that the wordform "which" should be preceded by this punctuation mark, in our error correction system step we generate two candidates: (a) one in which we insert a comma before "which" and (b) one in which we keep the word sequence untouched.

4 Results and Conclusions

The RACAI hybrid GEC system obtained a precision of 31.31%, a recall of 14.23% and an $F_{0.5}$ score of 25.25% on the test set provided by the CONLL shared task on Grammatical Error Correction.

We presented our system and the resources we used in the development process. All the data and tools required to run a similar experiment are available online and we are currently working on developing a self-contained GEC system that will be made publicly available.

Future development plans include the enhancement of the lexicons we use for English and the extension of this system for Romanian. Furthermore, we plan to include an extended method for solving collocations errors based on the synsets of Princeton WordNet (PWN) (Fellbaum, 1989).

References

Andreas Stolcke. 2002. SRILM: An extensible language modeling toolkit. In Proceedings of Interspeech

Boroş, T., Radu, I., & Tufiş, D. (2013). Large tagset labeling with Feed Forward Neural Networks. Case study on Romanian Language. In Proceedings of ACL

Boroş, T., & Dumitrescu, S. D. (2013). Improving the RACAI Neural Network MSD Tagger. In Engineering Applications of Neural Networks (pp. 42-51). Springer Berlin Heidelberg

Crammer, K., & Singer, Y. (2003). Ultraconservative online algorithms for multiclass problems. The Journal of Machine Learning Research, 3, 951-991.

Fellbaum, Ch. (1998, ed.) WordNet: An Electronic Lexical Database. Cambridge, MA: MIT Press

Hwee Tou Ng, Siew Mei Wu, Ted Briscoe, Christian Hadiwinoto, Raymond Hendy Susanto, and Christopher Bryant (2014). The CoNLL-2014 Shared Task on Grammatical Error Correction. Proceedings of the Eighteenth Conference on Computational Natural Language Learning: Shared Task (CoNLL-2014 Shared Task). Baltimore, Maryland, USA.

Thorsten Brants and Alex Franz. 2006. Google Web1T 5-gram corpus, version 1. In Linguistic Data Consortium, Philadelphia, Catalog Number LDC2006T13

Pauls, Adam, and Dan Klein. "Faster and smaller n-gram language models." Proceedings of the 49th Annual Meeting of the Association for Computational Linguistics: Human Language Technologies-Volume 1. Association for Computational Linguistics, 2011.

Grammatical Error Detection and Correction Using Tagger Disagreement

Anubhav Gupta
Université de Franche-Comté
anubhav.gupta@edu.univ-fcompte.fr

Abstract

This paper presents a rule-based approach for correcting grammatical errors made by non-native speakers of English. The approach relies on the differences in the outputs of two POS taggers. This paper is submitted in response to CoNLL-2014 Shared Task.

1 Introduction

A part-of-speech (POS) tagger, like any other software, has a set of inputs and outputs. The input for a POS tagger is a group of words and a tagset, and the output is a POS tag for a word (Jurafsky and Martin, 2009). Given that a software is bound to provide incorrect output for an incorrect input (garbage in, garbage out), it is quite likely that taggers trained to tag grammatically correct sentences (the expected input) would not tag grammatically incorrect sentences properly. Furthermore, it is possible that the output of two different taggers for a given incorrect input would be different.

For this shared task, the POS taggers used were the Stanford Parser, which was used to preprocess the training and test data (Ng et al., 2014) and the TreeTagger (Schmid, 1994). The Stanford Parser employs unlexicalized PCFG[1] (Klein and Manning, 2003), whereas the TreeTagger uses decision trees. The TreeTagger is freely available[2], and its performance is comparable to that of the Stanford Log-Linear Part-of-Speech Tagger (Toutanova et al., 2003). Since the preprocessed dataset was already annotated with POS tags, the Stanford Log-Linear POS Tagger was not used.

If the annotation of preprocessed data differed from that of the TreeTagger, it was assumed that the sentence might have grammatical errors. Once an error was detected it was corrected using the Nodebox English Linguistics library[3] (De Bleser et al., 2002).

2 Error Detection

The POS tag for each token in the data was compared with the tag given by the TreeTagger. Sentences were considered grammatically incorrect upon meeting the following conditions:

- The number of tags in the preprocessed dataset for a given sentence should be equal to the number of tags returned by the TreeTagger for the same sentence.
- There should be at least one token with different POS tags.

As an exception, if the taggers differed only on the first token, such that the Stanford Parser tagged it as **NNP** or **NNPS**, then the sentence was not considered for correction, as this difference can be attributed to the capitalisation of the first token, which the Stanford Parser interprets as a proper noun.

Table 1 shows the precision (P) and the recall (R) scores of this method for detecting erroneous sentences in the training and test data. The low recall score indicates that for most of the incorrect sentences, the output of the taggers was identical.

2.1 Preprocessing

The output of the TreeTagger was modified so that it had the same tag set as that used by the Stanford Parser. The differences in the output tagset is displayed in the Table 2.

2.2 Errors

Where the mismatch of tags is indicative of error, it does not offer insight into the nature of the error and thus does not aid in error correction per se. For example, the identification of a token as VBD

[1] Probabilistic Context-Free Grammar

[2] http://www.cis.uni-muenchen.de/~schmid/tools/TreeTagger/

[3] http://nodebox.net/code/index.php/Linguistics

Proceedings of the Eighteenth Conference on Computational Natural Language Learning: Shared Task, pages 49–52, Baltimore, Maryland, 26-27 July 2014.

Dataset	Total Erroneous Sentences	Sentences with Tag Mismatch	Erroneous Sentences Identified Correctly	P	R
Training	21860	26282	11769	44.77	53.83
Test	1176	642	391	60.90	33.24
Test (Alternative)†	1195	642	398	61.99	33.30

† consists of additional error annotations provided by the participating teams.

Table 1: Performance of Error Detection.

TreeTagger Tagset	Stanford Parser Tagset
(	-LRB-
)	-RRB-
NP	NNP
NPS	NNPS
PP	PRP
SENT	.

Table 2: Comparison of Tagsets.

(past tense) by one tagger and as VBN (past participle) another does not imply that the mistake is necessarily a verb tense (Vt) error. Table 4 lists some of the errors detected by this approach.

3 Error Correction

Since mismatched tag pairs did not consistently correspond to a particular error type, not all errors detected were corrected. Certain errors were detected using hand-crafted rules.

3.1 Subject-Verb Agreement (SVA) Errors

SVA errors were corrected with aid of dependency relationships provided in the preprocessed data. If a singular verb (VBZ) referred to a plural noun (NNS) appearing before it, then the verb was made plural. Similarly, if the singular verb (VBZ) was the root of the dependency tree and was referred to by a plural noun (NNS), then it was changed to the plural.

3.2 Verb Form (Vform) Errors

If a modal verb (MD) preceded a singular verb (VBZ), then the second verb was changed to the bare infinitive form. Also, if the preposition **to** preceded a singular verb, then the verb was changed to its bare infinitive form.

3.3 Errors Detected by POS Tag Mismatch

If a token followed by a noun is tagged as an adjective (JJ) in the preprocessed data and as an adverb (RB) by the TreeTagger, then the adverbial morpheme **-ly** was removed, resulting in the adjective. For example, **completely** is changed to **complete** in the second sentence of the fifth paragraph of the essay 837 (Dahlmeier et al., 2013). On the other hand, adverbs (RB) in the preprocessed dataset that were labelled as adjectives (JJ) by the TreeTagger were changed into their corresponding adverbs.

Dataset	P	R	$F_{\beta=0.5}$
Training	23.89	0.31	1.49
Test	70.00	1.72	7.84
Test (Alternative)	72.00	1.90	8.60

Table 3: Performance of the Approach.

A token preceded by the verb **to be**, tagged as JJ by the Stanford Parser and identified by the TreeTagger as a verb is assumed to be a verb and accordingly converted into its past participle. Finally, the tokens labelled NNS and VBZ by the Stanford Parser and the TreeTagger respectively are likely to be Mec[4] or Wform[5] errors. These tokens are replaced by plural nouns having same initial substring (this is achieved using the **get_close_matches** API of the difflib Python library).

The performance of this approach, as measured by the M2 scorer (Dahlmeier and Ng, 2012), is presented in Table 3.

4 Conclusion

The approach used in this paper is useful in detecting mainly verb form, word form and spelling errors. These errors result in ambiguous or incorrect input to the POS tagger, thus forcing it to produce incorrect output. However, it is quite likely that with a different pair of taggers, different rules

[4]Punctuation, capitalisation, spelling, typographical errors

[5]Word form

nid	829					
Sentence	This	caused	problem	like	the	appearance
Stanford Parser	DT	**VBD**	NN	IN	DT	NN
TreeTagger	DT	**VBN**	NN	IN	DT	NN
Error Type	Vt					
nid	829					
Sentence	but	also	to	reforms	the	land
Stanford Parser	CC	RB	TO	**VB**	DT	NN
TreeTagger	CC	RB	TO	**NNS**	DT	NN
Error Type	Wci					
nid	840					
Sentence	India	,	their	population	amount	to
Stanford Parser	NNP	,	PRP$	NN	**VB**	TO
TreeTagger	NNP	,	PRP$	NN	**NN**	TO
Error Type	Vform	(This was not an error in the training corpus.)				
nid	1051					
Sentence	Singapore	is	currently	a	develop	country
Stanford Parser	NNP	VBZ	RB	DT	**JJ**	NN
TreeTagger	NNP	VBZ	RB	DT	**VB**	NN
Error Type	Vform					
nid	858					
Sentence	Therefore	most	of	China	enterprisers	focus
Stanford Parser	RB	JJS	IN	NNP	**VBZ**	NN
TreeTagger	RB	RBS	IN	NNP	**NNS**	VBP
Error Type	Wform					
nid	847					
Sentence	and	social	constrains	faced	by	engineers
Stanford Parser	CC	JJ	**NNS**	VBN	IN	NNS
TreeTagger	CC	JJ	**VBZ**	VBN	IN	NNS
Error Type	Mec					

Table 4: Errors Detected.

would be required to correct these errors. Errors concerning noun number, determiners and prepositions, which constitute a large portion of errors committed by L2 learners (Chodorow et al., 2010; De Felice and Pulman, 2009; Gamon et al., 2009), were not addressed in this paper. This is the main reason for low recall.

Acknowledgments

I would like to thank Calvin Cheng for proofreading the paper and providing valuable feedback.

References

Martin Chodorow, Michael Gamon, and Joel Tetreault. 2010. The Utility of Article and Preposition Error Correction Systems for English Language Learners: Feedback and Assessment. *Language Testing* 27 (3): 419–436. doi:10.1177/0265532210364391.

Daniel Dahlmeier, Hwee Tou Ng, and Siew Mei Wu. 2013. Building a Large Annotated Corpus of Learner English: The NUS Corpus of Learner English. *Proceedings of the Eighth Workshop on Innovative Use of NLP for Building Educational Applications (BEA 2013).* 22–31. Atlanta, Georgia, USA.

Daniel Dahlmeier and Hwee Tou Ng. 2012. Better Evaluation for Grammatical Error Correction. *Proceedings of the 2012 Conference of the North American Chapter of the Association for Computational Linguistics: Human Language Technologies (NAACL 2012).* 568 – 572. Montreal, Canada.

Frederik De Bleser, Tom De Smedt, and Lucas Nijs 2002. NodeBox version 1.9.6 for Mac OS X.

Rachele De Felice and Stephen G Pulman. 2009. Automatic Detection of Preposition Errors in Learner Writing. *CALICO Journal* 26 (3): 512–528.

Michael Gamon, Claudia Leacock, Chris Brockett, William B. Dolan, Jianfeng Gao, Dmitriy Belenko, and Alexandre Klementiev. 2009. Using Statistical Techniques and Web Search to Correct ESL Errors. *CALICO Journal* 26 (3): 491–511.

Daniel Jurafsky and James H. Martin. 2009. Part-of-Speech Tagging. *Speech and Language Processing: An Introduction to Natural Language Processing, Speech Recognition, and Computational Linguistics*. Prentice-Hall.

Dan Klein and Christopher D. Manning. 2003. Accurate Unlexicalized Parsing. *Proceedings of the 41st Meeting of the Association for Computational Linguistics*. 423–430.

Hwee Tou Ng, Siew Mei Wu, Ted Briscoe, Christian Hadiwinoto, Raymond Hendy Susanto, and Christopher Bryant. 2014. The CoNLL-2014 Shared Task on Grammatical Error Correction. *Proceedings of the Eighteenth Conference on Computational Natural Language Learning: Shared Task (CoNLL-2014 Shared Task)*. Baltimore, Maryland, USA.

Helmut Schmid. 1994. Probabilistic Part-of-Speech Tagging Using Decision Trees. *Proceedings of International Conference on New Methods in Language Processing*. Manchester, UK.

Kristina Toutanova, Dan Klein, Christopher Manning, and Yoram Singer. 2003. Feature-Rich Part-of-Speech Tagging with a Cyclic Dependency Network. *Proceedings of HLT-NAACL 2003*. 252–259.

CoNLL 2014 Shared Task: Grammatical Error Correction with a Syntactic N-gram Language Model from a Big Corpora

S. David Hernandez
Centro de Investigación en
Computación - IPN / México
shernandez_b12@sagitario.cic.ipn.mx

Hiram Calvo
Centro de Investigación en
Computación - IPN / México
hcalvo@cic.ipn.mx

Abstract

We describe our approach to grammatical error correction presented in the CoNLL Shared Task 2014. Our work is focused on error detection in sentences with a language model based on syntactic tri-grams and bi-grams extracted from dependency trees generated from 90% of the English Wikipedia. Also, we add a naïve module to error correction that outputs a set of possible answers, those sentences are scored using a syntactic n-gram language model. The sentence with the best score is the final suggestion of the system.

The system was ranked 11th, evidently this is a very simple approach, but since the beginning our main goal was to test the syntactic n-gram language model with a big corpus to future comparison.

1 Introduction

Grammatical error correction is a difficult task to solve even for humans, because there are a lot of phenomena that can occur in a sentence. One example of the difficulty of the task is that the annotators of the training and test data in the NUCLE (Dahlmeier et al., 2013) differs in the corrections that they made to the sentences, those differences in the annotations are mostly because depend on uncontrolled conditions, such knowledge, emotional state and the environment of the annotator at the moment that the task is performed. This time the shared task is more difficult than the last year (Ng and Wu et al., 2013) that considered only five types of errors, and this time the task consist into correct all the grammatical errors in the NUCLE (Ng and Wu et al., 2014).

We are interested into test the behaviour of different methods used in different NLP task with the syntactic n-grams as a resource, in order to set a baseline to future work. There is work that probes that there is an improvement using syntactic n-grams in (Sidorov and Velasquez et al., 2014) where the author uses syntactic n-grams as machine learning features, another example of the use of syntactic n-grams occurred in the CoNLL 2013 Shared Task in (Sidorov and Gupta et al., CoNLL 2013), but they used a different approach from us.

Until the moment we do not have a comparison with the same method that we used in this task using normal n-grams, still our hypothesis is that syntactic n-grams allow us to relate words that in a common n-gram model wouldn't be related and that can outperform the results.

For example, in the sentence:

"Genetic risk refers more to your chance of inheriting a disorder or disease ."

Some common tri-grams are *"to your chance"*, *"your chance of"*, *"chance of inheriting"*. The word *chance* can not be related to the words *"disorder"* or *"disease"*, unless we use 5-grams or 7-grams, unlike with the syntactic tri-grams that as can be appreciated in the Table 3 the relation between this words are normally included.

Another hypothesis is that a low probability in a syntactic n-gram is an indicator that exist a wrong token in the portion of a dependency tree. A simple example of this intuition can be seen in the Table 1 for the sentence "This will , if not already , caused problems as there are very limited spaces for us ." from the training data in the NUCLE. The bold words are wrong tokens annotated in the training data and the numbers are the token number in the sentence.

As can be observed the low probability syntactic tri-grams include the wrong tokens. The problem is to establish a threshold in the prob-

Proceedings of the Eighteenth Conference on Computational Natural Language Learning: Shared Task, pages 53–59,
Baltimore, Maryland, 26-27 July 2014.

q_i	Syntactic tri-grams
0.0	'**are-12** **spaces-15** us-17 True'
0.0	'**spaces-15** limited-14 us-17 False'
0.00004	'**caused-8** will-2 **are-12** False'
0.00004	'**caused-8** will-2 not-5 False'
0.00004	'**caused-8** will-2 This-1 True'
0.00004	'**caused-8** will-2 problems-9 False'
0.00029	'**caused-8** not-5 **are-12** False'
0.00047	'**caused-8** **are-12** as-10 True'
0.00054	'**are-12** **spaces-15** limited-14 True'
0.00054	'**caused-8** **are-12** **spaces-15** True'
0.00057	'**caused-8** **are-12** there-11 True'
0.00065	'**caused-8** problems-9 **are-12** False'
0.00109	'**spaces-15** limited-14 very-13 True'
0.00194	'**caused-8** not-5 already-6 True'
0.00314	'**caused-8** not-5 problems-9 False'
0.00522	'**caused-8** not-5 if-4 True'
0.22841	'**are-12** as-10 there-11 False'
0.375	'**are-12** as-10 **spaces-15** False'
0.75510	'**are-12** there-11 **spaces-15** False'
1.0	'ROOT-0 **caused-8** **are-12** True'
1.0	'ROOT-0 **caused-8** not-5 True'
1.0	'ROOT-0 **caused-8** problems-9 True'
1.0	'ROOT-0 **caused-8** will-2 True'
1.0	'not-5 if-4 already-6 False'

Table 1: Ordered probabilities of syntactic tri-grams. The wrong tokens are *"caused"*, *"are"* and *"spaces"*.

abilities to consider as wrong a syntactic tri-gram and separate the wrong tokens from the correct ones.

2 Resources

For the language model we used a Wikipedia dump as training data (Wikipedia, 2013) and extracted the text with the Multithread Wikipedia Extractor (Souza, 2012) then was tokenized with the Stanford Tokenizer (Manning et al.,). There are about 87 millions of sentences and 1,480 millions of tokens.

To generate the dependency trees we used the Stanford Parser 3.2 (Socher et al., 2013), but for the syntactic n-gram language model we only took 90% of the sentences randomly chosen. The parsing task took a lot of time to be made with our computing resources and we had to use threads with the Stanford Parser, unfortunately this increases the amount of memory required by the software, so we had to exclude the sentences with more than one hundred token. At the end we parsed about 75 millions of sentences.

The dependency trees were generated as Stanford typed dependencies (Marneffe et al., 2006), in specific in the collapsed with propagation version as described in (Marneffe et al., 2008). One example of this kind of dependencies can be seen in the Figure 2. As can be observed the collapsed with propagation typed dependencies can break the tree, so strictly this is a directed graph with the grammatical relations in the edges and the words of the sentence in the nodes, though as convention we will continue referring it as a tree. In total there are about 1,166 million grammatical relations.

In the error detection phase we used the information provided with the NUCLE (Dahlmeier et al., 2013), specifically the tokens, POS and the grammatical relations from the test data in CoNLL style. From the training data we only made some calculations about the kinds of errors that occur with higher frequency and we used this information to include some rules in the correction phase.

3 System description

3.1 Syntactic n-gram language model

We used the dependency trees from Wikipedia corpus to generate the syntactic n-grams in the non-continuous form as described in (Sidorov, 2013) and in the book (Sidorov, Book 2013), but there is an significant difference, the current work with syntactic n-grams was made with the basic dependencies, and as we said before, we are using the dependencies that collapses the prepositions and propagates the conjunctions. The tree in Figure 1 is in the Basic representation and the differences with the collapsed and propagated dependencies can be appreciated in the Figure 2.

This change allow us to increase the scope of the relations between content words, but also it makes difficult to find preposition errors, so our system do not consider preposition correction.

The tables 2 and 3 show the syntactic tri-grams generated whit each one of the dependency representations, but without the relations for lack of space. As can be observed the

Genetic risk refers more to your chance of inheriting a disorder or disease

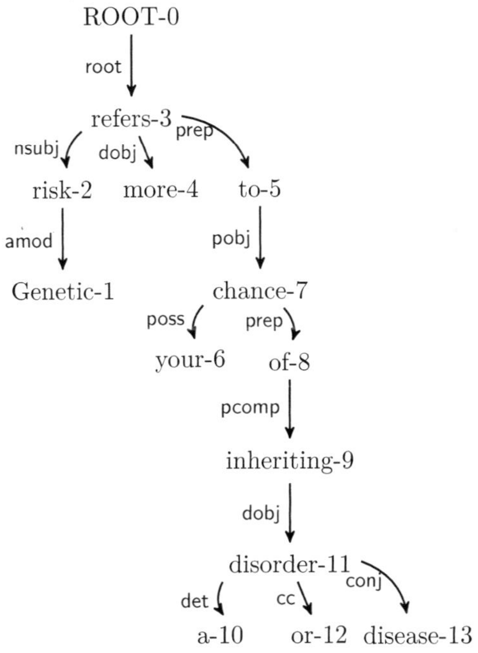

Figure 1: Basic dependencies.

Genetic risk refers more to your chance of inheriting a disorder or disease

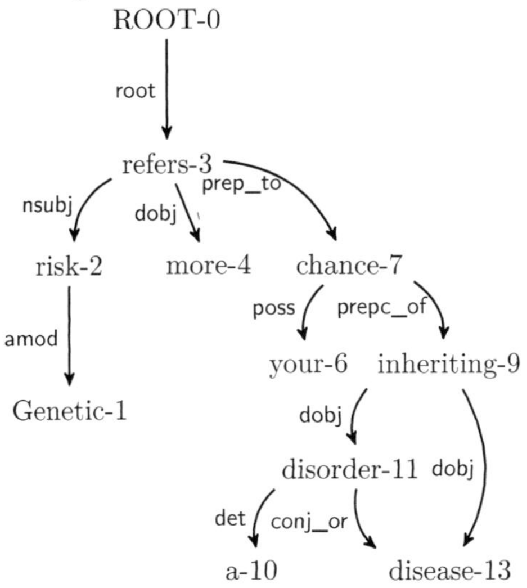

Figure 2: Collapsed dependencies with propagation.

word *"chance"* in the basic dependencies is not directly related with the words *"disorder"* and *"disease"*, on the contrary with the collapsed and propagated dependencies.

w_1	w_2	w_3	Continuous
to-5	chance-7	of-8	True
to-5	chance-7	your-6	True
refers-3	to-5	chance-7	True
refers-3	risk-2	Genetic-1	True
of-8	inheriting-9	disorder-11	True
inheriting-9	disorder-11	a-10	True
inheriting-9	disorder-11	disease-13	True
inheriting-9	disorder-11	or-12	True
chance-7	**of-8**	**inheriting-9**	True
ROOT-0	refers-3	to-5	True
ROOT-0	refers-3	risk-2	True
ROOT-0	refers-3	more-4	True
refers-3	risk-2	to-5	False
refers-3	risk-2	more-4	False
refers-3	more-4	to-5	False
disorder-11	a-10	disease-13	False
disorder-11	a-10	or-12	False
disorder-11	or-12	disease-13	False
chance-7	your-6	of-8	False

Table 2: Syntactic tri-grams from the basic dependencies.

w_1	w_2	w_3	Continuous
refers-3	chance-7	inheriting-9	True
refers-3	chance-7	your-6	True
refers-3	risk-2	Genetic-1	True
inheriting-9	disorder-11	a-10	True
inheriting-9	disorder-11	disease-13	True
chance-7	**inheriting-9**	**disorder-11**	True
chance-7	**inheriting-9**	**disease-13**	True
ROOT-0	refers-3	chance-7	True
ROOT-0	refers-3	risk-2	True
ROOT-0	refers-3	more-4	True
refers-3	risk-2	chance-7	False
refers-3	risk-2	more-4	False
refers-3	more-4	chance-7	False
inheriting-9	disorder-11	disease-13	False
disorder-11	a-10	disease-13	False
chance-7	your-6	inheriting-9	False

Table 3: Syntactic tri-grams from the collapsed with propagation dependencies.

Next we show the maximum likelihood estimations that we calculated for this language model. Where $w_1, w_2, w_3 \in W$ and W is the set of words of the sentence, $r_1, r_2 \in R$ with R as the set of grammatical relations between the words and $c \in \{True, False\}$, with True representing a continuous syntactic n-gram and False a non-continuous syntactic n-gram.

In equation (1) we take the maximum value between the probability estimation of the tri-gram with and without grammatical relations in order to favour the complete tri-gram.

Even with a big corpus as Wikipedia and with the non-continuous syntactic tri-grams these estimations can produce zeros in the probabilities, then we have to draw upon a back-off, so, we add other estimations.

$$q_1 = max(q(w_1|w_2, w_3; r_1, r_2; c), \quad q(w_1|w_2, w_3; c)) \tag{1}$$

$$q_2 = max(q(w_3|w_1, w_2; r_1, r_2; c), \quad q(w_3|w_1, w_2; c)) \tag{2}$$

Notice that equation (2) is similar to (1), both evaluate the same syntactic tri-gram, but with a different word of interest.

$$q_3 = \begin{cases} min(q(w_2|w_1; r_1), q(w_3|w_2; r_2)) & if \quad c = True \\ min(q(w_2|w_1; r_1), q(w_3|w_1; r_2)) & if \quad c = False \end{cases} \tag{3}$$

$$q_4 = \begin{cases} min(q(w_2|w_1), q(w_3|w_2)) & if \quad c = True \\ min(q(w_2|w_1), q(w_3|w_1)) & if \quad c = False \end{cases} \tag{4}$$

$$q_5 = max(q_3, q_4) \tag{5}$$

$$q_6 = \begin{cases} min(q(w_1|w_2; r_1), q(w_2|w_3; r_2)) & if \quad c = True \\ min(q(w_1|w_2; r_1), q(w_1|w_3; r_2)) & if \quad c = False \end{cases} \tag{6}$$

$$q_7 = \begin{cases} min(q(w_1|w_2), q(w_2|w_3)) & if \quad c = True \\ min(q(w_1|w_2), q(w_1|w_3)) & if \quad c = False \end{cases} \tag{7}$$

$$q_8 = max(q_6, q_7) \tag{8}$$

When the probabilities in equations (1) and (2) are equal to zero, we add a back-off estimation based in syntactic bi-grams, since a syntactic tri-gram is formed of two syntactic bi-grams or grammatical relations with different probabilities, but both or one of them can contain wrong tokens, so we decided to penalize the complete probability estimation of the syntactic tri-gram by choosing the min probability between the two relations. In the equations (3), (4), (6) and (7) a min operation is included to penalize the low probability in a syntactic bi-gram that corresponds to a syntactic tri-gram. In the equations (5) and (8) the max operation plays the same role as in equations (1) and (2).

The final expression of the model is shown in equation (9).

$$q_{stri} = \begin{cases} q_1 & if \quad q_1 > 0 \\ q_2 & if \quad q_1 = 0 \quad and \quad q_2 > 0 \\ q_5 & if \quad q_2 = 0 \quad and \quad q_5 > 0 \\ q_8 & if \quad q_5 = 0 \quad and \quad q_8 > 0 \\ 0 & Otherwise \end{cases} \tag{9}$$

Where $q_{stri} = q(w_1, w_2, w_3; r_1, r_2; c)$ and represents the probability of the syntactic trigram.

The syntactic tri-grams continuous and noncontinuous produced a vast amount of data, for that reason we only took about 1,660 millions of syntactic tri-grams to made the language model. This data can be downloaded from (Syntactic N-grams, 2014).

3.2 Detection and correction

In order to detect errors in the test data of NUCLE (Dahlmeier et al., 2013), we extract the Stanford typed dependencies from the conll-style file and to be congruent with the data of our language model excluded the *punct* grammatical relations. Then we obtain the syntactic tri-grams and probabilities of each sentence. The assumption is that low probability in a syntactic tri-gram makes it a candidate to be wrong, since grammatical errors could produce trees with portions where grammatical relations are unseen in the training data or with a low probability.

q_i	Syntactic tri-grams
0.0	refers-3 more-4 chance-7 False
0.0	refers-3 risk-2 chance-7 False
0.0	refers-3 chance-7 your-6 True
0.0	refers-3 chance-7 inheriting-9 True
0.00015	refers-3 risk-2 Genetic-1 True
0.00023	refers-3 risk-2 more-4 False
0.00355	chance-7 your-6 inheriting-9 False
0.00355	chance-7 inheriting-9 disorder-11 True
0.00609	inheriting-9 disorder-11 disease-13 True
0.00609	inheriting-9 disorder-11 a-10 True
0.00609	inheriting-9 disorder-11 disease-13 False
0.02128	disorder-11 a-10 disease-13 False
1.0	ROOT-0 refers-3 more-4 True
1.0	ROOT-0 refers-3 risk-2 True
1.0	ROOT-0 refers-3 chance-7 True
1.0	chance-7 inheriting-9 disease-13 True

Table 4: Ordered probabilities of the syntactic tri-grams.

To add the wrong syntactic tri-grams to a set E we include two parameters, $\alpha = 0.0001$

which is a threshold and $\xi = 0.5$ that is a percentage. To decide whose syntactic tri-grams must be in the set E, we sort them upwardly as in the table 4, if satisfy the condition $(q_i < \alpha)$ and $(q_i >= \xi q_{i+1})$ for $i \in \{1, 2, ...,$ until the first exception $\}$ the syntactic tri-gram is added to the set E. The fixed values of α and ξ were selected by experimentation.

w_1	w_2	w_3	Continuous
refers-3	more-4	chance-7	False
refers-3	risk-2	chance-7	False
refers-3	chance-7	your-6	True
refers-3	chance-7	inheriting-9	True

Table 5: Set of possible wrong syntactic tri-grams.

The syntactic tri-grams in the table 5 are the selected as suspicious to be wrong with the above considerations. All the tokens can be part of a grammatical error, but to get replacement candidates of all of them can increase the complexity of the task and with the window of time that we had to accomplish the task, so we decided to select words in the set E to be considered as wrong tokens. We counted the total amount of occurrences of each token in the set E and took the two with higher values.

Count	Tokens
4	refers-3
4	chance-7
1	more-4
1	risk-2
1	your-6
1	inheriting-9

Table 6: Possible wrong tokens.

We chose the best candidates that can replace each word in the sentence and generate new sentences with each one of the candidates in his different combinations. Is easy to see that can be a lot of sentences, considering that each word can have more than one candidate and that each sentence could have more than one wrong token to be replaced. To obtain the candidates to each suspicious token we search in our training data, words that start with the stemmed form of the selected token and that depends of the same word with the same relation, also we add the lemmatized word. The lemmatization was made with the WordNetLemmatizer and the stemming with LancasterStemmer, both from NLTK. Also we applied as we said some naïve rules based on the most frequent errors in the training corpus from NUCLE, for example, when the suspicious token is a pronoun or a common verb as *"have"* or *"do"* we replace them with their conjugations.

For the example in table 6, we have the respective candidates in table 7. Visibly the word *"chants"* has nothing to do with the original token to be replaced, it shows the main reason of why we have low score, the rules used in the correction phase are very simple. For this example, the word *"chance"* stemmed with the LancasterStemmer is *"chant"*, then the search of words in the grammatical relations that depends on the word *"refers"* and with the same relation, outputs the word *"chants"*.

Tokens	Candidates
refers	refers
chance-7	chance, chants

Table 7: Candidates.

The possible sentences generated for this example are *"Genetic risk **refers** more to your **chance** of inheriting a disorder or disease ."* and *"Genetic risk **refers** more to your **chants** of inheriting a disorder or disease ."*.

In this example the first sentence is the selected as the answer by the system. As can be appreciated the word *chants* just worsen the second sentence. This capacity to discriminate the wrong sentence is what draws our attention to continue with future work.

With this conditions our system produced 3613 new sentences from the original 1312. To choose the final answer from the set of proposed sentences for each sentence, we only sum all the probabilities of the syntactic tri-grams of each sentence, naturally the sentence with a higher mass of probability is the final proposed answer.

4 Evaluation

Our official results in the CoNLL 2014 Shared Task on grammatical error correction of the NUCLE and evaluated with the official scorer

(Dahlmeier and Ng, 2012) are shown in the table 8. The organizers provide all the resources.

Without alternative annotation	
Recall	2.85
Precision	11.28
F_0.5	7.09
With alternative annotation	
Recall	3.17
Precision	11.66
F_0.5	7.59

Table 8: Results in the CoNLL 2014 Shared Task .

The scoring without alternative answers was made with gold edits of the annotators and the scoring with alternative annotation includes answers proposed by 3 teams that participated on the Shared Task and were judged by the annotators.

5 Conclusions

The result of the system was not good or as we expected, first because our approach is simple and was motivated to test the use of a syntactic n-grams language model, second because the poor election of candidates to correct the errors. However, this task gave us the opportunity to test the behaviour in different conditions and now we have a reference to improve our system.

6 Future work

We have a lot of work to do, in order to support the use of this kind of resources. First we have to compare the same method that we used, but with a common n-gram language model. Second is necessary to make a more general language model that can be used with syntactic 4-grams or more, and analyse how this increase can affect the recall. Third find a way to made more efficient the consult of the resources.

Also we need to add a more wise method to correct the detected errors, including prepositions. The fact that we did not take into account this type of error does not mean that is not possible to do it with this resources, so we have to propose an alternative that takes into account this and other types of errors.

Acknowledgements

Work done under partial support of Mexican Government (CONACYT, SNI) and Instituto Politécnico Nacional, México (SIP-IPN, COFAA-IPN, PIFI-IPN).

References

Christopher Manning, Tim Grow, Teg Grenager, Jenny Finkel, and John Bauer. PTBTokenizer http://nlp.stanford.edu/software/tokenizer.shtml

Daniel Dahlmeier, Hwee Tou Ng, and Siew Mei Wu 2013. Building a Large Annotated Corpus of Learner English: The NUS Corpus of Learner English. *Proceedings of the Eighth Workshop on Innovative Use of NLP for Building Educational Applications (BEA 2013)* . (pp. 22 – 31). Atlanta, Georgia, USA.

Daniel Dahlmeier and Hwee Tou Ng 2012. Better Evaluation for Grammatical Error Correction. *Proceedings of the 2012 Conference of the North American Chapter of the Association for Computational Linguistics: Human Language Technologies (NAACL 2012)* . (pp. 568 – 572). Montreal, Canada.

Hwee Tou Ng, Siew Mei Wu, Yuanbin Wu, Christian Hadiwinoto and Joel Tetreault. 2013. The CoNLL-2013 Shared Task on Grammatical Error Correction. *Proceedings of the Seventeenth Conference on Computational Natural Language Learning: Shared Task (CoNLL-2013 Shared Task)* .

Hwee Tou Ng, Siew Mei Wu, Ted Briscoe, Christian Hadiwinoto, Raymond Hendy Susanto, and Christopher Bryant 2014. The CoNLL-2014 Shared Task on Grammatical Error Correction. *Proceedings of the Eighteenth Conference on Computational Natural Language Learning: Shared Task (CoNLL-2014 Shared Task)* . Baltimore, Maryland, USA.

Leonardo Souza (leonardossz@gmail.com). 2012. Multithread-Wikipedia-Extractor for SMP based architectures, Version: 1.0 (October 15, 2012). https://bitbucket.org/leonardossz/multithreaded-wikipedia-extractor/wiki/Home

Marie Catherine de Marneffe and Christopher D. Manning. 2008. Stanford Dependencies manual.

Marie Catherine de Marneffe, Bill MacCartney and Christopher D. Manning. 2006. Generating Typed Dependency Parses from Phrase Structure Parses. *In LREC 2006.*

Grigori Sidorov Book 2013. Non-linear construction of n-grams in computational linguistics: syntactic, filtered, and generalized n-grams. G. Sidorov. 2013, 166 p.

Grigori Sidorov, Francisco Velasquez, Efstathios Stamatatos, Alexander Gelbukh, Liliana Chanona-Hernández. 2014. Syntactic N-grams as Machine Learning Features for Natural Language Processing *I Expert Syst. Appl.*. vol. 41, no. 3, pp. 853-860, 2014.

Grigori Sidorov, 2013. Syntactic Dependency Based N-grams in Rule Based Automatic English as Second Language Grammar Correction. *International Journal of Computational Linguistics and Applications.* vol. 4, no. 2, pp. 169-188, 2013.

Grigori Sidorov, Anubhav Gupta, Martin Tozer, Dolors Catala, Angels Catena and Sandrine Fuentes. 2013. Rule-based System for Automatic Grammar Correction Using Syntactic N-grams for English Language Learning (L2). *Proceedings of the Seventeenth Conference on Computational Natural Language Learning: Shared Task.* pp. 96-101, 2013.

Non-continuous Syntactic N-grams from Wikipedia for the CoNLL 2014 Shared Task. 2014. http://iarp.cic.ipn.mx/~dhernandez/conll2014/ http://sdavidhernandez.com/conll2014/

Richard Socher, John Bauer, Christopher D. Manning, and Andrew Y. Ng. 2013. Parsing With Compositional Vector Grammars. *Proceedings of ACL 2013*

Wikipedia English dump. 2013. enwiki-20130904-pages-articles.xml.bz2 http://en.wikipedia.org/wiki/Wikipedia:Database_download

Tuning a Grammar Correction System for Increased Precision

Anoop Kunchukuttan*, **Sriram Chaudhury**†, **Pushpak Bhattacharyya***
* Department of Computer Science and Engineering, IIT Bombay, India
{anoopk,pb}@cse.iitb.ac.in

† Crimson Interactive Pvt. Limited, Mumbai, India
Sriram.Chaudhury@crimsoni.com

Abstract

In this paper, we propose two enhancements to a statistical machine translation based approach to grammar correction for correcting all error categories. First, we propose tuning the SMT systems to optimize a metric more suited to the grammar correction task (F-β score) rather than the traditional BLEU metric used for tuning language translation tasks. Since the F-β score favours higher precision, tuning to this score can potentially improve precision. While the results do not indicate improvement due to tuning with the new metric, we believe this could be due to the small number of grammatical errors in the tuning corpus and further investigation is required to answer the question conclusively. We also explore the combination of custom-engineered grammar correction techniques, which are targeted to specific error categories, with the SMT based method. Our simple ensemble methods yield improvements in recall but decrease the precision. Tuning the custom-built techniques can help in increasing the overall accuracy also.

1 Introduction

Grammatical Error Correction (GEC) is an interesting and challenging problem and the existing methods that attempt to solve this problem take recourse to deep linguistic and statistical analysis. In general, GEC may partly assist in solving natural language processing (NLP) tasks like Machine Translation, Natural Language Generation etc. However, a more evident application of GEC is in building automated grammar checkers thereby non-native speakers of a language. The goal is to have automated tools to help non-native speakers to generate good content by correcting grammatical errors made by them.

The CoNLL-2013 Shared Task (Ng et al., 2013) was focussed towards correcting some of the most frequent categories of grammatical errors. In contrast, the CoNLL-2014 Shared Task (Ng et al., 2014) set the goal of correcting all grammatical errors in the text. For correcting specific error categories, custom methods are generally developed, which exploit deep knowledge of the problem to perform the correction (Han et al., 2006; Kunchukuttan et al., 2013; De Felice and Pulman, 2008). These methods are generally the state-of-the-art for the concerned error categories, but a lot of engineering and research effort is required for correcting each error category. So, the custom development approach is infeasible for correcting a large number of error categories.

Hence, for correction of all the error categories, generic methods have been investigated - generally using language models or statistical machine translation (SMT) systems. The language model based method (Lee and Seneff, 2006; Kao et al., 2013) scores sentences based on a language model or count ratios of n-grams obtained from a large native text corpus. But this method still needs a candidate generation mechanism for each error category. On the other hand, the SMT based method (Brockett et al., 2006) formulates the grammar correction problem as a problem of translation of incorrect sentences to correct sentences. SMT provides a natural unsupervised method for identifying candidate corrections in the form of the translation model, and a method for scoring them with a variety of measures including the language model score. However, the SMT method requires a lot of parallel non-native learner corpora. In addition, the machinery in phrase based SMT is optimized towards solving the language translation problem. Therefore, the community has explored approaches to adapt the

Proceedings of the Eighteenth Conference on Computational Natural Language Learning: Shared Task, pages 60–64,
Baltimore, Maryland, 26-27 July 2014.

SMT method for grammar correction (Buys and van der Merwe, 2013; Yuan and Felice, 2013). These include use of factored SMT, syntax based SMT, pruning of the phrase table, disabling or re-ordering, etc. The generic SMT approach has performed badly as compared to the specific custom made approaches (Yuan and Felice, 2013).

Our system also builds upon the SMT methods and tries to address the above mentioned lacunae in two ways:

- Tuning the SMT model to a metric suitable for grammar correction (i.e.F-β metric), instead of the BLEU metric.
- Combination of custom-engineered methods and SMT based methods, by using classifier based for some error categories.

Section 2 describes our method for tuning the SMT system to optimize the F-β metric. Section 3 explains the combination of classifier based method with the SMT method. Section 4 lists our experimental setup. Section 5 analyzes the results of our experiments.

2 Tuning SMT system for F-β score

We model our grammar correction system as a phrase based SMT system which translates grammatically incorrect sentences to grammatically correct sentences. The phrase based SMT system selects the best translation for a source sentence by searching for a candidate translation which maximizes the score defined by the maximum entropy model for phrase based SMT defined below:

$$P(\mathbf{e}, \mathbf{a}|\mathbf{f}) = \exp \sum_i \lambda_i h_i(\mathbf{e}, \mathbf{a}, \mathbf{f})$$

where,
h_i: feature function for the ith feature. These are generally features like the phrase/lexical translation probability, language model score, etc.
λ_i: the weight parameter for the ith feature.

The weight parameters (λ_i) define the relative weights given to each feature. These parameter weights are learnt during a process referred to as *tuning*. During tuning, a search over the parameter space is done to identify the parameter values which maximize a measure of translation quality over a held-out dataset (referred to as the *tuning* set). One of the most widely used metrics for tuning is the BLEU score (Papineni et al., 2002), tuned using the Minimum Error Rate Training (MERT) algorithm (Och, 2003). Since BLEU is a form of weighted precision, along with a brevity penalty to factor in recall, it is suitable in the language translation scenario, where fidelity of the translation is an important in evaluation of the translation. Tuning to BLEU ensures that the parameter weights are set such that the fidelity of translations is high.

However, ensuring fidelity is not the major challenge in grammar correction since the meaning of most input sentences is clear and most don't have any grammatical errors. The metric to be tuned must ensure that weights are learnt such that the features most relevant to correcting the grammar errors are given due importance and that the tuning focuses on the grammatically incorrect parts of the sentences. The F-β score, as defined for the CoNLL shared task, is the most obvious metric to measure the accuracy of grammar correction on the tuning set. We choose the F-β metric as a score to be optimized using MERT for the SMT based grammar correction model. By choosing an appropriate value of β, it is possible to tune the system to favour increased recall/precision or a balance of both.

3 Integrating SMT based and error-category specific systems

As discussed in Section 1, the generic SMT based correction based systems are inferior in their correction capabilities compared to the error-category specific correction systems which have been custom engineered for the task. A reasonable solution to make optimum use of both the approaches is to develop custom modules for correcting high impact and the most frequent error categories, while relying on the SMT method for correcting other error categories. We experiment with two approaches for integrating the SMT based and error-category specific systems, and compare both with the baseline SMT approach:

- Correct all error categories using the SMT method, followed by correction using the custom modules.
- Correct only the error categories not handled by the custom modules using the SMT method, followed by correction using the custom modules.

The error categories for which we built custom modules are noun number, determiner and subject-verb agreement (SVA) errors. These errors are amongst the most common errors made by non-native speakers. The noun number and determiner errors are corrected using the classification model proposed by Rozovskaya and Roth (2013), where the label space is a cross-product of the label spaces of the possible noun number and determiners. We use the feature-set proposed by Kunchukuttan et al. (2013). SVA correction is done using a prioritized, conditional rule based system described by Kunchukuttan et al. (2013).

4 Experimental Setup

We used the NUCLE Corpus v3.1 to build a phrase based SMT system for grammar correction. The NUCLE Corpus contains 28 error categories, whose details are documented in Dahlmeier et al. (2013). We split the corpus into training, tuning and test sets are shown in Table 1.

Set	Document Count	Sentence Count
train	1330	54284
tune	20	854
test	47	2013

Table 1: Details of data split for SMT training

The phrase based system was trained using the *Moses*[1] system, with the *grow-diag-final-and* heuristic for extracting phrases and the *msd-bidirectional-fe* model for lexicalized reordering. We tuned the trained models using Minimum Error Rate Training (MERT) with default parameters (100 best list, max 25 iterations). Instead of BLEU, the tuning metric was the F-0.5 metric. We trained 5-gram language models on all the sentences from NUCLE corpus using the Kneser-Ney smoothing algorithm with *SRILM* [2].

The classifier for noun number and article correction is a Maximum Entropy model trained on the NUCLE v2.2 corpus using the MALLET toolkit. Details about the resources and tools used for feature extraction are documented in Kunchukuttan et al. (2013).

[1] `http://www.statmt.org/moses/`
[2] `http://goo.gl/4wfLVw`

5 Results and Analysis

Table 2 shows the results on the development set for different experimental configurations generated by varying the tuning metrics, and the method of combining the SMT model and custom correction modules. Table 3 shows the same results on the official CoNLL 2014 dataset without alternative answers.

5.1 Effect of tuning with F-0.5 score

We observe that both precision and recall drop sharply when the SMT model is tuned with the F-0.5 metric (system S2), as compared to tuning with the traditional BLEU metric (system S1). We observe that system S2 proposes very few corrections (82) as compared to system S1 (188), which contributes to the low recall of system S2. There are very few errors in the tuning set (202) which may not be sufficient to reliably tune the system to the F-0.5 score. It would be worth investigating the effect of number of errors in the tuning set on the accuracy of the system.

5.2 Effect of integrating the SMT and custom modules

Comparing the results of systems S1, S3 and S5, it is clear that using the SMT method alone gives the highest F-0.5 score. However, the recall is higher for systems which use the custom modules for some error categories. The recall is highest when custom modules as well as SMT method are used for the high impact error categories. The above observation is a consequence of the fact that the custom modules have higher recall for certain error categories compared to the SMT method. The lower precision of custom modules is due to the large number of false positives. If the custom modules are optimized for higher precision, then the overall ensemble can also achieve higher precision and consequently higher F-0.5 score. Thus, the integration of SMT method and custom modules can be beneficial in improving the overall accuracy of the SMT system.

6 Conclusion

We explored two approaches to adapting the SMT method for the problem of grammatical correction. Tuning the SMT system to the F-β metric did not improve performance over the BLEU-based tuning. However, we plan to further investigate to understand the reasons for this behaviour. We

Id	SMT Data	Custom Modules	Tuning Metric	%P	%R	%F-0.5
S1	All errors	No	BLEU	62.23	11.53	33.12
S2		No	F-0.5	55.32	5.13	18.71
S3		Yes	BLEU	10.99	26.33	12.44
S4		Yes	F-0.5	9.80	22.98	11.07
S5	All errors, except Nn, ArtOrDet, SVA	Yes	BLEU	10.15	23.96	11.47

Table 2: Experimental Results for various configurations on the development set

Id	SMT Data	Custom Modules	Tuning Metric	%P	%R	%F-0.5
S1	All errors	No	BLEU	38.81	4.15	14.53
S2		No	F-0.5	30.77	1.39	5.90
S3		Yes	BLEU	29.02	17.98	25.85
S4		Yes	F-0.5	28.23	16.72	24.81
S5	All errors, except Nn, ArtOrDet, SVA	Yes	BLEU	28.67	17.29	25.34

Table 3: Experimental Results for various configurations on the CoNLL-2014 test set without alternatives

also plan to explore tuning for recall and other alternative metrics which could be useful in some scenarios. An ensemble of the SMT method and custom methods for some high impact error categories was shown to increase the recall of the system, and with proper optimization of the system can also improve the overall accuracy of the correction system.

References

Chris Brockett, William B Dolan, and Michael Gamon. 2006. Correcting ESL errors using phrasal SMT techniques. In *Proceedings of the 21st International Conference on Computational Linguistics and the 44th annual meeting of the Association for Computational Linguistics*.

Jan Buys and Brink van der Merwe. 2013. A Tree Transducer Model for Grammatical Error Correction. In *Proceedings of the Seventeenth Conference on Computational Natural Language Learning: Shared Task*.

Daniel Dahlmeier and Hwee Tou Ng. 2012. Better Evaluation for Grammatical Error Correction. In *Proceedings of the 2012 Conference of the North American Chapter of the Association for Computational Linguistics*.

Daniel Dahlmeier, Hwee Tou Ng, and Siew Mei Wu. 2013. Building a large annotated corpus of learner english: The NUS Corpus of Learner English. In *To appear in Proceedings of the 8th Workshop on Innovative Use of NLP for Building Educational Applications*.

Rachele De Felice and Stephen G Pulman. 2008. A classifier-based approach to preposition and determiner error correction in L2 English. In *Proceedings of the 22nd International Conference on Computational Linguistics-Volume 1*.

Na-Rae Han, Martin Chodorow, and Claudia Leacock. 2006. Detecting errors in English article usage by non-native speakers. *Natural Language Engineering*.

Ting-hui Kao, Yu-wei Chang, Hsun-wen Chiu, Tzu-Hsi Yen, Joanne Boisson, Jian-cheng Wu, and Jason S. Chang. 2013. CoNLL-2013 Shared Task: Grammatical Error Correction NTHU System Description. In *Proceedings of the Seventeenth Conference on Computational Natural Language Learning: Shared Task*.

Anoop Kunchukuttan, Ritesh Shah, and Pushpak Bhattacharyya. 2013. IITB System for CoNLL 2013 Shared Task: A Hybrid Approach to Grammatical Error Correction. In *Proceedings of the Seventeenth Conference on Computational Natural Language Learning*.

J. Lee and S. Seneff. 2006. Automatic grammar correction for second-language learners. In *Proceedings of Interspeech*, pages 1978–1981.

Hwee Tou Ng, Siew Mei Wu, Yuanbin Wu, Christian Hadiwinoto, and Joel Tetreault. 2013. The CoNLL-2013 Shared Task on Grammatical Error Correction. In *Proceedings of the Seventeenth Conference on Computational Natural Language Learning*.

Hwee Tou Ng, Siew Mei Wu, Ted Briscoe, Christian Hadiwinoto, Raymond Hendy Susanto, and Christopher Bryant. 2014. The CoNLL-2014 Shared Task on Grammatical Error Correction. In *Proceedings of the Eighteenth Conference on Computational Natural Language Learning*.

Franz Josef Och. 2003. Minimum error rate training in statistical machine translation. In *Proceedings of the 41st Annual Meeting on Association for Computational Linguistics-Volume 1*.

Kishore Papineni, Salim Roukos, Todd Ward, and Wei-Jing Zhu. 2002. BLEU: a method for automatic evaluation of machine translation. In *Proceedings of the 40th annual meeting on association for computational linguistics*.

A. Rozovskaya and D. Roth. 2013. Joint Learning and Inference for Grammatical Error Correction. In *EMNLP*.

Zheng Yuan and Mariano Felice. 2013. Constrained Grammatical Error Correction using Statistical Machine Translation. In *Proceedings of the Seventeenth Conference on Computational Natural Language Learning: Shared Task*.

POSTECH Grammatical Error Correction System in the CoNLL-2014 Shared Task

Kyusong Lee, Gary Geunbae Lee
Department of Computer Science and Engineering
Pohang University of Science and Technology
Pohang, Korea
{Kyusonglee,gblee}@postech.ac.kr

Abstract

This paper describes the POSTECH grammatical error correction system. Various methods are proposed to correct errors such as rule-based, probability n-gram vector approaches and router-based approach. Google N-gram count corpus is used mainly as the correction resource. Correction candidates are extracted from NUCLE training data and each candidate is evaluated with development data to extract high precision rules and n-gram frames. Out of 13 participating teams, our system is ranked 4th on both the original and revised annotation.

1 Introduction

Automatic grammar error correction (GEC) is widely used by learners of English as a second language (ESL) in written tasks. Many methods have been proposed to correct grammatical errors; these include methods based on rules (Naber, 2003), on statistical machine translation (Brockett et al., 2006), on machine learning, and on n-grams (Alam et al., 2006). Early research (Han et al., 2006; De Felice, 2008; Knight & Chander, 1994; Nagata et al., 2006) on error correction for non-native text was based on well-formed corpora.

Most recent work (Cahill et al., 2013; Rozovskaya & Roth, 2011; Wu & Ng, 2013) has used machine learning methods that rely on a GE-tagged corpus such as NUCLE, Japanese English Learner corpus, and Cambridge Learner Corpus (Dahlmeier et al., 2013; Izumi et al., 2005; Nicholls, 2003), because well-formed and GE-tagged approaches are closely related to each other, can be synergistically combined. Therefore, research using both types of data has also been conducted (Dahlmeier & Ng, 2011). Moreover, a meta-classification method using several GE-tagged corpora and a native corpus has been proposed to correct the grammatical errors (Seo et al., 2012). A meta-classifier approach has been proposed to combine a language model and error-specific classification for correction of article and preposition errors (Gamon, 2010). Web-scale well-formed corpora have been successfully applied to grammar error correction tasks instead of using error-tagged data (Bergsma et al., 2009; Gamon et al., 2009; Hermet et al., 2008). Especially in the CoNLL-2013 grammar error correction shared task, many of the high-ranked teams (Kao et al., 2013; Mark & Roth, 2013; Xing et al., 2013) exploited the Google Web-1T n-gram corpus. The major advantage of using these web-scale corpora is that extremely large quantities of data are publicly available at no additional costs; thus fewer data sparseness problems arise compared to previous approaches based on error-tagged corpora.

We also use the Google Web-1T n-gram corpus. We extract the candidate pairs (original erroneous text and its correction) from NUCLE training data. We use a router to choose the best frame to compare the n-gram score difference between the original and replacement in a given candidate pair.

The intuition of our grammar error correction method is the following: First, if the uni-gram count is less than some threshold, we assume that the word is erroneous. Second, if the replacement word n-gram has more frequent than the original word n-gram, it presents strong evidence for correction. Third, depending on the candidate pair, tailored n-gram frames help to correct errors accurately. Fourth, only high precision method and rules are applied. If correction precision on a candidate pair is less than 30% in development data,

Proceedings of the Eighteenth Conference on Computational Natural Language Learning: Shared Task, pages 65–73,
Baltimore, Maryland, 26-27 July 2014.

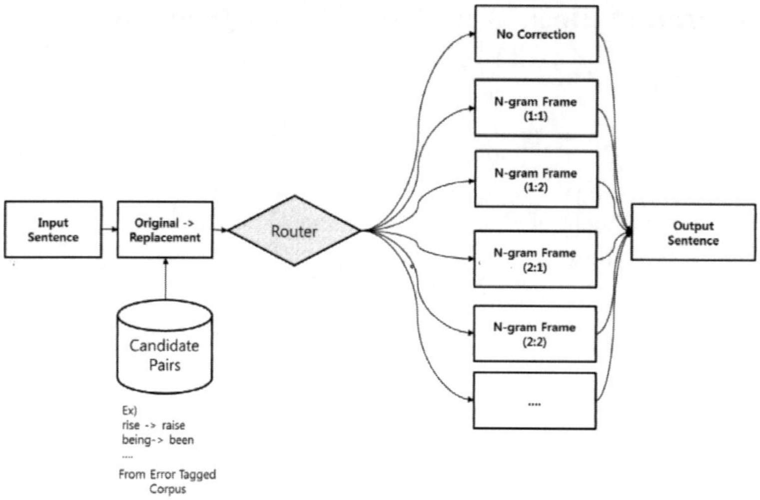

Figure 1. Overall Process of Router-based Correction

we do not make a correction for the candidate pair at runtime.

In the CoNLL-Shared Task, objectives were presented yearly. In 2012, the objective was to correct article and preposition errors; in 2013, it was to correct article, preposition, noun number, verb form, and subject-verb agreement errors. This year, the objective is to correct all errors. Thus, our method should also correct preprocessing and spelling errors. Detailed description of the shared task set up, data set, and evaluation about the CoNLL-2014 Shared Task is explained in (Ng et al., 2014)

2 Data and Recourse

The Google Web-1T corpus contains 10^{12} words of running text and the counts for all 10^9 five-word sequences that appear > 40 times (Brants & Franz, 2006). We used the NUS Corpus of Learner English (NUCLE) training data to extract the candidate pairs and CoNLL-2013 Official Shard Task test data as development data. We used the Stanford parser (De Marneffe & Manning, 2008) to extract part-of-speech, dependency, and constituency trees.

3 Method

3.1 Overall Process

We correct the errors in the following order:
Tokenizing → spelling error correction → punctuation error correction → N-gram Vector Approach for Noun number (Nn) → Router-based Correction (Deletion Correction → Insertion Correction → Replacement) for various error types → Rule-based method for verb errors. Between each pair of step, we parse, tag, and tokenize again using the Stanford parser because the previous correction affects parsing, tagging, and tokenizing results.

3.2 Preprocessing

Because the correction task is no longer restricted to five error types, tokenizing and spelling error correction have become critical for error correction. To detect tokenizing error such as "civilizations.It", a re-tokenzing process is necessary. If a word contains a comma, punctuation (e.g., ',' or '.') and the word count in Google n-gram is less than some threshold (here, 1000), we tokenize the word, e.g., as "civilizations . It". We also correct spelling errors by referring to the Google n-gram word count. If the word uni-gram count is less than a threshold (here, 60000) and the part-of-speech (POS) tag is not NNP or NNPS, we assume that the word has o ne or more errors. The threshold is set based on the development set. We use the Enchant Python Library to correct the spelling errors[1]. However, using only one best result is not very accurate. Thus, among the best results in the Enchant Python Library, we select the one best word, i.e. that word with the highest frequency in the Google n-gram corpus. Using NUCLE training data, rules are constructed for comma, punctuation, and other errors (Table 3).

[1] http://abisource.com/projects/enchant/

3.3 Candidate Generation

Selecting appropriate correction candidates is critical for the precision of the method. In article and noun number correction, the number of candidates is small: 'a','an','the' in article correction, 'plural' or 'singular' in noun number correction. However, the number of correction candidates can be unlimited in wrong collocation/idiom errors. Reducing the number of candidates is important in the grammar error correction task.

Nn Correction Candidate: noun number correction has just one replacement candidate. If the word is plural, its correction candidate is singular, and vice versa. The language tool[2] can perform these changes.

Other Correction Candidate: for corrections other than noun number, candidates are selected from the GE-tagged corpus. A total of 4206 pairs were extracted. We use the notation of candidate pair (o→r), which links the original word (o) and its correction candidate (r). In the deletion correction step, we determine whether or not the word should be deleted. In the insertion correction step, we select the insertion position in a sentence as a space between two words. If o is ∅, insertion correction is required; if r is ∅, the pair deletion correction is required. We use the Stanford constituency parser (De Marneffe & Manning, 2008) to extract a noun phrase; if it does not contain a determiner or article, we insert one in front of the noun phrase; if the noun in the noun phrase is singular, 'the', 'a', and, 'an' are selected an insertion candidates; if the noun is plural, only 'the' is selected as an insertion candidate. We only apply insertion correction at ArtOrDet, comma errors, and preposition; we skip insertion correction for other error types because selecting an insertion position is difficult and if every position is selected as insertion position, precision decrease.

4 N-gram Approach

We used the following notation.

N(o)	n-gram vector in original sentence
N(r)	n-gram vector in replacement sentence
$n(o)_i$	i th element in N(o)
$n(r)_i$	i th element in N(r)
N[i:j]	n-gram vector from i th element to j th element

[2]http://www.languagetool.org

Web-scale data have also been used successfully in many other research areas, such as lexical disambiguation (Bergsma et al., 2009). Most NLP systems resolve ambiguities with the help of a large corpus of text, e.g.:

- The system tried to decide {among, between} the two confusable words.

Disambiguation accuracy increases with the size of the corpus. Many systems incorporate the web count into their selection process. For the above example, a typical web-based system would query a search engine with the sequences "decide among the" and "decide between the" and select the candidate that returns the most hits. Unfortunately, this approach would fail when disambiguation requires additional context. Bergsma (2009) suggested using the context of samples of various lengths and positions. For example, from the above the example sentence, the following 5-gram patterns can be extracted:

- system tried to decide {among, between}
- tried to decide {among, between} the
- to decide {among, between} the two
- decide {among, between} the two confusable
- {among, between} the two confusable words

Similarly, four 4-gram patterns, three 3-gram patterns and two 2-gram patterns are extracted by spanning the target. A score for each pattern is calculated by summing the log-counts. This method was successfully applied in lexical disambiguation. Web-scale data were used with the count information specified as features. Kao et al. (2013) used a "moving window (MW)" :

$$MW_{i,k}(w) = \{w_{i-j}, \dots, w_{i-j+(k-1)}, j = 0, k-1\} \quad (1)$$

where i denotes the position of the word, k the window size and w the original or replacement word at position i. The window size is set to 2 to 5 words. MW is the same concept as the SUMLM:

$$S_{i,k}(w) = \sum_{ngram \in MW_k(w)} count(ngram) \quad (2)$$

Both approaches apply the sum of all MWs in (1). Our approach is based on the MW method. The difference is that instead of summing all the MWs, we consider only one best MW which is referred to here as a frame. The following sentences demonstrate the case when the following words are the crucial features to correct errors:

- I will do it (in→at) home.
- We need (an→∅) equipment to solve problems.

However, following sentences demonstrate the case when preceding words is the crucial feature to correct errors:

- One (are→is) deemed to death at a later stage .
- But data that (shows→show) the rising of life expectancies

We investigated which frame is the best based on the development set, then router is trained to decide on the frame depending on the candidate pair.

4.1 Router-based N-gram Correction

A frame is a sequence of words around the target position. A frame is divided into a preceding frame and a following frame. The target position can be either a position of a target word (Figure 2a) or a position in which a candidate word is judged to be necessary (Figure 2b). Once the size (i.e., number of words) of frames is chosen, several forms of frames (n; m) with different sizes of preceding (n) and following (m) words are possible.

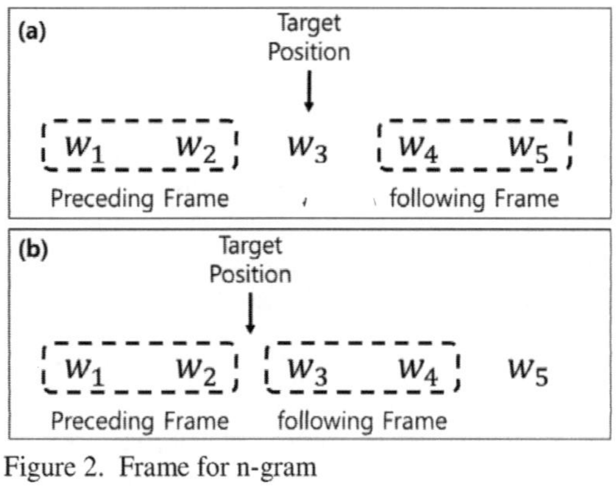

Figure 2. Frame for n-gram

The router is designed to take care of two stages (training, run-time) error correction. During training, the router selects the best frame for each candidate pair. By testing each candidate pair with each frame in the development data; the frame with the best precision is selected as the best frame among (1;1), (1;2), (1;3), (2;1),(2:2), etc.

At the end of the training stage, the router has a list of pairs (x) which matches the best frame (y) associated with it (Table 1) as a result of comparing each candidate pair with one in the development corpus.

During runtime, the router assigns each candidate pair to the best frame to produce the output sentence (Figure 1). For example, for a sentence "This ability is not seen 40 years **back** where the technology advances were not as good as now ." the candidate pair for correction (back→ ago) is suggested. The best frame assigned by the router for this pair (1;1), which is "years back where". The best candidate frame for this is "year ago where". At this point, we query the count of "years back where" and "years ago where" from the Google N-gram Count Corpus; these counts are 46 and 1815 respectively. Because the count

Table 1. Example of Trained Router

x (o→r)	y
(another→other)	(1;3)
(less→fewer)	(1;3)
(rise→raise)	(1;2)
(back→ago)	(1;1)
(could→can)	(2;1)
(well→good)	(2;1)
(near→∅)	No correction

of "years ago where" is greater than that of "years back where", the former is selected as the correct form. As a result, the sentence "This ability is not seen 40 years **back** where the technology advances were not as good as now." is corrected to "This ability is not seen 40 years **ago** where the technology advances were not as good as now."

Some words are allowed to have multiple best frames; in all the best frames, if a candidate word sequence is more frequent than an original word sequence in the Google count, then correction is made. The multiple frames are also trained from the development data set.

4.2 Probability n-gram Vector

We use the probability n-gram Vector approach to correct Nn. Most errors are corrected using the router-based method; however, training the router for every noun is difficult because the number of nouns is extremely large. Moreover, for noun number, we found that rather than considering one direction or one frame of n-gram, every direction of n-gram should be considered for better performance such as forward, backward, and two-way. Thus, the probability n-gram vector algorithm is applied only in the noun number error correction. We propose the probability n-gram vector method to correct grammatical errors to consider both directions, forward and backward. In a forward n-gram, the probability of each word is estimated depending on the preceding word. On the other hand, in a backward n-gram the probability of each word is estimated depending on the following words. When the probability of a candidate word is higher than original word, we replace the original with the candidate word in the correction step.

Probability n-gram vectors are generated from the original word and a candidate word (Figure 3). Rather than using a single sequence of n-gram probability, we apply contexts of various lengths and positions. We applied the probability information using the Google n-gram count information as in the following equation:

$$P(w_i|w_{i-2}, w_{i-1}) = \frac{C(w_{i-2}, w_{i-1} w_i)}{C(w_{i-2}, w_{i-1})}$$

Moreover, rather than calculating one word's probability given n words such as $P(w_i|w_{i-1}, w_{i-2}, w_{i-3})$, our model calculates the probability of m words given an n word sequence. The following is an example 4-gram with forward probability:

- m = 3, n = 1 $P(w_{i-2}, w_{i-1} w_i|w_{i-3})$
- m = 2, n = 2 $P(w_{i-1}, w_i|w_{i-3}, w_{i-2})$
- m = 1, n = 3 $P(w_i|w_{i-3}, w_{i-2}, w_{i-1})$.

We construct a 40-dimensional probability vector with forward and backward probabilities considering of twenty 5-grams, twelve 4-grams, six 3-gram, and two 2-gram. Additionally, the elements of the n-gram vector are detailed in Table 2.

Table 2: The elements of n-gram vector

5-GRAM
$n_0 = P(w_i\|w_{i+1} w_{i+2} w_{i+3} w_{i+4})$ backward
$n_1 = P(w_i\|w_{i-4} w_{i-3} w_{i-2} w_{i-1})$ forward
$n_2 = P(w_i w_{i+1}\|w_{i+2} w_{i+3} w_{i+4})$ backward
……..
4-GRAM
$n_{20} = P(w_i\|w_{i+1} w_{i+2} w_{i+3})$ backward
$n_{21} = P(w_i\|w_{i-3} w_{i-2} w_{i-1})$ forward
……..
3-GRAM
$n_{32} = P(w_i\|w_{i+1} w_{i+2})$ backward
$n_{33} = P(w_i\|w_{i-2} w_{i-1})$ forward
$n_{34} = P(w_i w_{i+1}\|w_{i+2})$ backward
$n_{35} = P(w_{i-1} w_i\|w_{i-2})$ forward
$n_{36} = P(w_{i-1} w_i\|w_{i+1})$ backward
$n_{37} = P(w_i w_{i+1}\|w_{i-1})$ forward
2-GRAM
$n_{38} = P(w_i\|w_{i+1})$ backward
$n_{39} = P(w_i\|w_{i-1})$ forward

Generate Candidates
- Original : work
- Candidate : works

Generate Probability N-gram Vector
- $n(o) = n_{\text{work}}$ =[0,0,0,0,0.2,0.3,……..,0]
- $n(r) = n_{\text{works}}$ =[0,0,0.7,0,0,0.4,0.2,……0]

Calculate each n-gram direction by back-off
- $P_{forward}$:$[\sum_{i=0}^{19} n(o)_{2i+1}, \sum_{i=0}^{20} n(r)_{2i+1}]$ =[0,3,0.4]
- $P_{backward}$:$[\sum_{i=0}^{20} n(o)_{2i}, \sum_{i=0}^{20} n(r)_{2i}]$=[0.2,0.9]
- $P_{two-way}$:$[\sum_{i=0}^{40} n(o)_i, \sum_{i=0}^{20} n(o)_i]$=[0.5,1.3]
- $fi = \text{argmax}_i P_{forward}$
- $bi = \text{argmax}_i P_{backward}$
- $fi = \text{argmax}_i P_{two-way}$
- If bi = 0 or fi =0 or ti = 0
  - then no correction
- else if bi=fi=ti then index= bi

Figure 3. Overall process of Nn Correction

Back-Off Model: A high-order n-gram is more effective than a low-order n-gram. Thus, we applied back-off methods (Katz, 1987) to assign higher priority to higher order probabilities. If all elements in 5-gram vectors are 0 for both the original and candidate sentence, which means $\sum_{i=0}^{19}\{n(o)_i + n(r)_i\} = 0$, we consider 4-gram vectors ($N_{[20:31]}$). If 4-gram vectors are 0, we consider 3-gram vectors. Moreover, when the proposed method calculates each of the forward, backward and two-way probabilities, the back-off method is used to get each score.

Correction: Here, we explain the process of error correction using n-gram vectors. First, we generate Nn error candidates. Second, we construct the n-gram probability vector for each candidate. The back-off method is applied in N(o)+N(r), The vector contains various directions and ranges of probabilities of words given a sample sentence. We then calculate forward n-gram score by summing even elements in the vector. We calculate the backward n-gram by summing odd elements in Table 2. Next, the two-way n-gram is calculated by summing all elements for both directions n-gram. If forward, backward, and two-way n-grams have higher probabilities for the candidate word, we select the candidate as corrected word (Figure 3).

Algorithm Rule1-Comma

```
function rule1( tok_sent, tok_pos)
  for i ← 0 ... len(tok_sent) do
    if tok_sent[i] in [ However', 'Therefore', 'Thus'] and not tok_sent[i + 1] == ',' then
      tok_sent[i]= tok_sent[i] + ','
```

Algorithm Rule2-preposition

```
function rule2( tok_sent, tok_pos)
  for i ← 0 ... len(tok_sent) do
    if tok_sent[i] = 'according' and not tok_sent [i+1] = 'to'
      tok_sent [i+1] = 'to '+ tok_sent [i+1]
```

Algorithm Rule3-Subject Verb Agreement

```
function rule3( tok_sent, tok_pos)
  for i ← 0 ... len(tok_sent) do
    if tok_sent[i] is 'which'
      if tok_pos[i − 1] == 'NNS' and tok_pos[i + 1] == 'VBZ' then
        tok_sent[i + 1]= changeWordForm (tok_sent[i + 1], 'VBP')
      else if tok_pos[i − 1] == 'NNS' and tok_pos[i + 1] == 'NNS' then
        tok_sent[i + 1]= =changeWordForm(tok_sent[i + 1], 'VBP')
      else if tok_pos[i − 1] == 'NN' and tok_pos[i + 1]== 'are' then
        tok_sent[i + 1]= = is
      else if tok_pos[i − 1] == 'NN' and tok_pos[i + 1] in ['VBP','VB','NN'] then
        tok_sent[i + 1]= = makePlural(tok_sent[i + 1])
```

Algorithm Rule4-Subject Verb Agreement

```
function rule4( tok_sent, tok_pos)
  for i ← 0 ... len(tok_sent) do
    if not ( tok_pos[i]is 'VBZ' and ['NN','this','it','one','VBG'] in tok_pos[i − 5: i]) then
      tok_cand ←changeWordForm( tok_word[i], 'VBP')
    else if not ( tok_pos[i]is 'VBP' and ['I','we','they','and'] in tok_sent[i − 5: i]) then
      tok_cand ←changeWordForm( tok_word[i], 'VBZ')
    else if not ( tok_pos[i]is 'NN' and ['be','ing'] in tok_sent[i − 5: i]) then
      tok_cand ←changeWordForm( tok_word[i], 'VBN')
    original = ngramCount( tok_sent), candidate =ngramCount(tok_cand)
    If original < candidate then
      Return tok_cand
```

Table 3. Examples of Rules

5 Verb Correction (Rule-based)

There are several types of verb errors in non-native text such as verb tense, verb modal, missing verb, verb form, and subject-verb-agreement (SVA). Among these errors, we attempt to correct SVA errors using rule-based methods (Table 3). In non-native text, parsing and tagging errors are inevitable, and it may cause false alarm. Thus, instead of dependency parsing to find subject and verb, we consider the preceding five words because erroneous sentences often contain dependency errors. Moreover, in erroneous sentences, POS tagging accuracy is lower than native text. Thus, NN and VB are misclassified, as are VBZ and NNS. A rule is used that encodes the relevant linguistic knowledge that these words or POSs should not occur in the five positions preceding the VBZ: 'NN', 'this', 'it' ,'one', 'VBG'. Moreover, words that preceded and follow 'which' should agree in verb form, as indicated in Rule3 and Rule4.

6 Experiment

The CoNLL-2014 training data consist of 1,397 articles together with gold-standard annotation.

Table 4. Performance on each error type

	Original annotation			Revised annotation		
	Precision	Recall	F0.5	Precision	Recall	F0.5
N-gram (Nn)	31.0	6.55	17.75	42.28	9.0	24.31
Rule (Verb)	28.95	1.12	4.86	31.17	1.29	5.52
Rule (Mec)	49.34	5.47	18.94	52.16	6.17	20.93
Router (Others)	28.11	12.49	22.49	35.29	15.45	28.08
All	**34.51**	**21.73**	**30.88**	**41.28**	**25.59**	**36.77**

The documents are a subset of the NUS Corpus of Learner English (NUCLE). We use the Max-Match (M2) scorer provided by the CoNLL-2014 Shared Task. The M2 scorer works by using the set that maximally matches the set of gold-standard edits specified by the annotator as being equal to the set of system edits that are automatically computed and used in scoring (Dahlmeier & Ng, 2012). The official evaluation metric is F0.5, weighting precision twice as much as recall. We achieve F0.5 of 30.88; precision of 34.51; recall of 21.73 in the original annotation (Table 4). After original official annotations announced by organizers (i.e., only based on the annotations of the two annotators), another set of annotations is offered based on including the additional answers proposed by the 3 teams (CAMB, CUUI, UMC). The improvement gap between the original annotation and the revised annotation of our team (POST) is 5.89%. We obtain the highest improvement rate except for the 3 proposed teams (Figure 4), F0.5 of 36.77; precision of 41.28; recall of 25.59 in the revised annotation. Our system achieves the 4th highest scores of 13 participating teams based on both the original and revised annotations. To analyze the scores of each of the error types and modules, we apply the method of n-gram vector (Nn), rule-based (Verb, Mec), and router-based (others) separately in both the original and the revised annotation of all error types. We achieve high precision by rules at the Mec which indicates punctuation, capitalization, spelling, and typos errors. Additionally, the Nn type has the highest improvement gap between the original and revised annotation (17% → 24.31 of F0.5). In order for our team to improve the high precision in the rule-based approach, we tested potential rules on the development data and kept a rule only if its precision on that data set was 30% or greater. When we trained router, the same strategy was conducted. If a frame could not achieve 30% precision, we assigned the candidate pair as "no correction" in the router. These constraints achieve precision of 30 % in most error types.

7 Discussion

Although preposition errors are frequently committed in non-native text, we mostly skip the correction of preposition error. This is because assigning prepositions correctly is extremely difficult, because (1) the preposition used can vary (e.g., Canada: 'on the weekend' vs. Britain 'at the weekend'); (2) in a given location, more than one preposition may be possible, and the choice affects the meaning (e.g., 'on the wall', vs. 'at the wall'). Verb errors can consist of many multi-

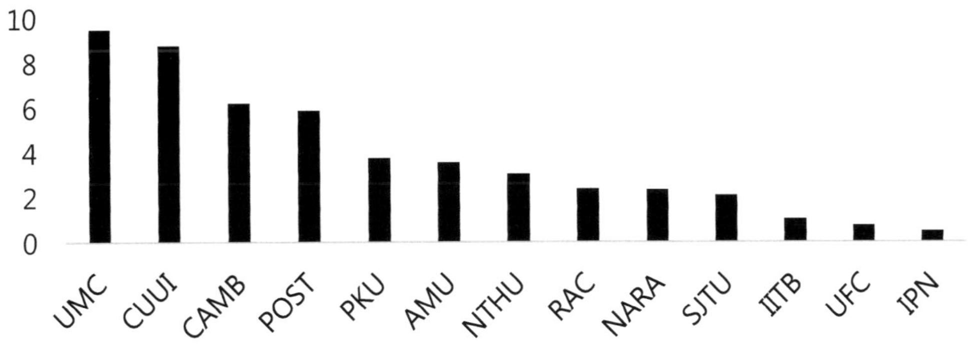

Figure 4. Improvement gap between the original annotation and revised annotation of each team

word errors due to errors of usages of passive and active voice. (e.g. release→be released). Our current system cannot correct these multi-words errors, for three reasons. First, if the original example consists of one word and the optimal replacement consists of two words, n-gram scores cannot be applied easily to compare probabilities between them. Second, the n-gram approach also fails if the distance between subject and verb is more than 5. Third, multiply dependent errors are critical for verb error correction. For example, noun number, determiner, and subject verb agreement are often dependent upon each other: e.g. "And once this happens, privacy does not exist any more and people's (life→lives) (is→are) under great threaten." The correction order will be important when all error type must be corrected simultaneously.

Grammar error correction is a challenging problem. In CoNNL-2013, more than half of the related teams obtained F-score < 10.0. This low performance in the grammar error correction can be explained by several reasons, which indicate the present limitations of grammar correction systems.

Among a total of 4206 pairs, we only use small amount of candidate pairs, 215 pairs are used for candidate pairs. The other 3991 pairs are discarded in the router training step because these pairs cannot be corrected by the n-gram approach. Various classification methods and statistical machine translation based methods will be investigated in the router-based approach to find the tailored methods for the given word. A demonstration and progress of our grammar error correction system is available to the public[3].

8 Conclusion

We have described the POSTECH grammatical error correction system. We use the Google N-gram count corpus to detect spelling errors, punctuation, and comma errors. A rule-based method is used to correct verb, punctuation, comma errors and preposition errors. The Google corpus is also used for an n-gram vector approach and a router-based approaches. Currently we use the router to select the best frame. In the future, we will train a router to select the best method among classification, n-gram approach, statistical machine translation-based method and pattern matching approaches. A machine learning method will be used to train the router with various features.

Acknowledgements

This research was supported by the MSIP(The Ministry of Science, ICT and Future Planning), Korea and Microsoft Research, under IT/SW Creative research program supervised by the NIPA(National IT Industry Promotion Agency) (NIPA-2013- H0503-13-1006) and this research was supported by the Basic Science Research Program through the National Research Foundation of Korea(NRF) funded by the Ministry of Education, Science and Technology(2010-0019523).

References

Han, Na-Rae, Chodorow, Martin, & Leacock, Claudia. (2006). Detecting errors in English article usage by non-native speakers.

Alam, Md Jahangir, UzZaman, Naushad, & Khan, Mumit. (2006). N-gram based statistical grammar checker for Bangla and English.

Bergsma, Shane, Lin, Dekang, & Goebel, Randy. (2009). *Web-Scale N-gram Models for Lexical Disambiguation.* Paper presented at the IJCAI.

Brants, Thorsten, & Franz, Alex. (2006). The Google Web 1T 5-gram corpus version 1.1. *LDC2006T13.*

Brockett, Chris, Dolan, William B, & Gamon, Michael. (2006). *Correcting ESL errors using phrasal SMT techniques.* Paper presented at the Proceedings of the 21st International Conference on Computational Linguistics and the 44th annual meeting of the Association for Computational Linguistics.

Cahill, Aoife, Madnani, Nitin, Tetreault, Joel, & Napolitano, Diane. (2013). *Robust Systems for Preposition Error Correction Using Wikipedia Revisions.* Paper presented at the Proceedings of NAACL-HLT.

Dahlmeier, Daniel, & Ng, Hwee Tou. (2011). *Grammatical error correction with alternating structure optimization.* Paper presented at the Proceedings of the 49th Annual Meeting of the Association for Computational Linguistics: Human Language Technologies-Volume 1.

Dahlmeier, Daniel, & Ng, Hwee Tou. (2012). *Better evaluation for grammatical error correction.* Paper presented at the Proceedings of the 2012 Conference of the North American Chapter of the Association for Computational Linguistics: Human Language Technologies.

[3] http://isoft.postech.ac.kr/grammar

Dahlmeier, Daniel, Ng, Hwee Tou, & Wu, Siew Mei. (2013). *Building a large annotated corpus of learner English: The NUS corpus of learner English.* Paper presented at the Proceedings of the Eighth Workshop on Innovative Use of NLP for Building Educational Applications.

De Felice, Rachele. (2008). *Automatic error detection in non-native English.* University of Oxford.

De Marneffe, Marie-Catherine, & Manning, Christopher D. (2008). *The Stanford typed dependencies representation.* Paper presented at the Coling 2008: Proceedings of the workshop on Cross-Framework and Cross-Domain Parser Evaluation.

Gamon, Michael. (2010). *Using mostly native data to correct errors in learners' writing: a meta-classifier approach.* Paper presented at the Human Language Technologies: The 2010 Annual Conference of the North American Chapter of the Association for Computational Linguistics.

Gamon, Michael, Leacock, Claudia, Brockett, Chris, Dolan, William B, Gao, Jianfeng, Belenko, Dmitriy, & Klementiev, Alexandre. (2009). Using statistical techniques and web search to correct ESL errors. *Calico Journal, 26*(3), 491-511.

Hermet, Matthieu, Désilets, Alain, & Szpakowicz, Stan. (2008). Using the web as a linguistic resource to automatically correct lexico-syntactic errors.

Izumi, Emi, Uchimoto, Kiyotaka, & Isahara, Hitoshi. (2005). *Error annotation for corpus of Japanese learner English.* Paper presented at the Proceedings of the Sixth International Workshop on Linguistically Interpreted Corpora.

Kao, Ting-Hui, Chang, Yu-Wei, Chiu, Hsun-Wen, & Yen, Tzu-Hsi. (2013). CoNLL-2013 Shared Task: Grammatical Error Correction NTHU System Description. *CoNLL-2013, 20.*

Katz, Slava. (1987). Estimation of probabilities from sparse data for the language model component of a speech recognizer. *Acoustics, Speech and Signal Processing, IEEE Transactions on, 35*(3), 400-401.

Knight, Kevin, & Chander, Ishwar. (1994). *Automated postediting of documents.* Paper presented at the AAAI.

Mark, Alla Rozovskaya Kai-Wei Chang, & Roth, Sammons Dan. (2013). The University of Illinois System in the CoNLL-2013 Shared Task. *CoNLL-2013, 51*, 13.

Naber, Daniel. (2003). A rule-based style and grammar checker. Diploma Thesis

Nagata, Ryo, Morihiro, Koichiro, Kawai, Atsuo, & Isu, Naoki. (2006). *A feedback-augmented method for detecting errors in the writing of learners of English.* Paper presented at the Proceedings of the 21st International Conference on Computational Linguistics and the 44th annual meeting of the Association for Computational Linguistics.

Ng, Hwee Tou , Wu, Siew Mei , Briscoe, Ted , Hadiwinoto, Christian , Susanto, Raymond Hendy, & Bryant, Christopher (2014). *The CoNLL-2014 Shared Task on Grammatical Error Correction.* Paper presented at the the Eighteenth Conference on Computational Natural Language Learning: Shared Task (CoNLL-2014 Shared Task), Baltimore, Maryland, USA.

Nicholls, Diane. (2003). *The Cambridge Learner Corpus: Error coding and analysis for lexicography and ELT.* Paper presented at the Proceedings of the Corpus Linguistics 2003 conference.

Rozovskaya, Alla, & Roth, Dan. (2011). Algorithm selection and model adaptation for ESL correction tasks. *Urbana, 51*, 61801.

Seo, Hongsuck, Lee, Jonghoon, Kim, Seokhwan, Lee, Kyusong, Kang, Sechun, & Lee, Gary Geunbae. (2012). *A meta learning approach to grammatical error correction.* Paper presented at the Proceedings of the 50th Annual Meeting of the Association for Computational Linguistics: Short Papers-Volume 2.

Wu, Yuanbin, & Ng, Hwee Tou. (2013). *Grammatical error correction using integer linear programming.* Paper presented at the Proceedings of the 51st Annual Meeting of the Association for Computational Linguistics.

Xing, Junwen, Wang, Longyue, Wong, Derek F, Chao, Lidia S, & Zeng, Xiaodong. (2013). UM-Checker: A Hybrid System for English Grammatical Error Cor-rection. *CoNLL-2013*, 34.

Yannakoudakis, Helen, Briscoe, Ted, & Medlock, Ben. (2011). *A New Dataset and Method for Automatically Grading ESOL Texts.* Paper presented at the ACL.

Grammatical Error Detection and Correction using a Single Maximum Entropy Model*

Peilu Wang, Zhongye Jia and Hai Zhao†
Key Laboratory of Shanghai Education Commission for
Intelligent Interaction and Cognitive Engineering,
Center for Brain-Like Computing and Machine Intelligence
Department of Computer Science and Engineering, Shanghai Jiao Tong University
800 Dongchuan Road, Shanghai 200240, China
{plwang1990, jia.zhongye}@gmail.com, zhaohai@cs.sjtu.edu.cn

Abstract

This paper describes the system of Shanghai Jiao Tong Unvierity team in the CoNLL-2014 shared task. Error correction operations are encoded as a group of predefined labels and therefore the task is formulized as a multi-label classification task. For training, labels are obtained through a strict rule-based approach. For decoding, errors are detected and corrected according to the classification results. A single maximum entropy model is used for the classification implementation incorporated with an improved feature selection algorithm. Our system achieved precision of 29.83, recall of 5.16 and F_0.5 of 15.24 in the official evaluation.

1 Introduction

The task of CoNLL-2014 is grammatical error correction which consists of detecting and correcting the grammatical errors in English essays written by non-native speakers (Ng et al., 2014). The research of grammatical error correction can potentially help millions of people in the world who are learning English as foreign language. Although there have been many works on grammatical error correction, the current approaches mainly focus on very limited error types and the result is far from satisfactory.

The CoNLL-2014 shared task, compared with the previous Help Our Own (HOO) tasks (Dale et al., 2012) considering only determiner and preposition errors and the CoNLL-2013 shared task focusing on five major types of errors, requires to correct all 28 types of errors (Ng et al., 2014).

One traditional strategy is designing a system combined of a set of sub-models, where each sub-model is specialized for a specific subtask, for example, correcting one type of errors. This strategy is computationally efficient and can adopt different favorable features for each subtask. Top ranked systems in CoNLL-2013 (Rozovskaya et al., 2013; Kao et al., 2013; Xing et al., 2013; Yoshimoto et al., 2013; Xiang et al., 2013) are based on this strategy. However, the division of the model relies on prior-knowledges and the designing of different features for each sub-model requires a large amount of manual works. This shortage is especially notable in CoNLL-2014 shared task, since the number of error types is much larger and the composition of errors is more complicated than before.

In contrast, we follow the work in (Jia et al., 2013a; Zhao et al., 2009a), integrating everything into one model. This integrated system holds a merit that a one-way feature selection benefits the whole system and no additional process is needed to deal with the conflict or error propagation of every sub-models. Here is a glance of this method: A set of more detailed error types are generated automatically from the original 28 types of errors. The detailed error type can be regarded as the label of a word, thus the task of grammatical error detection is transformed to a multi-label classification task using maximum entropy model (Berger et al., 1996; Zhao et al., 2013). A feature selection approach is introduced to get effective features from large amounts of feature candidates. Once errors are detected through word label classification, a rule-based method is used to make corrections according to their labels.

The rest of the paper is organized as follows. Section 2 describes the system architecture. Section 3 introduces the feature selection approach

*This work was partially supported by the National Natural Science Foundation of China (Grant No.60903119, Grant No.61170114, and Grant No.61272248), the National Basic Research Program of China (Grant No.2013CB329401), the Science and Technology Commission of Shanghai Municipality (Grant No.13511500200), and the European Union Seventh Framework Program (Grant No.247619).

†Corresponding author

Proceedings of the Eighteenth Conference on Computational Natural Language Learning: Shared Task, pages 74–82,
Baltimore, Maryland, 26-27 July 2014.

and the features we used. Experiments and results are presented in section 5, followed by conclusion.

2 System Architecture

In our approach, the grammatical error detection is regarded as a multi-label classification task. At first, each token in training corpus is assigned a label according to the golden annotation. The construction of labels is rule based using an extended version of Levenshtein edit distance algorithm which will be discussed in the following subsection. Each label maps an edit operation to do the correction, thus the generated labels are much more detailed than the originial 28 error types. Then, a maximum entropy (ME) model is adopted as the classifier. With the labeled data, the process of grammatical error correction is just applying the edit operation mapped by each label, which is basically the reverse of the labeling phase.

2.1 Data Labeling

In CoNLL-2014 shared task, there are 28 error types but they can not be used directly as class labels, since these types are too general that they can hardly be corrected by applying one rule-based edit. For example, the correction of *Vform* (verb form) error type includes all verb form inflections such as converting a verb to its infinitive form, gerund form, past form and past participle and so on. Previous works (Dahlmeier et al., 2012; Rozovskaya et al., 2012; Kochmar et al., 2012) manually decompose each error types to more detailed subtypes. For example, in (Dahlmeier et al., 2012), the determinater errors are decomposed into:

- replacement determiner (RD): { $a \rightarrow$ *the* }
- missing determiner (MD): { $\epsilon \rightarrow a$ }
- unwanted determiner (UD): { $a \rightarrow \epsilon$ }

For a task with a few error types such as merely determinative and preposition error in HOO 2012, manually decomposition may be sufficient. However, for CoNLL-2014, all 28 error types are required to be corrected and some of these types such as *Rloc-* (Local redundancy) and *Um* (Unclear meaning) are quite complex that the manual decomposition is time consuming and requires lots of grammatical knowledges. Therefore, an automatica decomposition method is proposed. It is extended from the Levenshtein edit distance algorithm and can divide error types into more detailed subtypes that each subtype can be corrected by applying one simple rule. How to calculate the extended Levenshtein edit distance is described in Algorithm 1.

Algorithm 1 Extended Levenshtein Edit Distance

```
INPUT:  toks_src, toks_dst
OUTPUT: 𝔼, ℙ
l_src, l_dst ← len(toks_src), len(toks_dst)
D[0...l_src][0...l_dst] ← 0
B[0...l_src][0...l_dst] ← (0, 0)
E[0...l_src][0...l_dst] ← φ
for i ← 1...l_src do
    D[i][0] ← i
    B[i][0] ← (i-1, 0)
    E[i][0] ← 𝒟
end for
for j ← 1...l_dst do
    D[0][j] ← j
    B[0][j] ← (0, j-1)
    E[0][j] ← 𝒜
end for
for i ← 1...l_src; do
    for j ← 1...l_dst do
        if toks_src[i-1] = toks_dst[j-1] then
            D[i][j] ← D[i-1][j-1]
            B[i][j] ← (i-1, j-1)
            E[i][j] ← 𝒰
        else
            m = min(D[i-1][j-1], D[i-1][j], D[i][j-1])
            if m = D[i-1][j-1] then
                D[i][j] ← D[i-1][j-1] + 1
                B[i][j] ← (i-1, j-1)
                if lemma(toks_src[i-1])
                  = lemma(toks_dst[j-1]) then
                    E[i][j] ← 𝒮
                else
                    E[i][j] ← ℐ
                end if
            else if m = D[i-1][j] then
                D[i][j] ← D[i-1][j] + 1
                B[i][j] ← (i-1, j)
                E[i][j] ← 𝒟
            else if m = D[i][j-1] then
                D[i][j] ← D[i][j-1] + 1
                B[i][j] ← (i, j-1)
                E[i][j] ← 𝒜
            end if
        end if
    end for
end for
i, j ← l_src, l_dst
while i > 0 ∨ j > 0 do
    insert E[i][j] into head of 𝔼
    insert toks_dst[j - 1] into head of ℙ
    (i, j) ← B[i][j]
end while
return (𝔼, ℙ)
```

In this algorithm, $toks_{src}$ represents the tokens that are annotated with one grammatical error and $toks_{dst}$ represents the corrected tokens of $toks_{src}$. At first, three two dimensional matrixes D, B and

E are initialized. For all i and j, $D[i][j]$ holds the Levenshtein distance between the first i tokens of $toks_{src}$ and first j tokens of $toks_{dst}$. B stores the path of the Levenshtein distance and E stores the edit operations in this path. The original Levenshtein edit distance has 4 edit operations: unchange ($\mathcal{U}$), addition ($\mathcal{A}$), deletion ($\mathcal{D}$) and substitution ($\mathcal{S}$). We extend the "substitution" edit into two types of edits: inflection ($\mathcal{I}$) and the original substitution ($\mathcal{S}$). If two different words have the same lemma, the substitution operation is $\mathcal{I}$, else is $\mathcal{S}$. $lemma(x)$ returns the lemma of token x. This algorithm returns the edit operations $\mathbb{E}$ and the parameters of these operations $\mathbb{P}$. Here is a simple sample illustrating this algorithm. For the golden edit {*a red apple is* $\rightarrow$ *red apples are*}, $toks_{src}$ is *a red apple is*, $toks_{dst}$ is *red apples are*, the output edits $\mathbb{E}$ will be $\{\mathcal{D}, \mathcal{U}, \mathcal{I}, \mathcal{S}\}$, and the parameters $\mathbb{P}$ will be {*-, red, apples, are*}.

Then with the output of this extended Levenshtein distance algorithm, labels can be generated by transforming these edit operations into readable symbols. For those tokens without errors, we directly assign a special label "$\odot$" to them. A tricky part of the labeling process is the problem of the edit "addition", $\mathcal{A}$. A new token can only be added before or after an existing token. Thus for edit operation with addition, we must find an existing token that the label can be assigned to, and this sort of token is defined as *pivot*. A pivot can be a token that is not changed in an edit operation, such as the "*apple*" in edit {*apple* $\rightarrow$ *an apple*}, or some other types of edit such as the inflection of "*look*" to "*looking*" in edit {*look* $\rightarrow$ *have been looking at*}.

The names of these labels are based on BNF syntax which is defined in Figure 1. The non-terminal ⟨*word*⟩ can be substituted by all words in the vocabulary. The non-terminal ⟨*inflection-rules*⟩ can be substituted by terminals of inflection rules that are used for correcting the error types of noun number, verb form, and subject-verb agreement errors. All the inflection rules are listed in Table 1.

With the output of extended Levenshtein edits distance algorithm, Algorithm 2 gives the process to generate labels whose names are based on the syntax defined in Figure 1. It takes the output $\mathbb{E}$, $\mathbb{P}$ of Algorithm 1 as inputs and returns the generated set of labels $\mathbb{L}$. Each label in $\mathbb{L}$ corresponds to one token in $toks_{src}$ in order. For our previous example of edit {*a red apple is* $\rightarrow$ *red apples are*},

⟨*label*⟩ ::= ⟨*simple-label*⟩ | ⟨*compound-label*⟩

⟨*simple-label*⟩ ::= ⟨*pivot*⟩ | ⟨*add-before*⟩ | ⟨*add-after*⟩

⟨*compound-label*⟩ ::= ⟨*add-before*⟩ ⟨*pivot*⟩
| ⟨*pivot*⟩ ⟨*add-after*⟩
| ⟨*add-before*⟩ ⟨*pivot*⟩ ⟨*add-after*⟩

⟨*pivot*⟩ ::= ⟨*unchange*⟩ | ⟨*substitution*⟩ | ⟨*inflection*⟩
| ⟨*deletion*⟩

⟨*add-before*⟩ ::= ⟨*word*⟩$\oplus$
| ⟨*word*⟩$\oplus$⟨*add-before*⟩

⟨*add-after*⟩ ::= $\oplus$⟨*word*⟩
| $\oplus$⟨*word*⟩⟨*add-after*⟩

⟨*substitution*⟩ ::= ⟨*word*⟩

⟨*inflection*⟩ ::= ⟨*inflection-rules*⟩

⟨*unchange*⟩ ::= $\odot$

⟨*deletion*⟩ ::= $\ominus$

Figure 1: BNF syntax of label

Rules	Description
LEMMA	change word to its lemma
NPLURAL	change noun to its plural form
VSINGULAR	change verb to its singular form
GERUND	change verb to its gerund form
PAST	change verb to its past form
PART	change verb to its past participle

Table 1: Inflection rules

the $\mathbb{L}$ returned by Algorithm 2 is {$\ominus$, $\odot$, NPLURAL, ARE} corresponding to the tokens {*a, red, apple, is*} in $toks_{src}$. Some other examples of the generated labels are presented in Table 2.

These labels are elaborately designed that each of them can be interpreted easily as a series of edit operations. Once the labels are determined by classifier, the correction of the grammatical errors is conducted by applying the edit operations interpreted from these labels.

Algorithm 2 Labeling Algorithm

INPUT: $\mathbb{E}, \mathbb{P}$
OUTPUT: $\mathbb{L}$
pivot $\leftarrow$ number of edits in $\mathbb{E}$ that are not $\mathcal{A}$
$\mathbb{L} \leftarrow \phi$
$L \leftarrow ''$
while $i <$ length($\mathbb{E}$) **do**
  if $\mathbb{E}[i] = \mathcal{A}$ **then**
    $L \leftarrow L+$ label of edit $\mathbb{E}[i]$ with $\mathbb{P}[i]$
    $i \leftarrow i+1$
  else
    $l \leftarrow L+$ label of edit $\mathbb{E}[i]$ with $\mathbb{P}[i]$
    $pivot \leftarrow pivot - 1$
    if $pivot = 0$ **then**
      $i \leftarrow i+1$
      while $i <$ length of $\mathbb{E}$ **do**
        $l \leftarrow l + \oplus + \mathbb{P}[i]$
        $i \leftarrow i+1$
      end while
    end if
    push l into $\mathbb{L}$
    $L \leftarrow ''$
  end if
end while
$\mathbb{L} \leftarrow$ upper case of $\mathbb{L}$
return $\mathbb{L}$

Tokens	Edit	Label
to reveal	{*to reveal→revealing*}	$\ominus$ GERUND
a woman	{*a woman→women*}	$\ominus$ NPLURAL
developing wold	{*developing world →the developing world*}	THE$\oplus$ $\odot$
a	{*a*→ ϵ}	$\ominus$
in	{*in→on*}	ON
apple	{*apple→an apple*}	AN$\oplus$

Table 2: Examples of labeling

2.2 Label Classification

Using the approach described above, the training corpus is converted to a sequence of words with labels. Maximum entropy model is used as the classifier. It allows a very rich set of features to be used in a model and has shown good performance in similiar tasks (Zhao et al., 2013). The features we used are discussed in the next section.

3 Feature Selection and Generation

One key factor affecting the performance of maximum entropy classifier is the features it used. A good feature that contains useful information to guide classification will significantly improve the performance of the classifier. One direct way to involve more good features is involving more features.

In our approach, large amounts of candidate features are collected at first. We carefully examine the factors involved in a wide range of features that have been or can be used to the word label classification task. Many features that are considered effective in various of previous works (Dahlmeier et al., 2012; Rozovskaya et al., 2012; Han et al., 2006; Rozovskaya et al., 2011; Tetreault, Joel R and Chodorow, Martin, 2008) are included. Besides, features that are used in the similar spell checking tasks (Jia et al., 2013b; Yang et al., 2012) and some novel features showing effectiveness in other NLP tasks (Wang et al., 2013; Zhang and Zhao, 2013; Xu and Zhao, 2012; Ma and Zhao, 2012; Zhao, 2009; Zhao et al., 2009b) are also included. However, using too many features is time consuming. Besides, it increases the probability of overfitting and may lead to a poor solution of the maximum-likelihood parameter estimate in the ME training.

Algorithm 3 Greedy Feature Selection

INPUT: all feature candidates F
OUTPUT: selected features S
$S = \{f_0, f_1, \ldots, f_k\}$, a random subset of F
while do
  C = RECRUITMORE(S)
  if $C = \{\}$ **then**
    return S
  end if
  S' = SHAKEOFF(S+C)
  if $scr(M(S)) \geq scr(M(S'))$ **then**
    return S
  end if
  $S = S'$
end while
function RECRUITMORE(S)
  $C = \{\}$, and $p = scr(M(S))$
  for each $f \in F - S$ **do**
    if $p < scr(M(S + \{f\}))$ **then**
      $C = C + \{f\}$
    end if
  end for
end function
function SHAKEOFF(S)
  while do
    $S' = S_0 = S$
    for each $f \in S$ **do**
      if $scr(M(S')) < scr(M(S' - \{f\}))$ **then**
        $S' = S' - \{f\}$
      end if
    end for
    $S = S'$
    if $S' = S_0$ **then**
      return S'
    end if
  end while
end function

Therefore a feature selection algorithm is introduced to filter out "bad" features at first and the remaining features will be used to generate new features. The feature selection algorithm has shown effectiveness in (Zhao et al., 2013) and is presented in Algorithm 3.

In this algorithm, $M(S)$ represents the model using feature set S and $scr(M)$ represents the evaluation score of model M on a development data set. It repeats two main steps until no further performance gain is achievable:

1. Include any features from the rest of F into the current set of candidate features if the inclusion would lead to a performance gain.

2. Exclude any features from the current set of candidate templates if the exclusion would lead to no deterioration in performance.

By repeatedly adding the useful and removing the useless features, the algorithm aims to return a better and smaller set of features for next round. Only 55 of the 109 candidate features remain after using this algorithm and they are presented in Table 4. Table 3 gives an interpretation of the abbreviations used in Table 4. Each feature of a word is set to that listed in **feature** column if the word satisfies the condition listed in **current word** column, else the feature is set to "NULL". For example, if the current word satisfies the condition in the first row of Table 4 which is the first word in the left of a *NC*, feature 1 of this word is set to all words in the *NC*, otherwise, feature 1 is set to "NULL".

4 Experiment

4.1 Data Sets

The CoNLL-2014 training data is a corpus of learner English provided by (Dahlmeier et al., 2013). This corpus consists of 1,397 articles, 12K sentences and 116K tokens. The official blind test data consists of 50 articles, 245 sentences and 30K tokens. More detailed information about this data is described in (Ng et al., 2014; Dahlmeier et al., 2013).

In development phase, the entire training corpus is splited by sentence. 80% sentences are picked up randomly and used for training and the rest 20% are used as the developing corpus. For the final submission, the entire corpus is used for training.

Abbreviation	Description
NP	*Noun Phrase*
NC	*Noun Compound* and is active if second to last word in *NP* is tagged as noun
VP	*Verb Phrase*
cw	*Current Word*
pos	part-of-speech of the current word
$X.l_i$	the ith word in the left of *X*
$X.r_i$	the ith word in the right of *X*
NP[0]	the first word of *NP*
NP.head	the head word of *NP*
NP.(DT or IN or TO)	word in *NP* whose pos is DT or IN or TO
VP.verb	word in *VP* whose pos is verb
VP.NP	*NP* in *VP*
dp	the dependency relation generated by standford dependency parser
dp.dep	the dependent in the dependency relation
dp.head	the head in the dependency relation
dp.rel	the type of the dependency relation

Table 3: The interpretation of the abbrevations in Table 4

4.2 Data Labeling

The labeling algorithm described in section 2.1 is firstly applied to the training corpus. Total 7047 labels are generated and those whose count is larger than 15 is presented in Table 5. Directly applying these 7047 labels for correction receives an M^2 score of precision=90.2%, recall=87.0% and F_0.5=89.5%. However, the number of labels is too large that the training process is time consuming and those labels appears only few times will hurt the generalization of the trained model. Therefore, labels with low frequency which appear less than 30 times are cut out and 109 labels remain. The M^2 score of the system using this refined labels is precision=83.9%, recall=64.0% and F_0.5=79.0%. Note that even applying all labels, the F_0.5 is not 100%. It is because some annotations in the training corpus are not consistency.

current word	**feature**
$NC.l_1$	*NC*
$NP.l_1$	*NP*
NP[0]	$NP.l_1$.pos
$NC.l_1$	*NC*
$NC.l_1$	$NC.l_1$.pos
$NC.l_1$ and *pos*=DT	*NC*
$NC.l_1$ and *pos*=VB	*NC*
$NP.l_1$ and *pos*=VB	*NP*
pos=VB	*cw*
pos=DT	*cw*
the	$cw.r_1$
a	$cw.r_1$
an	$cw.r_1$
NP[0]	*cw*
NP[0]	$NP.l_1$
NP[0]	$NP.l_2$
NP[0]	$NP.l_3$
NP[0]	$NP.l_1$.pos
NP[0]	$NP.l_2$.pos
NP[0]	$NP.l_3$.pos
$NP.l_1$	*NP*.head
$NP.l_1$	*NP*.head.pos
NP.head	*NP*. head
NP.head	*NP*. head.bag
NP.head	*NP*. head.pos
NP.head	*NP*. head.pos.bag
NP.head	*NP*. (JJ or CC)
NP.(DT or IN or TO)	*NP*
NP.(DT or IN or TO)	*NP*.head
NP.(DT or IN or TO)	*NP*.head.pos
dp.dep	*dp*.head
dp.head	*dp*.dep
dp.dep	*dp*.head.pos
dp.head	*dp*.dep.pos
dp.dep	*dp*.rel
dp.head	*dp*.rel
VP.verb	*VP*.*NP*
VP.verb	*VP*.*NP*.head
VP.*NP*.head	*VP*.verb
VP.verb	*VP*.*NP*.head.pos
VP.*NP*.head	*VP*.verb.pos
cw	$cw.l_i,\ i \in \{0,1,2,3\}$
cw	$cw.r_i,\ i \in \{1,2,3\}$
cw	$cw.l_i$.pos, $i \in \{0,1,2,3\}$
cw	$cw.r_i$.pos, $i \in \{1,2,3\}$

Table 4: Remained features after the feature selection.

Count	Label
1091911	⊙
31507	⊖
3637	NPLURAL
2822	THE⊕
2600	LEMMA
948	,⊕
300˜900	A⊕ PAST THE IN TO . IS OF ARE FOR GERUND ,
50˜100	AND ON AN⊕ A VSINGULAR WAS THEIR
20˜50	ELDERLY IT OF⊕ THEY WITH TO⊕ WERE THIS ; ITS .⊕ THAT 'S⊕ AND⊕ THAT⊕ HAVE⊕ CAN AS HAVE⊕PART FROM BE WOULD BY
15˜20	HAVE HAS⊕ WILL HAS AT AN THESE ⊕, THEM IN⊕ INTO #⊕ ARE⊕ WHICH PEOPLE HAS⊕PART ECONOMIC IS⊕ BE⊕ SO COULD TO⊕LEMMA MANY PART MAY LESS IT⊕ FOR⊕ BEING⊕
15˜20	NOT ABOUT WILL⊕LEMMA SHOULD HIS BECAUSE AGED SUCH ALSO WHICH⊕ HAVE⊕PAST WILL⊕ WHO WHEN MUCH
15˜20	ON⊕ ' THROUGH BE⊕PAST MORE IF HELP THE⊕ELDERLY 'S ONE AS⊕ THERE THEIR⊕ WITH⊕ HAVE⊕⊙ ECONOMY DEVELOPMENT CONCERNED PEOPLE⊕ PROBLEMS BUT MEANS THEREFORE HOWEVER BEING : UP PROBLEM '⊕ THE⊕LEMMA IN⊕ADDITION HOWEVER⊕,⊕ AMONG ;⊕ WHERE THUS ONLY HEALTH HAS⊕PAST FUNDING EXTENT ALSO⊕ TECHNOLOGICAL " OR HAD WOULD⊕ VERY .⊕THIS ITS⊕ IMPORTANT DEVELOPED ⊕BEEN AGE ABOUT⊕ WHO⊕ USE THEY⊕ THAN NUMBER HOWEVER⊕, GOVERNMENT FURTHERMORE DURING BUT⊕ YOUNGER RIGHT POPULATION PERSON⊕ FEWER ENVIRONMENTALLY WOULD⊕LEMMA OTHER MAY⊕ LIMITED HE COULD⊕HAVE BEEN STILL SPENDING SAFETY OVER ONE⊕'S MAKE MADE LIFE HUMAN HAD⊕ FUNDS CARE ARGUED ALL "⊕ WHEN⊕ TIME THOSE SOCIETY RESEARCH PROVIDE OLD NEEDS INCREASING DEVELOPING BECOME BE⊕⊙ ADDITION

Table 5: Labels whose count is larger than 15.

current word	**feature**
$NC.l_1$	*NC*, *cw*, $cw.l_1$, $cw.l_1$.pos, $cw.r_1$, $cw.r_1$.pos
NP[0]	*NP*.head, $NP.l_1$, $NP.l_2$, *cw*, $cw.l_1$, $cw.l_1$.pos,
NP.head	*NP*[0], $NP.l_1$, $NP.l_2$, *cw*, $cw.l_1$, $cw.l_1$.pos,
dp.head	*cw*, $cw.l_1$, $cw.l_2$ *dp*.dep, *dp*.dep.pos, *dp*.rel

Table 6: Examples of the new generated features.

4.3 Data Refinement

The training corpus is refined before used that sentences which do not contain errors are filtered out. Only 38% of the total sentences remain. With less training corpus, it takes less time to train the ME model. Table 7 presents the performance of systems using the unrefined training corpus and refined corpus.

System	Presicion	Recall	F_0.5
unrefined	26.99%	1.67%	6.71%
refined	11.17%	3.1%	7.34%

Table 7: Comparison of systems with different training corpus.

All sets of these systems are kept the same except the training corpus they use. It can be seen that the refinement also improves the performance of the system.

4.4 Feature Selection

Figure 2 shows the results of systems with different feature sets. *sys_10* is the system with

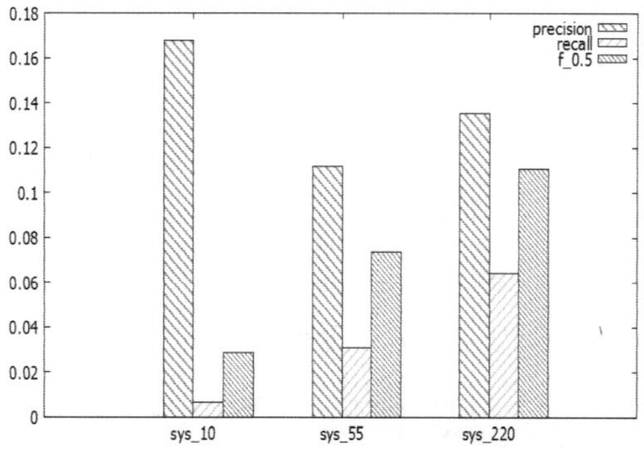

Figure 2: Performance of systems with different features.

10 randomly chosen features which are used as the initial set of features in Algorithm 3, *sys_55* is the system with the refined 55 features. With these refined features, various of new features are generated by combining different features. This combination is conducted empirically that features which are considered having relations are combined to generate new features. Using this method, 165 new features are generated and total 220 features are used in *sys_220*. Table 6 gives a few of examples showing the combined features. The performance is evaluated by the precision, recall and F_0.5 score of the M^2 scorer according to (Dahlmeier and Ng, 2012). It can be seen that *sys_220* with the most number of features achieves the best performance.

4.5 Evaluation Result

The final system we use is *sys_220* with refined training data, the performance of our system on the developing corpus and the blind official test data is presented in Table 8. The score is calculated using M^2 scorer.

Data Set	Precision	Recall	F_0.5
DEV	13.52%	6.41%	11.07%
OFFICIAL	29.83%	5.16%	15.24%

Table 8: Evaluation Results

5 Conclusion

In this paper, we describe the system of Shanghai Jiao Tong Univerity team in the CoNLL-2014 shared task. The grammatical error detection is regarded as a multi-label classification task and the correction is conducted by applying a rule-based approach based on these labels. A single maximum entropy classifier is introduced to do the multi-label classification. Various features are involved and a feature selection algorithm is used to refine these features. Finally, large amounts of feature templates that are generated by the combination of the refined features are used. This system achieved precision of 29.83%, recall of 5.16% and F_0.5 of 15.24% in the official evaluation.

References

Adam L Berger, Vincent J Della Pietra, and Stephen A Della Pietra. 1996. A maximum entropy approach to natural language processing. *Computational linguistics*, 22(1):39–71.

Daniel Dahlmeier and Hwee Tou Ng. 2012. Better evaluation for grammatical error correction. In *Proceedings of the 2012 Conference of the North American Chapter of the Association for Computational Linguistics: Human Language Technologies (NAACL 2012)*, pages 568–572, Montreal, Canada.

Daniel Dahlmeier, Hwee Tou Ng, and Eric Jun Feng Ng. 2012. NUS at the HOO 2012 Shared Task. In *Proceedings of the Seventh Workshop on Building Educational Applications Using NLP*, pages 216–224, Montréal, Canada, June. Association for Computational Linguistics.

Daniel Dahlmeier, Hwee Tou Ng, and Siew Mei Wu. 2013. Building a large annotated corpus of learner english: The nus corpus of learner english. In *Proceedings of the Eighth Workshop on Innovative Use of NLP for Building Educational Applications (BEA 2013)*, pages 22–31, Atlanta, Georgia, USA.

Robert Dale, Ilya Anisimoff, and George Narroway. 2012. Hoo 2012: A report on the preposition and determiner error correction shared task. In *Proceedings of the Second Workshop on Building Educational Applications Using NLP*, pages 54–62, Montréal, Canada, June. Association for Computational Linguistics.

NA-RAE Han, Martin Chodorow, and Claudia Leacock. 2006. Detecting Errors in English Article Usage by Non-Native Speakers. *Natural Language Engineering*, 12:115–129, 5.

Zhongye Jia, Peilu Wang, and Hai Zhao. 2013a. Grammatical error correction as multiclass classification with single model. In *Proceedings of the Seventeenth Conference on Computational Natural Language Learning: Shared Task*, pages 74–81, Sofia, Bulgaria, August. Association for Computational Linguistics.

Zhongye Jia, Peilu Wang, and Hai Zhao. 2013b. Graph model for chinese spell checking. In *Proceedings of the Seventh SIGHAN Workshop on Chinese Language Processing*, pages 88–92, Nagoya, Japan, October. Asian Federation of Natural Language Processing.

Ting-hui Kao, Yu-wei Chang, Hsun-wen Chiu, Tzu-Hsi Yen, Joanne Boisson, Jian-cheng Wu, and Jason S. Chang. 2013. Conll-2013 shared task: Grammatical error correction nthu system description. In *Proceedings of the Seventeenth Conference on Computational Natural Language Learning: Shared Task*, pages 20–25, Sofia, Bulgaria, August. Association for Computational Linguistics.

Ekaterina Kochmar, Øistein Andersen, and Ted Briscoe. 2012. HOO 2012 Error Recognition and Correction Shared Task: Cambridge University Submission Report. In *Proceedings of the Seventh Workshop on Building Educational Applications Using NLP*, pages 242–250, Montréal, Canada, June. Association for Computational Linguistics.

Xuezhe Ma and Hai Zhao. 2012. Fourth-order dependency parsing. In *Proceedings of COLING 2012: Posters*, pages 785–796, Mumbai, India, December. The COLING 2012 Organizing Committee.

Hwee Tou Ng, Siew Mei Wu, Ted Briscoe, Christian Hadiwinoto, Raymond Hendy Susanto, and Christopher Bryant. 2014. The conll-2014 shared task on grammatical error correction. In *Proceedings of the Eighteenth Conference on Computational Natural Language Learning: Shared Task (CoNLL-2014 Shared Task)*, Baltimore, Maryland, USA.

Alla Rozovskaya, Mark Sammons, Joshua Gioja, and Dan Roth. 2011. University of Illinois System in HOO Text Correction Shared Task. In *Proceedings of the 13th European Workshop on Natural Language Generation*, pages 263–266. Association for Computational Linguistics.

Alla Rozovskaya, Mark Sammons, and Dan Roth. 2012. The UI System in the HOO 2012 Shared Task on Error Correction. In *Proceedings of the Seventh Workshop on Building Educational Applications Using NLP*, pages 272–280, Montréal, Canada, June. Association for Computational Linguistics.

Alla Rozovskaya, Kai-Wei Chang, Mark Sammons, and Dan Roth. 2013. The university of illinois system in the conll-2013 shared task. In *Proceedings of the Seventeenth Conference on Computational Natural Language Learning: Shared Task*, pages 13–19, Sofia, Bulgaria, August. Association for Computational Linguistics.

Tetreault, Joel R and Chodorow, Martin. 2008. The Ups and Downs of Preposition Error Detection in ESL Writing. In *Proceedings of the 22nd International Conference on Computational Linguistics-Volume 1*, pages 865–872. Association for Computational Linguistics.

Rui Wang, Masao Utiyama, Isao Goto, Eiichro Sumita, Hai Zhao, and Bao-Liang Lu. 2013. Converting continuous-space language models into n-gram language models for statistical machine translation. In *Proceedings of the 2013 Conference on Empirical Methods in Natural Language Processing*, pages 845–850, Seattle, Washington, USA, October. Association for Computational Linguistics.

Yang Xiang, Bo Yuan, Yaoyun Zhang, Xiaolong Wang, Wen Zheng, and Chongqiang Wei. 2013. A hybrid model for grammatical error correction. In *Proceedings of the Seventeenth Conference on Computational Natural Language Learning: Shared Task*, pages 115–122, Sofia, Bulgaria, August. Association for Computational Linguistics.

Junwen Xing, Longyue Wang, Derek F. Wong, Lidia S. Chao, and Xiaodong Zeng. 2013. Um-checker: A hybrid system for english grammatical error correction. In *Proceedings of the Seventeenth Conference on Computational Natural Language Learning: Shared Task*, pages 34–42, Sofia, Bulgaria, August. Association for Computational Linguistics.

Qiongkai Xu and Hai Zhao. 2012. Using deep linguistic features for finding deceptive opinion spam. In *Proceedings of COLING 2012: Posters*, pages 1341–1350, Mumbai, India, December. The COLING 2012 Organizing Committee.

Shaohua Yang, Hai Zhao, Xiaolin Wang, and Bao liang Lu. 2012. Spell checking for chinese. In Nicoletta Calzolari (Conference Chair), Khalid Choukri, Thierry Declerck, Mehmet Uğur Doğan, Bente Maegaard, Joseph Mariani, Jan Odijk, and

Stelios Piperidis, editors, *Proceedings of the Eighth International Conference on Language Resources and Evaluation (LREC-2012)*, pages 730–736, Istanbul, Turkey, May. European Language Resources Association (ELRA). ACL Anthology Identifier: L12-1423.

Ippei Yoshimoto, Tomoya Kose, Kensuke Mitsuzawa, Keisuke Sakaguchi, Tomoya Mizumoto, Yuta Hayashibe, Mamoru Komachi, and Yuji Matsumoto. 2013. Naist at 2013 conll grammatical error correction shared task. In *Proceedings of the Seventeenth Conference on Computational Natural Language Learning: Shared Task*, pages 26–33, Sofia, Bulgaria, August. Association for Computational Linguistics.

Jingyi Zhang and Hai Zhao. 2013. Improving function word alignment with frequency and syntactic information. In *Proceedings of the Twenty-Third international joint conference on Artificial Intelligence*, pages 2211–2217. AAAI Press, August.

Hai Zhao, Wenliang Chen, and Chunyu Kit. 2009a. Semantic dependency parsing of nombank and propbank: An efficient integrated approach via a large-scale feature selection. In *Proceedings of the 2009 Conference on Empirical Methods in Natural Language Processing*, pages 30–39, Singapore, August. Association for Computational Linguistics.

Hai Zhao, Yan Song, Chunyu Kit, and Guodong Zhou. 2009b. Cross language dependency parsing using a bilingual lexicon. In *Proceedings of the Joint Conference of the 47th Annual Meeting of the ACL and the 4th International Joint Conference on Natural Language Processing of the AFNLP*, pages 55–63, Suntec, Singapore, August. Association for Computational Linguistics.

Hai Zhao, Xiaotian Zhang, and Chunyu Kit. 2013. Integrative semantic dependency parsing via efficient large-scale feature selection. *Journal of Artificial Intelligence Research*, 46:203–233.

Hai Zhao. 2009. Character-level dependencies in chinese: Usefulness and learning. In *Proceedings of the 12th Conference of the European Chapter of the ACL (EACL 2009)*, pages 879–887, Athens, Greece, March. Association for Computational Linguistics.

Factored Statistical Machine Translation for Grammatical Error Correction

Yiming Wang, Longyue Wang, Derek F. Wong, Lidia S. Chao, Xiaodong Zeng, Yi Lu
Natural Language Processing & Portuguese-Chinese Machine Translation Laboratory,
Department of Computer and Information Science,
University of Macau, Macau S.A.R., China
{wang2008499,vincentwang0229}@gmail.com,derekfw@umac.mo,
lidiasc@umac.mo,nlp2ct.samuel@gmail.com,mb25435@umac.mo

Abstract

This paper describes our ongoing work on grammatical error correction (GEC). Focusing on all possible error types in a real-life environment, we propose a factored statistical machine translation (SMT) model for this task. We consider error correction as a series of language translation problems guided by various linguistic information, as factors that influence translation results. Factors included in our study are morphological information, i.e. word stem, prefix, suffix, and Part-of-Speech (PoS) information. In addition, we also experimented with different combinations of translation models (TM), phrase-based and factor-based, trained on various datasets to boost the overall performance. Empirical results show that the proposed model yields an improvement of 32.54% over a baseline phrase-based SMT model. The system participated in the CoNLL 2014 shared task and achieved the 7th and 5th $F_{0.5}$ scores[1] on the official test set among the thirteen participating teams.

1 Introduction

The task of grammatical error detection and correction (GEC) is to make use of computational methods to fix the mistakes in a written text. It is useful in two aspects. For a non-native English learner it may help to improve the grammatical quality of the written text. For a native speaker the tool may help to remedy mistakes automatically. Automatic correction of grammatical errors is an active research topic, aiming at improving the writing process with the help of artificial intelligent techniques. Second language learning is a user group of particular interest.

Recently, Helping Our Own (HOO) and CoNLL held a number of shared tasks on this topic (Dale et al., 2012, Ng et al., 2013, Ng et al., 2014). Previous studies based on rules (Sidorov et al., 2013), data-driven methods (Berend et al., 2013, Yi et al., 2013) and hybrid methods (Putra and Szabó, 2013, Xing et al., 2013) have shown substantial gains for some frequent error types over baseline methods. Most proposed methods share the commonality that a sub-model is built for a specific type of error, on top of which a strategy is applied to combine a number of these individual models. Also, detection and correction are often split into two steps. For example, Xing et al. (2013) presented the UM-Checker for five error types in the CoNLL 2013 shared task. The system implements a cascade of five individual *detection-and-correction* models for different types of error. Given an input sentence, errors are detected and corrected one-by-one by each sub-model at the level of its corresponding error type. The specifics of an error type are fully considered in each sub-model, which is easier to realize for a single error type than for multiple types in a single model. In addition, dividing the error detection and correction into two steps alleviates the application of machine learning classifiers. However, an approach that considers error types individually may have negative effects:

- This approach assumes independence between each error type. It ignores the interaction of neighboring errors. Results (Xing et al., 2013) have shown that

[1] These two rankings are based on gold-standard edits without and with alternative answers, respectively.

Proceedings of the Eighteenth Conference on Computational Natural Language Learning: Shared Task, pages 83–90,
Baltimore, Maryland, 26-27 July 2014.

consecutive errors of multiple types tend to hinder solving these errors individually.

- As the number of error types increases, the complexities of analyzing, designing, and implementing the model increase, in particular when combinatorial errors are taken into account.
- Looking for an optimal model combination becomes complex. A simple pipeline approach would result in interference and the generation of new errors, and hence to propagating those errors to the subsequent processes.
- Separating the detection and correction tasks may result in more errors. For instance, once a candidate is misidentified as an error, it would be further revised and turned into an error by the correction model. In this scenario the model risks losing precision.

In the shared task of this year (Ng et la., 2014), two novelties are introduced: 1) all types of errors present in an essay are to be detected and corrected (i.e., there is no restriction on the five error types of the 2013 shared task); 2) the official evaluation metric of this year adopts $F_{0.5}$, weighting precision twice as much as recall. This requires us to explore an alternative universal joint model that can tackle various kinds of grammatical errors as well as join the detection and correction processes together. Regarding grammatical error correction as a process of translation has been shown to be effective (Ehsan and Faili, 2013, Mizumoto et al., 2011, Yoshimoto et al., 2013, Yuan and Felice, 2013). We treat the problematic sentences and golden sentences as pairs of source and target sentences. In SMT, a translation model is trained on a parallel corpus that consists of the source sentences (i.e. sentences that may contain grammatical errors) and the targeted translations (i.e. the grammatically well-formed sentences). The challenge is that we need a large amount of these parallel sentences for constructing such a data-driven SMT system. Some researches (Brockett et al., 2006, Yuan and Felice, 2013) explore generating artificial errors to resolve this sparsity problem. Other studies (Ehsan and Faili, 2013, Yoshimoto et al., 2013, Yuan and Felice, 2013) focus on using syntactic information (such as PoS or tree structure) to enhance the SMT models.

In this paper, we propose a factored SMT model by taking into account not only the surface information contained in the sentence, but also morphological and syntactic clues (i.e., word stem, prefix, suffix and finer PoS information). To counter the sparsity problem we do not use artificial or manual approaches to enrich the training data. Instead we apply factored and transductive learning techniques to enhance the model on a small dataset. In addition, we also experimented with different combinations of translation models (TM), phrase- and factor-based, that are trained on different datasets to boost the overall performance. Empirical results show that the proposed model yields an improvement of 32.54% over a baseline phrase-based SMT model.

The remainder of this paper is organized as follows: Section 2 describes our proposed methods. Section 3 reports on the design of our experiments. We discuss the result, including the official shared task results, in Section 4,. We summarize our conclusions in Section 5.

2 Methodology

In contrast with phrase-based translation models, factored models make use of additional linguistic clues to guide the system such that it generates translated sentences in which morphological and syntactic constraints are met (Koehn and Hoang, 2007). The linguistic clues are taken as factors in a factored model; words are represented as vectors of factors rather than as a single token. This requires us to pre-process the training data to factorize all words. In this study, we explore the use of various types of morphological information and PoS as factors. For each possible factor we build an individual translation model. The effectiveness of all factors is analyzed by comparing the performance of the corresponding models on the grammatical error correction task. Furthermore, two approaches are proposed to combine those models. One adopts the model cascading method based on transductive learning. The second approach relies on learning and decoding multiple factors learning. The details of each approach are discussed in the following sub-sections.

2.1 Data Preparation

In order to construct a SMT model, we convert the training data into a parallel corpus where the problematic sentences that ought to be corrected are regarded as source sentences, while the reference sentences are treated as the corresponding target translations. We discovered that a number of sentences is absent at the target side due to incorrect annotations in the golden data. We removed these unparalleled sentences from the data. Secondly, the initial capitalizations of sentences are converted to their most probable casing using the Moses *truecaser*[2]. URLs are quite common in the corpus, but they are not useful for learning and even may cause the model to apply unnecessary correction on it. Thus, we mark all of the ULRs with XML markups, signaling the SMT decoder not to analyze an URL and output it as is.

2.2 Model Construction

In this study we explore four different factors: prefix, suffix, stem, and PoS. This linguistic information not only helps to capture the local constraints of word morphologies and the interaction of adjacent words, but also helps to prevent data sparsity caused by inflected word variants and insufficient training data.

Word stem: Instead of lemmas, we prefer word stemming as one of the factors, considering that stemming does not requires deep morphological analysis and is easier to obtain. Second, during the whole error detection and correction process, stemming information is used as auxiliary information in addition to the original word form. Third, for grammatical error correction using word lemmas or word stems in factored translation model shows no significant difference. This is because we are translating text of the same language, and the translation of this factor, stem or lemma, is straightforwardly captured by the model. Hence, we do not rely on the word lemma. In this work, we use the English Porter stemmer (Porter, 1980) for generating word stems.

Prefix: The second type of morphological information we explored is the word prefix. Although a prefix does not present strong evidence to be useful to the grammatical error correction, we include it in our study in order to fully investigate all types of morphological information. We believe the prefix can be an important factor in the correction of initial capitalization, e.g. "*In this era,* engineering *designs...*" should be changed to "*In this era,* engineering *designs...*" In model construction, we take the first three letters of a word as its prefix. If the length of a word is less than three, we use the word as the prefix factor.

Suffix: Suffix, one of the important factors, helps to capture the grammatical agreements between predicates and arguments within a sentence. Particularly the endings of plural nouns and inflected verb variants are useful for the detection of agreement violations that shown up in word morphologies. Similar to how we represent the prefix, we are interested in the last three characters of a word.

	Examples
Sentence	this card contains biometric data *to* add security and reduce *the* risk *of* falsification
Original POS	DT NN BVZ JJ NNS **TO** VB NN CC VB **DT** NN **IN** NN
Specific POS	DT NN VBZ JJ NNS **TO_to** VB NN CC VB **DT_the** NN **IN_of** NN

Table 1: Example of modified PoS.

According to the description of factors, Figure 1 illustrates the forms of various factors extracted from a given example sentence.

Surface	*constantly combining ideas will result in better solutions being formulated*
Prefix	*con com ide wil res in bet sol bei for*
Suffix	*tly ing eas ill ult in ter ons ing ted*
Stem	*constantli combin idea will result in better solut be formul*
Specific POS	RB VBG NNS MD VB IN JJR NNS VBG VBN

Figure 1: The factorized sentence.

PoS: Part-of-Speech tags denote the morpho-syntactic category of a word. The use of PoS sequences enables us to some extent to recover missing determiners, articles, prepositions, as well as the modal verb in a sentence. Empirical studies (Yuan and Felice, 2013) have demonstrated that the use of this information can greatly improve the accuracy of the grammatical error correction. To obtain the PoS, we adopt the Penn Treebank tag set (Marcus et al., 1993), which contains 45 PoS tags. The Stanford parser (Klein and Manning, 2002) is used to extract the PoS information. Inspired by Yuan and Felice (2013), who used preposition-specific tags to fix the problem of being unable to distinguish between prepositions and obtained good performance, we create specific tags both for determiners (i.e., *a*, *an*, *the*) and prepositions. Table 1 provides an example of this modification, where prepositions, **TO** and **IN**, and determiner,

[2] After decoding, we will de-truecase all these words.

DT, are revised to **TO_to**, **IN_of** and **DT_the,** respectively.

2.3 Model Combination

In addition to the design of different factored translation models, two model combination strategies are designed to treat grammatical error correction problem as a series of translation processes, where an incorrect sentence is translated into the correct one. In both approaches we pipeline two translation models, tm^1 and tm^2. In the first approach, we derive four combinations of different models that trained on different sources.

- In case I, tm_f^1 and tm_f^2 are both factored models but trained on different factors, e.g. for $tm_{f_i}^1$ training on "*surface + factor$_i$*" and $tm_{f_j}^2$ on "*surface + factor$_{i \neq j}$*". Both models use the same training sentences, but different factors.
- In case II, $tm_{f_j}^2$ is trained on sentences that paired with the output from the previous model, $tm_{f_i}^1$, and the golden correct sentences. We want to create a second model that can also tackle the new errors introduced by the first model.
- In case III, similar to case II, the second translation model, tm_p^2 is replaced by a phrase-based translation model.
- In case IV, the quality of training data is considered vital to the construction of a good translation model. The present training dataset is not large enough. To complement this, the second model, $tm_{f_j}^2$, is trained on an enlarged data set, by combining the training data of both models, i.e. the original parallel data (official incorrect and correct sentence pairs) and the supplementary parallel data (sentences output from the first model, $tm_{f_i}^1$, and the correct sentences). Note that we do not de-duplicate sentences.

In all cases, the testing process is carried out as follows. The test set is translated by the first translation model, $tm_{f_i}^1$. The output from the first model is then fed into the second translation model, $tm_{f_j}^2$. The output of the second model is used as the final corrections.

The second combination approach is to make use of multiple factors for model construction. The question is whether multiple factors when used together may improve the correction results. In this setting we combine two factors together with the word surface form to build a multi-factored translation model. All pairs of factors are used, e.g. stem and PoS. The decoding sequence is as follows: translate the input stems into target stems; translate the PoS; and generate the surface form given the factors of stem and PoS.

3 Experiment Setup

3.1 Dataset

We pre-process the NUCLE corpus (Dahlmeier et al., 2013) as described in Section 2 for training different translation models. We use both the official golden sentences and additional WMT2014 English monolingual data[3] to train an in-domain and a general-domain language model (LM), respectively. These language models are linearly interpolated in the decoding phase. We also randomly select a number of sentence pairs from the parallel corpus as a development set and a test set, disjoint from the training data. Table 2 summarizes the statistics of all the datasets.

Corpus	Sentences	Tokens
Parallel Corpus	55,503	1,124,521 / 1,114,040
Additional Monolingual	85,254,788	2,033,096,800
Dev. Set	500	10,532 / 10,438
Test Set	900	18,032 / 17,906

Table 2: Statistics of used corpora.

The experiments were carried out with MOSES 1.0[4] (Philipp Koehn et al., 2007). The translation and the re-ordering model utilizes the "*grow-diag-final*" symmetrized word-to-word alignments created with GIZA++[5] (Och and Ney, 2003) and the training scripts of MOSES. A 5-gram LM was trained using the SRILM toolkit[6] (Stolcke et al., 2002), exploiting the improved modified Kneser-Ney smoothing (Kneser and Ney, 1995), and quantizing both probabilities and back-off weights. For the log-linear model training, we take minimum-error-rate training (MERT) method as described in (Och, 2003). The result is evaluated by M^2 Scorer (Dahlmeier and Ng, 2012) computing precision, recall and $F_{0.5}$.

---

[3] http://www.statmt.org/wmt14/translation-task.html.
[4] http://www.statmt.org/moses/.
[5] http://code.google.com/p/giza-pp/.
[6] http://www.speech.sri.com/projects/srilm/.

In total, one baseline system, five individual systems, and four combination systems are evaluated in this study. The baseline system (**Baseline**) is trained on the words-only corpus using a phrase-based translation model. For the individual systems we adopt the factored translation model that are trained respectively on 1) surface and stem factors (**Sys$_{+stem}$**), 2) surface and suffix factors (**Sys$_{+suf}$**), 3) surface and prefix factors (**Sys$_{+pref}$**), 4) surface and PoS factors (**Sys$_{+PoS}$**), and 5) surface and modified-PoS factors (**Sys$_{+MPoS}$**). The combination systems include: 1) the combination of "factored + phrase-based" and "factored + factored" for models cascading; and 2) the factors of surface, stem and modified-PoS (**Sys$_{+stem+MPoS}$**) are combined for constructing a correction system based on a multi-factor model.

4 Results and Discussions

We report our results in terms of the precision, recall and $F_{0.5}$ obtained by each of the individual models and combined models.

4.1 Individual Model

Table **3** shows the absolute measures for the baseline system, while the other individual models are listed with values relative to the baseline.

Model	Precision	Recall	$F_{0.5}$
Baseline	25.58	3.53	11.37
Sys$_{+stem}$	-14.84	+13.00	+0.18
Sys$_{+suf}$	-14.57	+14.77	+0.60
Sys$_{+pref}$	-15.74	+12.20	-0.77
Sys$_{+PoS}$	-11.63	+9.79	+2.45
Sys$_{+MPoS}$	-10.25	+10.60	+3.70

Table 3: Performance of various models.

The baseline system has the highest precision score but the lowest recall. Nearly all individual models except **Sys$_{+pref}$** show improvements in the correction result ($F_{0.5}$) over the baseline. Overall, **Sys$_{+MPoS}$** achieves the best result for the grammatical error correction task. It shows a significant improvement over the other models and outperforms the baseline model by 3.7 $F_{0.5}$ score. The **Sys$_{+stem}$** and **Sys$_{+suf}$** models obtain an improvement of 0.18 and 0.60 in $F_{0.5}$ scores, respectively, compared to the baseline. Although the differences are not significant, it confirms our hypothesis that morphological clues do help to improve error correction. The $F_{0.5}$ score of **Sys$_{+pref}$** is the lowest among the models including the baseline, showing a drop of 0.77 in $F_{0.5}$ score against the baseline. One possible reason is that few errors (in the training corpus) involve word prefixes. Thus, the prefix does not seem to be a suitable factor for tackling the GEC problem.

Type	Sys$_{+stem}$ (%)	Sys$_{+suf}$ (%)	Sys$_{+MPoS}$ (%)	Error Num.
Vt	17.07	12.20	12.20	41
ArtOrDet	37.65	36.47	29.41	85
Nn	33.33	19.61	23.53	51
Prep	10.26	10.26	12.82	39
Wci	9.10	10.61	6.10	66
Rloc-	15.20	13.92	10.13	79

Table 4: The capacity of different models in handling six frequent error types.

We analyze the capacities of the models on different types of errors. **Sys$_{+PoS}$** and **Sys$_{+MPoS}$** are built by using the PoS and modified PoS. Both of them yield an improvement in $F_{0.5}$ score. Overall, **Sys$_{+MPoS}$** produces more accurate results than **Sys$_{+pref}$**. Therefore, we specifically compare and evaluate the best three models, **Sys$_{+stem}$**, **Sys$_{+suf}$** and **Sys$_{+MPoS}$**. Table 4 presents evaluation scores of these models for the six most frequent error types, which take up a large part of the training and test data. Among them, **Sys$_{+stem}$** displays a powerful capacity to handle determiner and noun/number agreement errors, up to 37.65% and 33.33%. **Sys$_{+suf}$** shows the ability to correct determiner errors at 36.47%; **Sys$_{+MPoS}$** yields a similar performance to **Sys$_{+suf}$**. All three individual models exhibit a relatively high capacity to handle determiner errors. The likely reason is that this mistake constitutes the largest portion in training data and test set, giving the learning models many examples to capture this problem well. In the case of preposition errors, **Sys$_{+MPoS}$** demonstrates a better performance. This, once again, confirms the result (Yuan and Felice, 2013) that the modified PoS factor is effective for every preposition word. For these six error types, the individual models show a weak capacity to handle the word collocation or idiom error category (Wci). Although **Sys$_{+MPoS}$** achieves the highest $F_{0.5}$ score in the overall evaluation, it only achieves 6.10% in handling this error type. The likely reason is that idioms are not frequent in the training data, and also that in most of the cases they contain out-of-vocabulary words never seen in training data.

4.2 Model Combination

We intend to further boost the overall performance of the correction system by combining the strengths of individual models through model combination, and compare against the baseline. The systems compared here cover three pipelined models and a multi-factored model, as described earlier in Section 3. The combined systems include: 1) **CSys$_{suf+phrase}$**: the combination of **Sys$_{+suf}$** and the baseline phrase-based translation model; 2) **CSys$_{suf+suf}$**: we combine two similar factored models with suffix factors, **Sys$_{+suf}$**, which is trained on the same corpus; and 3) **TSys$_{suf+phrase}$**: similar to **CSys$_{suf+phrase}$**, but the training data for the second phrase-based model is augmented by adding the output sentences from the previous model (paired with the correct sentences). Our intention is to enlarge the size of the training data. The evaluation results are presented in Table 5.

Model	Precision	Recall	$F_{0.5}$
Baseline	25.58	3.53	11.37
CSys$_{suf+phrase}$	-14.70	+14.61	+0.45
CSys$_{suf+suf}$	-15.04	+14.13	+0.09
TSys$_{suf+phrase}$	-14.76	+14.61	+0.40
Sys$_{+stem+MPoS}$	-15.87	+11.72	-0.90

Table 5: Evaluation results of combined models.

In Table 5 we observe that **Sys$_{+stem+MPoS}$** hurts performance and shows a drop of 0.9% in $F_{0.5}$ score. Both the **CSys$_{suf+phrase}$** and **CSys$_{suf+suf}$** show minor improvements over the baseline system. Even when we enrich the training data for the second model in **TSys$_{suf+phrase}$**, it cannot help in boosting the overall performance of the system. One of the problems we observe is that, with this combination structure, new incorrect sentences are introduced by the model at each step. The errors are propagated and accumulated to the final result. Although **CSys$_{suf+phrase}$** and **CSys$_{suf+suf}$** produce a better $F_{0.5}$ score over the baseline, they are not as good as the individual models, **Sys$_{+PoS}$** and **Sys$_{+MPoS}$**, which are trained on PoS and modified-PoS, respectively.

4.3 The Official Result

After fully evaluating the designed individual models as well as the integrated ones, we adopt **Sys$_{+MPoS}$** as our designated system for this grammatical error correction task. The official test set consists of 50 essays, and 2,203 errors. Table 6 shows the final result obtained by our submitted system.

Table 7 details the correction rate of the five most frequent error types obtained by our system. The result suggests that the proposed system has a better ability in handling the verb, article and determiner error than other error types.

Criteria	Result	Alt. Result
P	0.3127	0.4317
R	0.1446	0.1972
$F_{0.5}$	0.2537	0.3488

Table 6: The official correction results of our submitted system.

Type	Error	Correct	%
Vt	203/201	21/22	10.34/10.94
V0	57/54	9/9	15.79/16.67
Vform	156/169	11/18	7.05/10.65
ArtOrDet	569/656	84/131	14.76/19.97
Nn	319/285	31/42	9.72/10.91

Table 7: Detailed error information of evaluation system (with alternative result).

5 Conclusion

This paper describes our proposed grammatical error detection and correction system based on a factored statistical machine translation approach. We have investigated the effectiveness of models trained with different linguistic information sources, namely morphological clues and syntactic PoS information. In addition, we also explore some ways to combine different models in the system to tackle the correction problem. The constructed models are compared against the baseline model, a phrase-based translation model. Results show that PoS information is a very effective factor, and the model trained with this factor outperforms the others. One difficulty of this year's shared task is that participants have to tackle all 28 types of errors, which is five times more than last year. From the results, it is obvious there are still many rooms for improving the current system.

Acknowledgements

The authors are grateful to the Science and Technology Development Fund of Macau and the Research Committee of the University of Macau for the funding support for their research, under the Reference nos. MYRG076 (Y1-L2)-FST13-WF and MYRG070 (Y1-L2)-FST12-CS. The authors also wish to thank the anonymous reviewers for many helpful comments with special thanks to Antal van den Bosch for his generous help on this manuscript.

References

Gábor Berend, Veronika Vincze, Sina Zarriess, and Richárd Farkas. 2013. LFG-based Features for Noun Number and Article Grammatical Errors. *CoNLL-2013.*

Chris Brockett, William B. Dolan, and Michael Gamon. 2006. Correcting ESL errors using phrasal SMT techniques. *Proceedings of the 21st International Conference on Computational Linguistics and the 44th annual meeting of the Association for Computational Linguistics* pages 249–256.

Daniel Dahlmeier, Hwee Tou Ng, and Siew Mei Wu. 2013. Building a Large Annotated Corpus of Learner English: The NUS Corpus of Learner English. *Proceedings of the Eighth Workshop on Innovative Use of NLP for Building Educational Applications.* pages 22-31.

Robert Dale, Ilya Anisimoff, and George Narroway. 2012. HOO 2012: A report on the preposition and determiner error correction shared task. *Proceedings of the Seventh Workshop on Building Educational Applications Using NLP* pages 54–62.

Nava Ehsan, and Heshaam Faili. 2013. Grammatical and context-sensitive error correction using a statistical machine translation framework. *Software: Practice and Experience.* Wiley Online Library.

D. Klein, and C. D. Manning. 2002. Fast exact inference with a factored model for natural language parsing. *Advances in neural information processing systems.*

Reinhard Kneser, and Hermann Ney. 1995. Improved backing-off for m-gram language modeling. *Acoustics, Speech, and Signal Processing, 1995. ICASSP-95., 1995 International Conference on* Vol. 1, pages 181–184.

P. Koehn, and H. Hoang. 2007. Factored translation models. *Proceedings of the Joint Conference on Empirical Methods in Natural Language Processing and Computational Natural Language Learning (EMNLP-CoNLL)* Vol. 868, pages 876–876.

Philipp Koehn, Hieu Hoang, Alexandra Birch, Chris Callison-Burch, Marcello Federico, Nicola Bertoldi, Brooke Cowan, et al. 2007. Moses: Open source toolkit for statistical machine translation. *Proceedings of the 45th Annual Meeting of the ACL on Interactive Poster and Demonstration Sessions* pages 177–180.

M. P. Marcus, M. A. Marcinkiewicz, and B. Santorini. 1993. Building a large annotated corpus of English: The Penn Treebank. *Computational linguistics.* MIT Press.

Tomoya Mizumoto, Mamoru Komachi, Masaaki Nagata, and Yuji Matsumoto. 2011. Mining Revision Log of Language Learning SNS for Automated Japanese Error Correction of Second Language Learners. *IJCNLP* pages 147–155.

Hwee Tou Ng, Siew Mei Wu, Ted Briscoe, Christian Hadiwinoto, Raymond Hendy Susanto, and Bryant Christopher. 2014. The conll-2014 shared task on grammatical error correction. *Proceedings of CoNLL.* Baltimore, Maryland, USA.

Hwee Tou Ng, Siew Mei Wu, Yuanbin Wu, Christian Hadiwinoto, and Joel Tetreault. 2013. The conll-2013 shared task on grammatical error correction. *Proceedings of CoNLL.*

Franz Josef Och. 2003. Minimum Error Rate Training in Statistical Machine Translation, 160–167.

Franz Josef Och, and Hermann Ney. 2003. A systematic comparison of various statistical alignment models. *Computational linguistics.* MIT Press.

Martin F. Porter. 1980. An algorithm for suffix stripping. *Program: electronic library and information systems.* MCB UP Ltd.

Desmond Darma Putra, and Lili Szabó. 2013. UdS at the CoNLL 2013 Shared Task. *CoNLL-2013.*

Grigori Sidorov, Anubhav Gupta, Martin Tozer, Dolors Catala, Angels Catena, and Sandrine Fuentes. 2013. Rule-based System for Automatic Grammar Correction Using Syntactic N-grams for English Language Learning (L2). *CoNLL-2013.*

Andreas Stolcke, and others. 2002. SRILM-an extensible language modeling toolkit. *INTERSPEECH.*

Junwen Xing, Longyue Wang, Derek F. Wong, Lidia S. Chao, and Xiaodong Zeng. 2013. UM-Checker: A Hybrid System for English Grammatical Error Correction. *Proceedings of the Seventeenth Conference on Computational Natural Language Learning: Shared Task,* 34–42. Sofia, Bulgaria: Association for Computational Linguistics. Retrieved from http://www.aclweb.org/anthology/W13-3605

Bong-Jun Yi, Ho-Chang Lee, and Hae-Chang Rim. 2013. KUNLP Grammatical Error Correction System For CoNLL-2013 Shared

Task. *CoNLL-2013*.

Ippei Yoshimoto, Tomoya Kose, Kensuke Mitsuzawa, Keisuke Sakaguchi, Tomoya Mizumoto, Yuta Hayashibe, Mamoru Komachi, et al. 2013. NAIST at 2013 CoNLL grammatical error correction shared task. *CoNLL-2013*.

Zheng Yuan, and Mariano Felice. 2013. Constrained grammatical error correction using Statistical Machine Translation. *CoNLL-2013*.

NTHU at the CoNLL-2014 Shared Task

Jian-Cheng Wu*, Tzu-Hsi Yen*, Jim Chang*, Guan-Cheng Huang*,
Jimmy Chang*, Hsiang-Ling Hsu+, Yu-Wei Chang+, Jason S. Chang*

* Department of Computer Science
+ Institute of Information Systems and Applications

National Tsing Hua University
HsinChu, Taiwan, R.O.C. 30013
{wujc86, joseph.yen, cwebb.tw, a2961353,
rocmewtwo, ilovecat6717, teer1990, jason.jschang}@gmail.com

Abstract

In this paper, we describe a system for correcting grammatical errors in texts written by non-native learners. In our approach, a given sentence with syntactic features are sent to a number of modules, each focuses on a specific error type. A main program integrates corrections from these modules and outputs the corrected sentence. We evaluated our system on the official test data of the CoNLL-2014 shared task and obtained 0.30 in F-measure.

1 Introduction

Millions of non-native learners are using English as their second language (ESL) or foreign language (EFL). These learners often make different kinds of grammatical errors and are not aware of it. With a grammatical error corrector applies rules or statistical learning methods, learners can use the system to improve the quality of writing, and become more aware of the common errors. It may also help learners improve their writing skills.

The CoNLL-2014 shared task is aimed at promoting research on correcting grammatical errors. Types of errors handled in the shared task are extended from the five types in the previous shared task to include all common errors present in an essay.

In this paper, we focus on the following errors made by ESL writers:

- Spelling and comma
- Article and determiner
- Preposition
- Preposition + verb (interactive)
- Noun number
- Word form
- Subject-verb-agreement

For each error type, we developed and tuned a module based on the official development data. A main program combines the correction hypotheses from these modules and produces the final correction. If multiple modules propose different corrections to the same word/phrase, the correction proposed by the module with the highest precision will be chosen.

2 Method

2.1 Spelling and Comma module

In this section, we correct comma errors and spelling errors, including missing/extraneous hyphens. For simplicity, we adopt Aspell[1] and GingerIt[2] to detect spelling errors and generate possible replacements, considered as confusable words, which might contain the word with correct spelling. Then, we replace the word being checked with confusable words to generate sentences. Language models trained on well-formed texts are used to measure the probability of these

[1] `http://aspell.net/`

[2] `https://pypi.python.org/pypi/gingerit` We use GingerIt only for correcting missing/extraneous hyphens

Proceedings of the Eighteenth Conference on Computational Natural Language Learning: Shared Task, pages 91–95, Baltimore, Maryland, 26-27 July 2014.

candidates. Candidate with the highest probability is chosen as correction.

Omitted commas form a large proportion of punctuation errors. We apply the CRF model proposed by Israel, et. al. (2012) with some modification. We replace distance features with syntactic features. More specifically, we do not use features such as distances to the start of sentence or last comma. And we add two features, one indicates whether a word is at the end of a clause, and the other indicates whether the current clause starts with a prepositional phrase.

2.2 Subject-verb-agreement module

This module corrects subject-verb-agreement errors in a given sentence. Consider the sentence "*The boy in blue pants are my brother*". The correct sentence should be "*The boy in blue pants is my brother*". Since a verb could be far from it's subject, using ngram counts may fail to detect and correct such an error.

We use a rule-based method in this module. In the first stage, we identify the subject of each clause by using information from the parser. Both the dependency relation and syntactic structure are used in this stage. Dependency relations such as `nsubj` and `rcmod` indicate subjects of subject-verb relation. If there is a verb that has not been assigned a subject via dependency relations, head of noun phrase in the same clause will be used instead. And in the second stage, we check whether subject and verbs agree, for each clause in the sentence.

Here we explain our correction process in more detail. For each clause, the singular and plural forms of verbs in the clause must be consistent with the subject of the clause unless the subject is a quantifier. Consider the following sentences:

The number of cats *is* ten.
A number of cats *are* playing.

Since our judgment only depends on the subject *number*, it's hard to tell whether should we use a plural verb or not in this case. The quantifiers we do not handle are listed as follow: *number, lot, quantity, variety, type, amount, neither*.

2.3 Number module and Forms module

We correct noun number error in two stages. In the first stage, we generate a confusion set for each word. While constructing confusion set for noun number, both of the singular form and plural form are included in the set. While constructing confusion set for word forms, we use the word families in Academic Word List (AWL)[3] and British National Corpus (BNC4000) [4]. Given a content word, all the words in the same family except antonyms are entered into the confusion set. However, comparative form and superlative form of an adjective are eliminated from the confusion set, since replacing an adjective with these forms is a semantic rather than syntactic decision. The following examples illustrate what kinds of alternatives are eliminated:

antonyms: *misleading* for the word *lead*
semantics: *higher* for the word *high*

Additionally, in the forms module, a correction is ignored, if it is actually correcting a verb tense, subject-verb-agreement, or noun number error. We use part-of-speech (POS) tag to check this. More specifically, any corrections that changes a word with a *VBZ* tag to a word with a *VBP* or *VBD* tag is ignored, and vice versa. And any corrections that switches a noun between it's singular form and plural form is also ignored.

With the confusion sets, we proceed to the second stage. In this stage, we use words in the confusion set to attempt to replace potential errors. Language models trained on well-formed text are used to validate the replacement decisions. Given a word *w*, If there is an alternative *w'* that fits in the context better, *w* is flagged as an error and *w'* is returned as a correction.
Here is our formula for correcting errors

$$P(O) = \frac{P_{ngram}(O) + P_{rnn}(O)}{2}$$

$$P(R) = \frac{P_{ngram}(R) + P_{rnn}(R)}{2}$$

$$Promotion = \frac{P(R) - P(O)}{|O|}$$

While checking a content word *w*, we replace *w* in the original sentence *O* with alternatives and generate candidates *C*. We then generate the candidate *R* with the highest probability among all

[3]`http://www.victoria.ac.nz/lals/resources/academicwordlist/sublists`

[4]`http://simple.wiktionary.org/wiki/Wiktionary:BNC_spoken_freq`

candidates. We use an interpolated probability[5] of ngram language model P_{ngram} and recurrent neural network language model P_{rnn}. *Promotion* indicates the increase in probability per word after we replace sentence O with the candidate R. We use word number to normalize *Promotion* following Dahlmeier, et al. (2012). Corrections are made only if *Promotion* is higher than a empirically determined threshold.[6]

2.4 Article and Determiner module

In this subsection, we describe how we correct errors of omitting a determiner or adding a spurious determiner. The language models mentioned in the last subsection are also used in this module. We tune our thresholds for making corrections on development data[7], and found that deleting a determiner should have a lower threshold while inserting one should have a higher one, so we set different thresholds accordingly. [8]

To cope with the situation where a determiner/article is far ahead of the head of the noun phrase, we apply another constraint while making correction decision.

First, we calculate statistics on the head of noun phrases. We extract the most frequent 100,000 terms in Web-1T 5-gram corpus. These terms are used to search their definitions in Wikipedia (usually at the first paragraph). The characteristic of a definition is that it has no prior context and most of the noun phrases with a determiner are unique or known to the general public. Heads of these nouns phrases are likely to always appear with a determiner.

Heads that tend to appear with a determiner `the` help us to decide whether a determiner should be added to a noun phrase. We add a determiner using two constraints. We only insert a determiner or an article, if the statistics indicate that head of a noun phrase tends to have a determiner, or the promotion of log probability is much higher than the threshold. A similar constraint is also applied, for deleting a determiner or an article.

[5]the probabilities present in the formula are log probabilities

[6]the threshold for noun number module is 0.035 and 0.050 for word form module. These threshold were set empirically after testing on development data

[7]test data of the CoNLL-2013 shared task

[8]the threshold for insertion is 0.035 and 0.040 for deletion

2.5 Preposition module

For preposition errors, we focus on handling two types of errors: REPLACE and DELETE. A preposition, which should be deleted from the given sentence, is regarded as a DELETE error, whereas for a preposition, which should be replaced with a more appropriate alternative, is regarded as a REPLACE error. In this work, we correct the two types of errors based on the assumption that the usage of preposition often depends on the collocation relations with a verb or noun. Therefore, we use the dependency relations such as `dobj` and `pobj`, and `prep` to identify the related words, and then we validate the usage of prepositions, and correct the preposition errors.

A dependency-based model is proposed in this paper to handle the preposition errors. The model consists of two stages: detecting the possible preposition errors and correcting the errors.

In the first stage, we use the Stanford dependency parser (Klein and Manning, 2003) to extract the dependency relations for each preposition. The relation tuples, which contain the preposition, verb or noun, and prepositional object. For example, the tuple of verb-prep-object (listen, to, music), or the tuple of noun-prep-object (point, of, view) are extracted for validation. We identify a preposition containing as an error, if the tuple containing the preposition does not occur in a reference list built using a reference corpus. In order to resolve the data sparseness and false alarm problems, we need a sufficiently large list of validated tuples. In this study, the reference tuple lists are generated from the Google Books Syntactic N-grams (Goldberg and Orwant, 2013)[9]. For example, we can find (come, to, end, 236864) and (lead, to, result, 57632) in the verb-preposition-object reference list. We have generated 21,773,752 different dependency tuples for our purpose.

In the second stage, we attempt to correct all potential preposition errors. At first, a list of candidate tuples is generated by substituting the original preposition in the error tuple with alternative prepositions. For example, the generated candidate tuples for the error tuple (join, at, party) will include (join, in, party), (join, on, party), etc. On the other hand, the tuple, (join, party), which

[9]Data sets available from `http://commondatastorage.googleapis.com/books/syntactic-ngrams/index.html`

deletes the preposition, is also taken into consideration. All candidates are ranked according to the frequency provided by the reference lists. The preposition in the tuple with the highest frequency is returned as the correction suggestion.

VPV, *accuse be*, accused of being	230,600
VPV, *accuse kill*, accused of killing	83,100
VPV, *accuse have*, accused of having	78,500
VPV, *accuse use*, accuse of using	45,200
VPV, *accuse* murder, accused of murdering	40,032
VPV, *accuse be*, accused to be	10,200
VPV, *accuse prove*, accused to prove	3,600

Figure 1: Sample annotated trigrams

VPV, *accuse be*, accused of being	230,600
VPV, *accuse be*, accused to be	10,200
VPV, *accuse be*, accused of is	2,841
VPV, *accuse be*, accuse of being	2,837
VPV, *accuse be*, accused as being	929
VPV, *accuse be*, accused of was	676
VPV, *accuse be*, accused from being	535

Figure 2: Sample trigram group

accused to be	||| accused of being	||| 0.93
accused of is	||| accused of being	||| 0.93
accuse of being	||| accused of being	||| 0.93
accused as being	||| accused of being	||| 0.93
accuse of was	||| accused of being	||| 0.93
accused from being	||| accused of being	||| 0.93

Figure 3: Sample phrase translation for a trigram group

2.6 Interactive errors module

This module uses a new method for correcting serial grammatical errors in a given sentence in learners writing. A statistical translation model is generated to attempt to translate the input with serial and interactive errors into a grammatical sentence. The method involves automatically learning translation models based on Web-scale n-gram. The model corrects trigrams containing serial preposition-verb errors via translation. Evaluation on a set of sentences in a learner corpus shows that the method corrects serial errors reasonably well.

Consider an error sentence *"I have difficulty to understand English."* The correct sentence for this should be *"I have difficulty in understanding English."* It is hard to correct these two errors one by one, since the errors are dependent on each other. Intuitively, by identifying *difficulty to understand* as containing serial errors and correct it to *difficulty in understanding*, we can handle this kind of problem more effectively.

First, we generate translation phrase table as follows. We begin by selecting trigrams related to serial errors and correction from Web 1T 5-gram. Figure 1 shows some sample annotation trigrams. Then, we group the selected trigrams by the first and last word in the trigrams. See Figure 2 for a sample VPV group of trigrams. Finally, we generate translation phrase table for each group. Figure 3 shows a sample translation phrase table.

At run time, we tag the input sentence with part of speech information in order to find trigrams that fit the type of serial errors. Then, we search phrase table and generate translations for the input phrases in a machine translation decoder to produce a corrected sentence.

3 Experiment

Two types of trigram language models, ngram model and recurrent neural network (RNN) model, are used in correcting spelling, noun number, word form, and determiner errors. We trained the ngram language model on English Gigaword and BNC corpus, using the SRILM tool (Stolcke, 2002). We train the RNN model with RNNLM toolkit (Mikolov et al., 2011). Complexity of training the RNN language model is much higher, so we train it on a smaller corpus, the British National Corpus (BNC).

We used the Stanford Parser (Klein and Christopher D. Manning, 2003) to obtain dependency relations in the preposition module, and to obtain POS tags for the word form module. The subject-verb-agreement module also uses dependency relations contained in test data. Dependency relations in Google Books Syntactic N-grams (Goldberg and Orwant, 2013) were also used to develop our dendepency-based model in the preposition module.

To assess the effectiveness of the proposed method, we used the official training, development, and test data of the CoNLL-2014 shared task. On the test data, our system obtained the precision, recall and $F_{0.5}$ score of 0.351, 0.189, and 0.299. The following table shows the performance breakdown by module.

	Precision	Recall	$F_{0.5}$
Article or Determiner	39.81	5.91	18.55
Noun Numbers	46.08	4.79	16.93
Preposition	16.91	2.81	8.44
Preposition + Verb	23.17	0.94	4.05
Word form	36.84	3.46	12.56
Subject Verb Agreement	53.44	4.82	17.71
Spelling and hyphen*	53.12	4.11	15.69
Punctuation	50.00	0.69	3.29

Figure 4: The performance breakdown by module. (Displayed in %)

In the spelling and hyphen module, candidates from *Aspell* include words that only differ from the original word in one character, `s`. Language models are then used to choose the candidate with highest probability as our correction. The module therefore gives some corrections about noun numbers or subject-verb-agreement. As a result, some corrections made by this module overlap with corrections made by the noun numbers module and the subject-verb-agreement module, which makes the recall of correcting spelling and hyphen errors, 4.11%, overestimated.

4 Conclusion

In this work, we have built several modules for error detection and correction. For different types of errors, we developed modules independently using different features and thresholds. If multiple modules propose different corrections to a word/phrase, the one proposed by the module with higher precision will be chosen. Many avenues for future work present themselves. We plan to integrate modules in a more flexible way. When faced with different corrections made by different modules, the decision would better be based on the confidence of each correction with a uniform standard, but not on the confidence of modules.

Acknowledgments

We would like to acknowledge the funding supports from Delta Electronic Corp and National Science Council (contract no: NSC 100-2511-S-007-005-MY3), Taiwan. We are also thankful to anonymous reviewers and the organizers of the shared task.

References

Daniel Dahlmeier, Hwee Tou Ng, and Eric Jun Feng Ng 2012. NUS at the HOO 2012 Shared Task. In *Proceedings of the Seventh Workshop on Building Educational Applications Using NLP*, Association for Computational Linguistics, June 7.

Daniel Dahlmeier and Hwee Tou Ng, 2012. Better Evaluation for Grammatical Error Correction. In *Proceedings of the 2012 Conference of the North American Chapter of the Association for Computational Linguistics (NAACL 2012).*,568-672

Daniel Dahlmeier, Hwee Tou Ng, Siew Mei Wu. 2013. Building a Large Annotated Corpus of Learner English: The NUS Corpus of Learner English. In *Proceedings of the 8th Workshop on Innovative Use of NLP for Building Educational Applications(BEA 2013)*

Yoav Goldberg and Jon Orwant 2013. A dataset of syntactic-ngrams over time from a very large corpus of English books. In *Proceedings of the Second Joint Conference on Lexical and Computational Semantics*, Atlanta, GA, 2013.

Ross Israel, Joel Tetreault, and Martin Chodorow 2012. Correcting Comma Errors in Learner Essays, and Restoring Commas in Newswire Text. In *Proceeding of the 2012 Conference of the North America Chapter of the Association for Computational Linguistics: Human Language Technologies*,284-294, Montreal Canada, June. Association for Computational Linguistics

Dan Klein and Christopher D. Manning. 2003. Accurate unlexicalized parsing. In *Proceedings of the 41st Meeting of the Association for Computational Linguistics*, 423-430.

Tomas Mikolov, Anoop Deoras, Dan Povey, Lukar Burget, and Jan Honza Cernocky 2011. Strategies for Training Large Scale Neural Network Language Models *Proceedings of ASRU 2011*

Andreas Stolcke 2002. SRILM-An Extensible Language Modeling Toolkit In *Proceedings of the International Conference on Spoken Language Processing*, vol 2, 901-904

A Unified Framework for Grammar Error Correction

Longkai Zhang Houfeng Wang
Key Laboratory of Computational Linguistics (Peking University) Ministry of Education, China
zhlongk@qq.com, wanghf@pku.edu.cn

Abstract

In this paper we describe the PKU system for the CoNLL-2014 grammar error correction shared task. We propose a unified framework for correcting all types of errors. We use unlabeled news texts instead of large amount of human annotated texts as training data. Based on these data, a tri-gram language model is used to correct the replacement errors while two extra classification models are trained to correct errors related to determiners and prepositions. Our system achieves 25.32% in $f_{0.5}$ on the original test data and 29.10% on the revised test data.

1 Introduction

The task of grammar error correction is difficult yet important. An automatic grammar error correction system can help second language(L2) learners improve the quality of their writing. Previous shared tasks for grammar error correction, such as the HOO shared task of 2012 (HOO-2012) and the CoNLL-2013 shared task(CoNLL-2013), focus on limited types of errors. For example, HOO-2012 only considers errors related to determiners and prepositions. CoNLL-2013 further considers errors that are related to noun number, verb form and subject-object agreement. In the CoNLL-2014 shared task, all systems should consider all the 28 kinds of errors, including errors such as spelling errors which cannot be corrected using a single classifier.

Most of the top-ranked systems in the CoNLL-2013 shared task(Ng et al., 2013) train individual classifiers or language models for each kind of errors independently. Although later systems such as Wu and Ng (2013); Rozovskaya and Roth (2013) use Integer Linear Programming (ILP) to decode a global optimized result, the input scores for ILP still come from the individual classification confidence of each kind of errors. It is hard to adapt these methods directly into the CoNLL-2014 shared task. It will be both time-consuming and impossible to train individual classifiers for all the 28 kinds of errors.

Besides the classifier and language model based methods, some systems(Dahlmeier and Ng, 2012a; Yoshimoto et al., 2013; Yuan and Felice, 2013) also use the machine translation approach. Because there are a limited amount of training data, this kind of approaches often need to use other corpora of L2 learners, such as the Cambridge Learner Corpus. Because these corpora use different annotation criteria, the correction systems should figure out ways to map the error types from one corpus to another. Even with these additions and transformations, there are still too few training data available to train a good translation model.

In contrast, we think the grammar error correction system should 1) correct most kinds of errors in a unified framework and 2) use as much unlabeled data as possible instead of using large amount of human annotated data. To be specific, our system do not need to train individual classifiers for each kind of errors, nor do we need to use manually corrected texts. Following the observation that a correction can either replace a wrong word or delete/insert a word, our system is divided into two parts. Firstly, we use a Language Model(LM) to correct errors with respect to the wrongly used words. The LM only uses the statistics from a large corpus. All errors related to wrongly used words can be examined in this unified model instead of designing individual systems for each kind of errors. Secondly, we train extra classifiers for determiner errors and preposition errors. We further consider these two kinds of errors because many of the deletion and insertion errors belongs to determiner or preposition errors. The

Proceedings of the Eighteenth Conference on Computational Natural Language Learning: Shared Task, pages 96–102,
Baltimore, Maryland, 26-27 July 2014.

training data of the two classification models also come from a large unlabeled news corpus therefore no human annotation is needed.

Although we try to use a unified framework to get better performance in the grammar error correction task, there are still a small portion of errors we do not consider. The insertion and deletion of words are not considered if the word is neither a determiner nor a preposition. Our system is also incapable of replacing a word sequence into another word sequence. We do not consider these kinds of errors because we find some of them are hard to generate correction candidates without further understanding of the context, and are not easy to be corrected even by human beings.

The paper is structured as follows. Section 1 gives the introduction. In section 2 we describe the task. In section 3 we describe our algorithm. Experiments are described in section 4. We also give a detailed analysis of the results in section 4. In section 5 related works are introduced, and the paper is concluded in the last section.

2 Task Description

The CoNLL-2014 shared task focuses on correcting all errors that are commonly made by L2 learners of English. The training data released by the task organizers come from the NUCLE corpus(Dahlmeier et al., 2013). This corpus contains essays written by L2 learners of English. These essays are then corrected by English teachers. Details of the CoNLL-2014 shared task can be found in Ng et al. (2014).

3 System Overview

3.1 Overview

It is time-consuming to train individual models for each kind of errors. We believe a better way is to correct errors in a unified framework. We assume that each word in the sentence may be involved in some kinds of errors. We generate a list of correction candidates for each word. Then a Language Model (LM) is used to find the most probable word sequences based on the original sentence and the correction candidates for each word. An illustrative example is shown in figure 1.

Because the LM is designed for the replacement errors rather than insertion and deletion errors, we train two extra classifiers for determiners and prepositions. The determiner model and the preposition model can improve the performance in our experiment.

3.2 Correction Candidate Generation

The correction candidate generation phase aims to generate a list of correction candidates for each word in the original sentence. We generate correction candidates based on the following rules:

1. Words with the same stem
2. Similar words based on edit distance

The first rule includes the words with the same stem as candidates. These candidates can be used later to correct the errors related to word form. For example, candidates for the word 'time' in the original sentence 'This is a timely rain indeed.' may include 'timed','time','timed','times','timings','timely', 'timees' and 'timing', which all have the stem 'time'. The correct candidate 'timely' is also included in the candidate list and can be detected through further processing.

The candidate generated by the second rule are mainly used for spelling correction. For example, a such candidate for 'beleive' may be 'belive' or 'believe'. To generate meaningful candidates while guarantee accuracy, we require that the candidate and the original word should have the same initial character. By examining the training data we experimentally find that very few L2 learners make spelling errors on the initial characters. For example, they may spell "believe" as "belive". However, very few of them may spell "believe" as "pelieve" or "delieve".

In our system, we generate 10 candidates for each word. To keep the decoding of the best word sequence controllable, we do not generate candidates for every word in the original sentence. We only generate the edit distance based candidates for the following words:

1. Words that never appear in the English gigaword corpus[1]
2. Words that appear in the gigaword corpus but with frequency below a threshold (we use 10 in the experiment)

Besides, we do not generate candidates for the words whose POS tags are "NNP" or "NNPS".

[1] `http://catalog.ldc.upenn.edu/LDC2003T05`

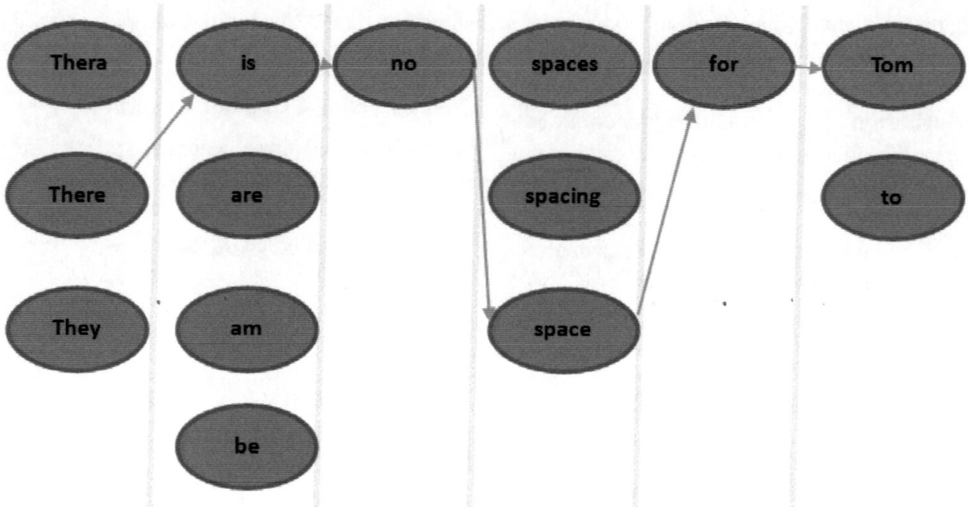

Figure 1: Correction of the original sentence "Thera is no spaces for Tom". We use red nodes to represent the original words in the sentence, and use blue nodes below each word to represent the candidate list of each word. We use arrows to show the final corrected word sequence with the highest probability.

These words are proper nouns. The correction of this kind of words should depend on more contextual information. For the stemming tools we use the snowball stemmer[2]. To generate candidates based on edit distance, we use the org.apache.lucene.search.spell.SpellChecker in Lucene[3]. Note that unlike other context based spell checkers such as the one in Microsoft Office, the SpellChecker class in Lucene is actually not a spell checker. For an input word w, it can only suggest words that are similar to w given a predefined dictionary. We build the dictionary using all words collected from the English Gigaword corpus.

3.3 Language Model for Candidate Selection

After given each word a list of candidates, we can now find the word sequence which is most likely to be the correct sentence. The model we use is the language model. The probability $P(s)$ of a sentence $s = w_0 w_1 ... w_{n-1}$ is calculated as:

$$P(s) = \prod_{i=0}^{n-1} P(w_i | w_0, ..., w_{i-1}) \tag{1}$$

The transition probability $P(w_i | w_0, ..., w_{i-1})$ is calculated based on language model. In our system we use a tri-gram language model trained on the gigaword corpus. Therefore, $P(w_i | w_0, ..., w_{i-1})$ is reduced to $P(w_i | w_{i-2}, w_{i-1})$. We do not use a fixed smoothing method. We just set the probability of an unseen string to be a positive decimal which is very close to zero.

The decoding of the word sequence that maximize $p(s)$ can be tackled through dynamic programming using Viterbi algorithm(Forney Jr, 1973). One useful trick is that to multiply $p(w_i | w_{i-2}, w_{i-1})$ with a coefficient (4 in our system) if w_{i-2}, w_{i-1} and w_i are all words in the original sentence. This is because most of the original word sequences are correct. If the system needs to make a correction, the corrected sequence should have a much higher score than the original one.

We do not generate candidates for determiners and prepositions. Firstly, they are all frequent words that are excluded by the rules we mentioned in this section. Secondly, the determiner and preposition errors are the main kinds of errors made by L2 learners. Some of the errors are related to the wrong deletions or insertions. Therefore we choose to take special care of determiners and prepositions to correct all their replacement, deletion and insertion errors instead of generating candidates for them in this stage.

3.4 Determiner Correction

After using LM, the spelling errors as well as ordinary word form errors such as noun numbers, verb

[2] `http://snowball.tartarus.org/`

[3] `https://lucene.apache.org/`

forms are supposed to be corrected. As we mentioned in the introduction, we should now handle the deletion and insertion errors. We choose to use special models for determiner and prepositions because many of the deletion and insertion errors are related to determiner errors or preposition errors. Also, these two kinds of errors have been considered in HOO-2012 and CoNLL2013. Therefore it's easier to make meaningful comparison with previous works. We use Maximum Entropy (ME) classifiers to correct the determiner and preposition errors. In this section we consider the determiner errors. The preposition errors will be considered in the next section. For both of the two parts, we use the open source tool MaxEnt[4] as the implementation of ME.

We consider the determiner correction task as a multi-class classification task. The input instances for classification are the space between words. We consider whether the space should keep empty, or insert 'a' or 'the'. Therefore, 3 labels are considered to indicate 'a', 'the' and 'NULL'. We use ''NULL' to denote that the correct space does not need an article. We leave the clarification between 'a' and 'an' as a post-process by manually designed rules. We do not consider other determiners such as 'this' or ''these' because further information such as the coreference resolution results is needed.

Instead of considering all spaces in a sentence, some previous works(AEHAN et al., 2006; Rozovskaya and Roth, 2010; Rozovskaya et al., 2013) only consider spaces at the beginning of noun phrases. Compared to these methods, our system do not need a POS tagger or a phrase chunker (which is sometimes not accurate enough) to filter the positions. All the operations are done on the word level. We list the features we use in table 1. Note that for 3-grams and 4-grams we do not use all combinations of characters because it will generate more sparse features while the performance is not improved.

Because there are limited amount of training data, we choose to use the English Gigaword corpus to generate training instances instead of using the training data of CoNLL-2014. Because the texts in the Gigaword corpus are all news texts, most of them are well written by native speakers and are proofread by the editors. Therefore they can serve as implicit gold annotations. We generate the training instances from the sentences in the Gigaword corpus with the following rules:

1-gram	w_{-3}, w_{-2}, w_{-1}, w_1, w_2, w_3
2-gram	all combinations of $w_i w_j$ where $i, j \in \{-3, -2, -1, 1, 2, 3\}$
3-gram	$w_{-3}w_{-2}w_{-1}$,$w_{-2}w_{-1}w_1$, $w_{-1}w_1w_2$, $w_1w_2w_3$
4-gram	$w_{-3}w_{-2}w_{-1}w_1$, $w_{-2}w_{-1}w_1w_2$,$w_{-1}w_1w_2w_3$

Table 1: The features used in our system. For a given blank(space), w_i means the next ith word and w_{-i} means the previous ith word. For the example of "I do not play balls .", if the current considered instance is the space between 'play' and 'balls', then w_{-2} means 'not' and w_1 means 'balls'.

1. for each space between words, we treat it as an instance with label 'NULL', which means no article is needed. We use the 3 words before the space as w_{-3}, w_{-2}, w_{-1} and the 3 words after the space as w_1, w_2, w_3 to generate features. We name this kind of instances 'Space Instance' to indicate we operate on a space. This kind of training instances can convey the information that in this context no article is needed.

2. for each word that is an article, we assume it as an instance, with the label 'a' or 'the' depending on itself. We use the 3 words before it as w_{-3}, w_{-2}, w_{-1} and the 3 words after is as w_1, w_2, w_3. In this case we do not use the article itself as the context. We name this kind of instances 'article Instance' to indicate we operate on an article. This kind of training instances can convey the information that in this context a particular article should be added.

The testing instance are also generated following the previously mentioned rules. The decoding process is as follows. If an instance is a 'space instance' and is predicted as 'a' or 'the', we then add 'a' or 'the' in this space. If an instance is an 'article instance', the situation is a bit complex. If it is predicted as another article, we replace it with the predicted one. If it is predicted as 'NULL', we should delete the article to make it a space.

[4] http://homepages.inf.ed.ac.uk/lzhang10/maxent_toolkit.html

To guarantee a certain level of precision, we require the decoding should only be based on confident predictions. We use the probability calculated by the classifier as the confidence score and require the probability of the considered predictions should exceed a threshold.

3.5 Preposition Correction

The preposition model is similar to the article model. We use the same set of features as in table 1. The training and testing instance generation is similar except now we consider prepositions instead of articles. The decoding phase is also identical to the determiner model.

3.6 Post Processing

The post processing in our system is listed as follows:

1. Distinguish between "a" and "an". We use rule based method for this issue.
2. Splitting words. If a word is not in the dictionary but one of its splitting results has a high frequency, we will split the word into two words. For example, "dailylife" is an out of vocabulary word and the splitting result "daily life" is common in English. Then we split "dailylife" into "daily life".
3. We capitalize the first character of each sentence.

4 Experiment and Analysis

We experiment on the CoNLL-2014 test data. We evaluate our system based on the M2 scorer which is provided by the organizers. Details of the M2 scorer can be found in Dahlmeier and Ng (2012b). We tune the additional parameters like all the thresholds on the CoNLL-2014 official training data. We use all the text in the Gigaword corpus to train the language model. We use 2.5 million sentences in the Gigaword corpus to train the extra two classifier.

Results of our system are shown in table 2. LM refers to using language model alone. LM+det refers to using a determiner classifier after using a language model. LM+prep refers to using a preposition classifier after using a language model. LM+det+preposition refers to using a preposition classifier after LM+det, which is the method used in our final system.

Model	P	R	F0.5
LM	29.89%	10.04%	21.42%
LM+det	32.23%	13.64%	25.33%
LM+prep	29.73%	10.04%	21.35%
LM+det+prep(all)	32.21%	13.65%	25.32%

Table 2: The experimental results of our system in the CoNLL-2014 shared task. The threshold for determiner model and preposition model is 0.99 and 0.99. Parameters are tuned on the CoNLL-2014 training data.

Model	P	R	F0.5
LM+det+prep(all)	36.64%	15.96%	29.10%

Table 3: The experimental results of our system in the CoNLL-2014 shared task on the revised annotations. The threshold for determiner model and preposition model is 0.99 and 0.99. Parameters are tuned on the CoNLL-2014 training data.

From the results we can see that the main contribution comes from the LM model and determiner model. The preposition model can correct part of the errors while introduce new errors. The preposition model may harm the overall performance. But considering the fact that the grammar error correction systems are always used for recommending errors, we still keep the preposition model in real applications and suggest the errors predicted by the preposition model.

One limitation of our system is that we only use a tri-gram based language model as well as up to 4-gram features for limited instances. Previous works(Rozovskaya et al., 2013; Kao et al., 2013) have shown that other resources like the Google 5-gram statistics can help improve performance. For the determiner and preposition models, we experiment on different size of training data, from near zero to the upper bound of our server's memory limit (about 72GB). We find that under this limitation, the performance is still improving when adding more training instances. We believe the performance can be further improved.

Scores based on the revised annotations is shown in table 3.

For the convenience of future meaningful comparison, we report the result of our system on the CoNLL-2013 data set in table 4. We tune the additional parameters like all the thresholds on the CoNLL-2013 official training data. Note that in CoNLL-2013 the scorer considers F1 score in-

Model	P	R	F1
CoNLL13 1st	23.49%	46.45%	31.20 %
CoNLL13 2nd	26.35%	23.80%	25.01 %
LM	18.92%	14.55%	16.45%
LM+det	23.76%	36.15%	28.67%
LM+prep	18.89%	14.55%	16.44%
LM+det+prep	**23.74%**	**36.15%**	**28.66%**

Table 4: The experimental results of our system on the CoNLL-2013 shared task data. The threshold for determiner model and preposition model is 0.75 and 0.99. Parameters are tuned on the CoNLL-2013 training data. CoNLL13 1st is Rozovskaya et al. (2013) and the 2nd is Kao et al. (2013)

stead of F0.5. Therefore some of the thresholds are different with the ones in the CoNLL-2014 system. Because the CoNLL-2013 shared task only considers 5 types of errors, it will be much easier to design components specially for each kind of errors. Therefore our system is a bit less accurate than the best system. In this system, we restrict the candidates to be either noun or verb, and omit the spell checking model. We also omit some post-processings like deciding whether a word should be split into two words, because these kinds of errors are not included.

5 Conclusion

In this paper we describe the PKU system for the CoNLL-2014 grammar error correction shared task. We propose a unified framework for correcting all types of errors. A tri-gram language model is used to correct the replacement errors while two extra classification models are trained to correct errors related to determiners and prepositions. Our system achieves 25.32% in $f_{0.5}$ on the original test data and 29.10% on the revised test data.

Acknowledgments

This research was partly supported by National Natural Science Foundation of China (No.61370117, No.61333018), National High Technology Research and Development Program of China (863 Program) (No.2012AA011101) and Major National Social Science Fund of China(No.12&ZD227).

References

AEHAN, N., Chodorow, M., and LEACOCK, C. L. (2006). Detecting errors in english article usage by non-native speakers.

Dahlmeier, D. and Ng, H. T. (2012a). A beam-search decoder for grammatical error correction. In *Proceedings of the 2012 Joint Conference on Empirical Methods in Natural Language Processing and Computational Natural Language Learning*, pages 568–578. Association for Computational Linguistics.

Dahlmeier, D. and Ng, H. T. (2012b). Better evaluation for grammatical error correction. In *Proceedings of the 2012 Conference of the North American Chapter of the Association for Computational Linguistics: Human Language Technologies*, pages 568–572. Association for Computational Linguistics.

Dahlmeier, D., Ng, H. T., and Wu, S. M. (2013). Building a large annotated corpus of learner english: The nus corpus of learner english. In *Proceedings of the Eighth Workshop on Innovative Use of NLP for Building Educational Applications*, pages 22–31.

Forney Jr, G. D. (1973). The viterbi algorithm. *Proceedings of the IEEE*, 61(3):268–278.

Kao, T.-h., Chang, Y.-w., Chiu, H.-w., Yen, T.-H., Boisson, J., Wu, J.-c., and Chang, J. S. (2013). Conll-2013 shared task: Grammatical error correction nthu system description. In *Proceedings of the Seventeenth Conference on Computational Natural Language Learning: Shared Task*, pages 20–25, Sofia, Bulgaria. Association for Computational Linguistics.

Ng, H. T., Wu, S. M., Briscoe, T., Hadiwinoto, C., Susanto, R. H., and Bryant, C. (2014). The conll-2014 shared task on grammatical error correction. In *Proceedings of the Eighteenth Conference on Computational Natural Language Learning: Shared Task (CoNLL-2014 Shared Task)*, pages 1–12, Baltimore, Maryland, USA. Association for Computational Linguistics.

Ng, H. T., Wu, S. M., Wu, Y., Hadiwinoto, C., and Tetreault, J. (2013). The conll-2013 shared task on grammatical error correction. In *Proceedings of the Seventeenth Conference on Computational Natural Language Learning: Shared*

Task, pages 1–12, Sofia, Bulgaria. Association for Computational Linguistics.

Rozovskaya, A., Chang, K.-W., Sammons, M., and Roth, D. (2013). The university of illinois system in the conll-2013 shared task. In *Proceedings of the Seventeenth Conference on Computational Natural Language Learning: Shared Task*, pages 13–19, Sofia, Bulgaria. Association for Computational Linguistics.

Rozovskaya, A. and Roth, D. (2010). Training paradigms for correcting errors in grammar and usage. In *Human language technologies: The 2010 annual conference of the north american chapter of the association for computational linguistics*, pages 154–162. Association for Computational Linguistics.

Rozovskaya, A. and Roth, D. (2013). Joint learning and inference for grammatical error correction. In *Proceedings of the 2013 Conference on Empirical Methods in Natural Language Processing*, pages 791–802, Seattle, Washington, USA. Association for Computational Linguistics.

Wu, Y. and Ng, H. T. (2013). Grammatical error correction using integer linear programming. In *Proceedings of the 51st Annual Meeting of the Association for Computational Linguistics (Volume 1: Long Papers)*, pages 1456–1465, Sofia, Bulgaria. Association for Computational Linguistics.

Yoshimoto, I., Kose, T., Mitsuzawa, K., Sakaguchi, K., Mizumoto, T., Hayashibe, Y., Komachi, M., and Matsumoto, Y. (2013). Naist at 2013 conll grammatical error correction shared task. *CoNLL-2013*, 26.

Yuan, Z. and Felice, M. (2013). Constrained grammatical error correction using statistical machine translation. *CoNLL-2013*, page 52.

Author Index